AF555923

THE MAKING OF A CATASTROPHE

THE MAKING OF A CATASTROPHE

The Disastrous Economic Fallout of the Covid-19 Pandemic in India

JAYATI GHOSH

ALEPH

ALEPH BOOK COMPANY
An independent publishing firm
promoted by ***Rupa Publications India***

First published in India in 2022
by Aleph Book Company
7/16 Ansari Road, Daryaganj
New Delhi 110 002

ISBN: 978-93-90652-96-9

1 3 5 7 9 10 8 6 4 2

Printed in India

CONTENTS

Introduction

THE POLICY-DRIVEN CATASTROPHE

The incidence of the novel Coronavirus, or Covid-19, was first noticed in Wuhan, China, in November 2019, and notified to the World Health Organization (WHO) at the end of that month. At that time, it appeared to follow the pattern of other zoonotic diseases (like H1N1 and avian flu) that have been appearing with increasing frequency in recent years, but have not raised major ripples beyond certain parts of Asia. However, by March 2020, the World Health Organization declared Covid-19 to be a pandemic, and since then, it has swept across the world. By early February 2022, there were more than 406 million recorded Covid-19 cases worldwide, with around 6 million recorded deaths of those infected with the virus.[1] Despite some abatement of infection in 2021 and the spread of rapidly developed vaccines, even in early 2022 the emergence of new mutant variants, with greater transmission powers, was still creating concern. Meanwhile, the disease had already created widespread and unprecedented disruptions of normal life and economic activity even as governments and individuals sought to fend off the disease through various, often extreme, measures.

The Covid-19 pandemic has been the worst health calamity in India for at least a century. But beyond the direct health

---

[1]'Cumulative Confirmed COVID-19 Deaths', *Our World in Data*, https://ourworldindata.org/explorers/Coronavirus-data-explorer, accessed 13 February 2022.

and mortality impacts, the economic and social devastation experienced by the country over this period had even worse results, being so severe as to merit the description 'catastrophe'. This catastrophe cannot be ascribed only to the disease. Rather, it is argued in the rest of this book that much of the damage resulted from government action and inaction. Very significant policy failures—acts of both commission and omission—were responsible for the widespread and pronounced decline in people's livelihoods and in many of the basic indicators of well-being among the population, and caused major setbacks to the development project of the country.[2]

This may seem like an excessively harsh judgement. After all, the pandemic was certainly not of the Indian government's making; several other countries have had worse experiences with the spread of the disease; and most countries have suffered severe economic declines, to varying degrees. So, what makes India different from other countries? Why should the outcomes that have been seen as the result of 'an act of God' be ascribed to government policies? How can it be argued that, even more than the disease, these policies and the processes they set in train, have been responsible for economic declines and humanitarian disasters?

Indeed, while Coronavirus certainly affected the Indian population and caused increased morbidities and death, the impact of the illness over the first year was less acute than in countries like the US and some countries in Europe. This was also true in much of the Asian continent, although the Indian experience has been significantly worse than that in China (where the virus originated) or other countries like Vietnam, and even worse than in some South Asian neighbours. So, while

---

[2]A note on this chapter: this introduction simply summarizes arguments developed later in the book, where they are presented in more detail and with appropriate references.

the Covid-19 spread in India has been severe and worrying, it cannot account for the terrible economic and other outcomes experienced by the population. Rather, as will be shown later in this book, the damage to living and working conditions in India resulted principally from the way the central government first attempted to control the disease through a brutal national lockdown, which also had an impact on essential public services, and then did next to nothing to ensure basic protection for the hundreds of millions of people who were denied income for several months. Since around 95 per cent of all workers in India are informal, with no legal or social protection, many of whom already functioned at the margin of subsistence, this had devastating consequences.

These consequences are so severe that they are unlikely to be simply wished away once the pandemic recedes. The setback to social and economic progress is enormous. Economic recovery for the greater proportion of the population—rather than simply of formal enterprises or the stock market, which typically do not reflect the material conditions of most Indians—will require major changes in economic policies and a reversal of several tendencies set in train by the ruling party, which currently threaten to destroy the socio-political fabric and federal economic structure of the country.

The pandemic and the associated policies did not create the many fissures, vulnerabilities, and fault lines in Indian society and economy; but they definitely exposed them, brought them to the surface, and enabled them to become even more significant. Inequalities of incomes, assets, and opportunities, which were already very severe in India before the pandemic, have now reached unimaginable extremes. In this period of crisis, money and resources have defied gravity to flow from the poor and the middle classes to the richest corporations and high-net-worth individuals, who have become richer than ever, even as working people face hunger, destitution, and ever-greater material insecurity. And the intersecting inequalities of caste, gender, religion, and migration status have become even more marked and oppressive. Before the pandemic, there was an uneasy sense that, far from progressing, Indian economy, society, and polity were spiralling downwards; the pandemic seems to have intensified and accelerated these tendencies.

Nevertheless, these catastrophic outcomes were not inevitable. Many other countries, including those at similar levels of per capita income and development, managed to handle both the pandemic and the resulting economic crisis differently, and with better results in terms of both people's health and livelihoods. In this book, I explore what went wrong, consider what could have been done differently, and finally consider what can still be done to salvage the economy and enable a just and sustainable recovery of livelihoods.

The big difference in India is the extent of the economic collapse and the massive impact it has had on the lives of people, bringing millions to absolute destitution and creating economic insecurity for the majority of workers, which is likely to persist for several years. Several aspects of the Indian government's policy responses were responsible for this combination of adverse outcomes. To begin with, the unplanned and brutal lockdown and the unthinking adoption of containment strategies not suited to the Indian context had immediate and direct effects on employment and livelihoods. The most stringent lockdown in the world was imposed across the nation, without notice or consultation even with state governments, at a time when it was not needed because there were very few cases, limited to some pockets. The more expensive (but more effective) strategy of testing, tracing, isolating, and treating those infected, was not implemented as a national strategy, although some states like Kerala did do so, in the initial phases. Instead, the onus was put on the population to restrict their own activity, even at the cost of losing whatever little incomes they had, and with little to no compensation. The restrictions assumed that people would be able to maintain 'social distancing' (more accurately physical distancing) and hygiene, when this was not really possible for around half of the population. The government did not use the breathing space provided by the lockdown to prepare health systems; rather, it left state governments to manage as best they could with very limited and inadequate resources. When the economic disaster became too extreme, the central government proceeded to 'unlock' the economy even as cases mounted and infections spread more rapidly, thereby putting more people at risk.

While hundreds of millions of people were deprived of their livelihoods for several months, they were provided very little in terms of compensation or social protection. This is both astounding and inexcusable in a country where around 95 per cent of all workers are informal, and around half of those are self-employed, where median wages provide only the most basic subsistence and where loss of income beyond even a week can lead to absolute starvation for millions who are already at the margin of survival. There was some distribution of free foodgrain for some months to those with ration cards, but this excluded at least 100 million of the needy, and the amounts distributed were inadequate. The government continued to hold excess food stocks, adding to stock levels through more procurement but releasing only small amounts even as absolute hunger among the people increased massively, and stopping the distribution of some free foodgrains even as employment continued to slump and millions faced much worsening levels of nutrition and even starvation. The denial of basic food items to hundreds of millions of people is, undoubtedly, more than a human tragedy: it will reflect in maternal, infant, and child undernutrition with terrible consequences for the future.

What is worse, at a time when governments across the world were significantly increasing public spending to respond to the twin crises of pandemic and livelihood collapses, the Indian government actually controlled and even reduced its expenditure as its revenues declined. This conservative fiscal stance during a downswing added to the shock of the lockdown that had already affected economic activity, prevented wage incomes from increasing, and set in motion additional contractionary tendencies that will damage economic prospects in the medium term.

Not only did the central government refuse to spend more itself; at first it also refused to let the state governments spend more either. (In India the central government has the power to control borrowing limits of the states.) After invoking the centralizing National Disaster Management Act to declare a national lockdown, without consulting or informing the states, the centre then minimized its obligations to deal with the pandemic or the consequences of its own actions. Instead, it left the state governments to deal with the additional health spending and other measures required to deal with the increased economic distress as best they could. The centre even first refused to pay and then delayed paying dues that it owed to the states because of a prior agreement on the implementation of the Goods and Services Tax (GST). When it became evident that this was completely unfeasible and would lead to a major humanitarian crisis, in late July 2020, state governments were allowed to borrow more—but knowing that they would have to repay later. This was part of a peculiar pattern, whereby state governments had to agree to often arbitrary decisions by the centre (including with regard to purchase of testing kits and vaccine distribution) on which they were not consulted, while receiving only the most minimal financial assistance.

This curtailment of public spending, at a time when it should have been massively increased, had disastrous effects. Of course, it affected public services, including health services that were already overstretched due to the pandemic. But it also meant that people were generally not afforded any compensation for the loss of incomes during the lockdown, and most did not recover their incomes even when the economy was allowed to open. It generated a severe humanitarian crisis that was most starkly evident in the desperate conditions faced by migrant workers, but extended to the majority of the population to varying degrees.

There was a deep and pervasive display of inequality in both official and societal responses to the pandemic and the lockdown. These inequalities operated on different levels. India is not known as a country that values and respects ordinary workers and the poor; nevertheless, the extent to which leaders, the elite, and the middle classes abandoned the poor, while seeking to protect themselves, was startling. The disease was brought into the country by the relatively better-off who could travel abroad; but to stop its proliferation, the most extreme containment policies were visited upon those less fortunate, with little thought for their well-being or even survival, and with almost vicious implementation of rules that were then intermittently abandoned even as the spread of the pandemic and the potential risks of infection were much greater than before.

The class divide was most evident in the fiscal response: in the previous year, the central government had lost more than ₹2 lakh crore in revenue foregone after bringing in corporate tax cuts[3] that essentially benefited a few large companies and pushed up their retained profits. By contrast, during the pandemic, increased government spending on social sectors that would directly affect the poor came to less than half that amount. The disease prevention measures that were imposed on the population, like physical distancing and frequent handwashing,

[3]PTI, 'Govt stares at tax shortfall of ₹2 lakh crore; little room for income tax cut', *Economic Times*, 27 January 2020.

presumed living conditions that were actually available only to middle classes and elites, and could not be implemented among the urban poor and many rural dwellers. The denial of livelihood to informal workers without providing compensatory social protection was another indication of the class orientation of policy. The refusal to release foodgrains for the hungry even as grains accumulated in public storage facilities was compounded by the travesty of allowing open market sales of some food stocks to convert into ethanol for making hand sanitizers. One stark example of unequal treatment came from controls on mobility and subsequent provision of transport to migrants. Throughout the period of lockdown, special evacuation flights were arranged for Indian citizens stranded abroad, who are typically among the better-off. However, stranded workers within India got little or no assistance. At first, movement was completely prohibited, and those who desperately attempted to walk hundreds of kilometres to their homes were detained, attacked, and humiliated in various ways for 'breaking the curfew'. When some trains for internal migrants were finally arranged, impoverished workers were made to pay full fares, and conditions on these trains were often appalling, with prolonged and delayed journeys in intense heat during which food and water were not provided, adding to distress, ill-health, and spread of Covid-19 infections to far-flung and less developed parts of the country.

The still pervasive caste system in India justifies hierarchies and discrimination, and also relies on 'social distancing', which became a natural fit in the current pandemic for those on top of the socio-economic hierarchy. This added further layers to the impact of pervasive patriarchy. Many of the frontline workers in the fight against Covid-19, especially basic health workers and sanitation workers, come from lower castes and more of them tend to be women. They are poorly remunerated, most not even receiving minimum wages. During the pandemic, they typically had to work without adequate protection (with a disproportionate number getting infected), faced social discrimination and physical threats, and in many cases did not receive their full pay. Meanwhile, among other workers the impact of job losses and food insecurity was significantly higher for women, as well as for Muslims and Dalits. As in many other countries, the lockdown was also associated with significant increases in complaints of domestic violence on women, yet there was no administrative effort to ensure that affected women had access to help and support. Gender blindness was also evident in many official decisions during the pandemic, such as the initial exclusion of sanitary napkins from the original list of essential items whose production and distribution was permitted during the lockdown.

Instead of providing more support to the population during this devastating period, the central government used the pandemic to advance its agenda of centralizing power and suppressing dissent. Just before the lockdown, there were many peaceful protests across the country, against the new citizenship law that effectively gave lower status to Muslims. Some of these peaceful gatherings had been met with violence on the part of police and armed supporters of the ruling party. The central government used the opportunity presented by the lockdown not just to prohibit any kind of public protest but to arrest several of those who had participated in the non-violent protests, while protecting supporters of the ruling party. The crackdown on dissent has affected students, lawyers, human rights activists, journalists, and academics, many of whom were forced into prisons in which Covid-19 infections were proliferating. The purpose of such continued repression during a period of national calamity appeared to be to teach a lesson to those who had interrogated the government's intentions and actions, and to intimidate others. Unfortunately, this also meant that the government's own ability to create a widespread social consensus and atmosphere of trust in which to combat the pandemic was correspondingly reduced.

The health, nutrition, and economic consequences of this strategy have been devastating, with very adverse implications for the future. Nutrition and hunger affect people's lives today, but they also impact children particularly badly, creating conditions for inadequate development. The digital divide, more pronounced than ever, now extends into all aspects of life, including education and the ability to participate as citizens. A particular betrayal has been that of the youth, whose dreams and aspirations to somehow achieve a middle-class existence were among the factors propelling Narendra Modi to his first national electoral victory. These had already been battered by the falls in total employment and worsening labour market conditions for educated youth over the previous six years, but the pandemic's impact was even more direct and brutal, decimating productive income opportunities.

Meanwhile it became apparent that the government would use the lockdown not only to crack down on dissenters and increase its surveillance of all actual and potential dissenters, but also to suppress the existing institutional checks and balances on its own functioning. Covid-19 was used as the excuse to truncate both Budget and Monsoon sessions of both houses of Parliament, which had historically the lowest number of sittings in 2020—only thirty-three days for the entire year. Demands by Opposition parties to convene virtual sessions of Parliament, or at least allow online meetings of the various Parliamentary panels that are supposed to monitor the executive and consider specific proposed legislation, were ignored or rejected. The refusal to convene Parliament was particularly egregious as the central government progressively eased lockdown restrictions through the course of the year, forcing people (especially the poor) to put themselves at risk at a time of high spread of the disease, because of the need to earn their livelihood; but elected representatives were not enabled or required to attend

Parliament even with appropriate restrictions and distancing norms put in place. The truncated sessions were used to rush through controversial legislation like the farm bills and labour codes, without any consultation, discussion, or consideration by the appropriate Parliamentary committees. Not surprisingly, these moves generated massive public protests subsequently, which were typically sought to be suppressed with a heavy hand.

All of this could have been done very differently, even within the economic and political constraints existing in India. Even now, there is scope—and the urgent need—for a reversal of these policies and a different economic strategy that would enable a just, more sustainable and less unequal recovery, especially with regard to lives and livelihoods of the bulk of the population.

These arguments are developed in more detail in the chapters that follow. I begin in Chapter 1 with a brief overview of how the Covid-19 pandemic has affected the global economy, and the implications especially for developing countries. One striking fact is that certain regions (notably Europe and the USA) have been much more affected by the spread of the disease than all the other regions. But even more striking may be the dramatic inequality of official response, with the advanced economies suddenly willing to make massive fiscal outlays to cope with the economic consequences of the pandemic, while developing countries have been much less willing or able to do so. The economic inequalities that were accentuated by these differing fiscal responses were made much worse by the ongoing 'nationalist' attempts at a vaccine grab by the governments of rich countries, effectively excluding much of the world's population.

In Chapter 2, I consider how India was poorly placed to deal with a calamity of this scale because of the vulnerabilities of the economy and the health system. The economy was already fragile and on the verge of crisis, with decelerating output, falling employment, consumption, and investment, and evidence of increased material distress among the poorest groups—but also evidence of greater wealth among the tiny handful of extremely wealthy individuals. Health conditions were also dire, on the whole: successive Indian governments have ignored public health concerns and provided very little money for it, such that government health spending per capita and as a share of national income have been among the lowest in the world and people have been forced to engage in out-of-pocket spending, making access to decent health services unaffordable for most. Nutrition indicators were poor, especially for women, adding to health vulnerabilities. There were substantial differences across states, with some like Kerala showing much better health indicators and others like Tamil Nadu showing improvement; but in most of the country, health indicators showed the effect of continuous official neglect and inadequate public funding. This in turn meant that the disruptions brought about by the disease and the lockdowns had even worse impacts than they would have had on a more buoyant economy and a population in better health overall.

In Chapter 3, I provide a short account of the trajectory of the disease in India, and how this has played out in conjunction with public health policies over this period. India may be the only country in the world where the virus was given religious overtones, with government officials, ruling party members, and pliant media attempting to link the initial spread of the infection with a particular religious gathering organized by Muslims. Thereafter, the lockdown and subsequent policies perversely operated to spread the infection across the country as migrant workers deprived of incomes were forced to go back to their homes in whichever ways they could. While the incidence of infection and fatality from Covid-19 first peaked in September 2020, from late January 2021, the emergence of the Delta variant of the virus created a devastating second wave of the disease. The spread of newer variants like Omicron in the second half of 2021 was not associated with as many deaths, but suggested that the pandemic would not simply fade away easily. The official approval of some vaccines was met with both relief and some controversy. This resulted from the unorthodox procedures adopted in approval of one vaccine before all clinical trials were complete, which resulted in some doubts and scepticism, even though the Indian population has been very accepting of vaccination in the past; and because of the confused policies that underfunded public provision and for some time allowed private players to distribute vaccines at higher prices.

Macroeconomic and sectoral policies and their impacts are taken up in Chapter 4. In the first instance, the lockdown affected supply, and then, by impacting on employment and incomes, it affected demand, creating a wide range of anticipated and unanticipated effects that were aggravated by the nature of the government response. Immediately, the economy fell off a cliff, with a precipitous decline in GDP in the period April–June 2020, by at least one-fourth compared to the previous year according to official data, and possibly more in actuality. The 'recovery' thereafter was concentrated in some segments of the organized sector and in the stock market, which appeared to move in the opposite direction from indicators like consumption and employment that continued to decline or stagnate. This was reflected in two striking outcomes: significant increases in economic inequality in an already very unequal society; and a generalized collapse in mass demand that was already depressed before the pandemic. Agriculture benefited from good weather conditions, but farmers were impacted by distribution and marketing problems, as well as other concerns, such as the threatened imposition of controversial farm laws.

In Chapter 5, I consider the outcomes for employment and workers, as well as how these processes affected the lives of people in other ways. The dramatic falls in aggregate employment were followed by only partial recovery, while wage incomes remained well below pre-pandemic levels (and in some cases even below the levels of several years earlier, before the 2016 demonetization). The particularly extreme plight of migrant workers is discussed in some detail, because it went beyond being a major failure of governance, especially at the central government level, and provided evidence of the absence of social cohesion, pointing to a breakdown of the social contract of hitherto unimaginable proportions. Food insecurity and absolute hunger increased sharply, with both immediate and possibly far-reaching adverse consequences. Certain categories of workers, like the self-employed, women, youth, and workers belonging to disadvantaged social groups (especially Dalits and Muslims), were particularly badly affected. Women faced multiple disadvantages as paid and unpaid workers, and because of relational inequalities that spilled over into domestic violence; these issues were made worse by the gender-blindness of official policies. Education—so critical for India's future—was effectively subverted by the hasty and ill-planned attempt to shift entirely to online learning without reckoning for the country's immense digital divide, which not only excluded the bulk of students but did not really enable genuine instruction. In this generally dark scene, a crucial role was played by the rural employment guarantee programme as a cushion for household survival and as an automatic stabilizer, despite still-inadequate budgetary allocations.

In the last chapter, I discuss what can still be done to get the Indian economy and the Indian people out of this mess. Redemption requires a reversal of these unjust and counterproductive policies. Immediately, this means a significant increase in public expenditure, especially in areas with high multiplier effects, such as health, nutrition, social services like education, economic sectors like agriculture, and expansion of the employment guarantee in rural areas as well as its introduction in urban areas; as well as more spending in areas that would help overcome any supply bottlenecks that have emerged because of the breakdown of supply chains resulting from the poorly planned and aggressively implemented lockdowns. Some of this increase in spending could be immediately financed through solidarity taxes imposed on the extremely wealthy and reforming tax systems to prevent multinational companies from shifting profits out of the country and thus avoiding paying their fair share of taxes in India even at the existing tax rates. Over time, other 'reforms' are clearly required, but not the kinds of reforms that seek to privilege capital over workers and citizens; rather, reforms that stress greater public spending on green and sustainable activities with a focus on good quality employment generation, and with much greater public accountability.

chapter 1

COVID-19 AND THE GLOBAL ECONOMY

The Covid-19 pandemic swept across the world more rapidly than any epidemic in human history, aided by the processes of globalization that enabled the virus to be carried across borders by travellers, after it first emerged in the Wuhan province of China. The word 'unprecedented' has been used very often about this pandemic; but it is not entirely so. Previous epidemics have also been global in sweep, such as the Spanish influenza of 1918—a form of avian flu that apparently originated in the Great Plains of the USA but spread across the world over fifteen months, infecting at least 500 million people and killing between 3–5 per cent of the global population of the time.[1] The HIV-AIDS epidemic has infected around 76 million people since it was first detected in the early 1980s. More recently, other epidemics have also spread rapidly and initially had much higher fatality rates than Covid-19,[2] such as the Severe Acute Respiratory Syndrome (SARS) virus that affected East Asia in 2003; the Middle East Respiratory Syndrome Coronavirus (MERS-CoV) that affected at least twenty-seven countries in Africa, the Middle East, and Asia, since it was first identified in Saudi Arabia in 2012; the Ebola virus disease that ravaged West Africa over 2014–2016, the largest outbreak since the virus was first discovered in 1976; the Nipah virus that was first recognized in 1999 in an outbreak in Malaysia; and Zika virus infections

[1]Robert Kessler, 'Outbreak: Pandemic Strikes', *EcoHealth Alliance*, 2018.

[2]'The Global HIV/AIDS Epidemic', KFF (Kaiser Family Foundation), 2 March 2021.

that have been reported from 86 countries and territories, etc. However, these mostly affected developing countries, and were contained to specific regions, and so attracted less international attention, even though they were more lethal in nature. The novel Coronavirus has three critical features that makes it different from the others: the speed with which it has spread; its disproportionate impact on people living in rich countries; and the sheer scale of the policy response for containment of the spread.

Figures 1.1 and 1.2 indicate how the pandemic has impacted the major regions of the world, in terms of the number of those infected and the number of deaths from the disease, as rolling seven-day averages of these numbers per million population. But they should be interpreted with caution because the assessment of numbers of people infected depends on the extent of testing, which has varied across countries and over time. Similarly, the cause of death may not be accurately identified. In many countries (especially including India as discussed in Chapter 3) deaths from Covid-19 are likely to be underestimated, sometimes quite significantly. Nevertheless, these figures point to some notable features of this pandemic, which by late February 2022 had infected around 430 million people worldwide, with many more probably not identified as having been infected, and around 6 million recorded deaths. North America and Europe were disproportionately affected, both in terms of Covid-19 infections and deaths per population, while South America showed the highest death rate per population. By late February 2022, these three continents accounted for 70 per cent of the total number of recorded cases and 74 per cent of Covid-19 deaths, though they comprise less than 20 cent of the world's population.[3] Asia (where the disease originated) and Africa were apparently relatively less affected, although this could reflect lower rates of testing and recording of deaths. The pandemic spread in waves in different regions. It is worth noting that each wave seems to have been more damaging than the previous one, despite the faster rollout of vaccinations in Europe and North America.

Figure 1.1

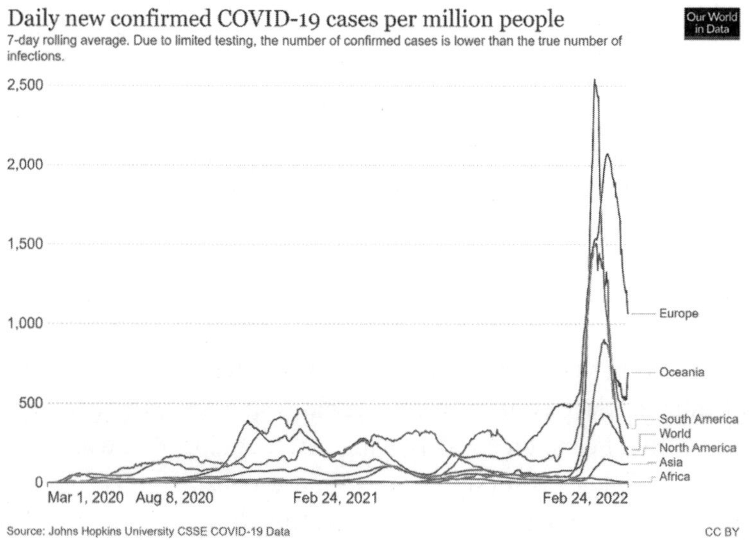

Source: *Our World in Data*, retrieved 25 February 2022.

[3]*Our World in Data*, accessed on 25 February 2022.

Figure 1.2

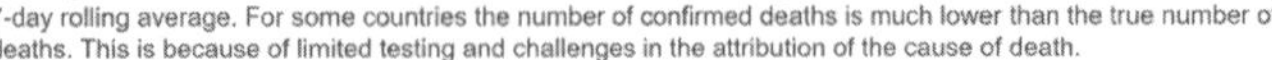

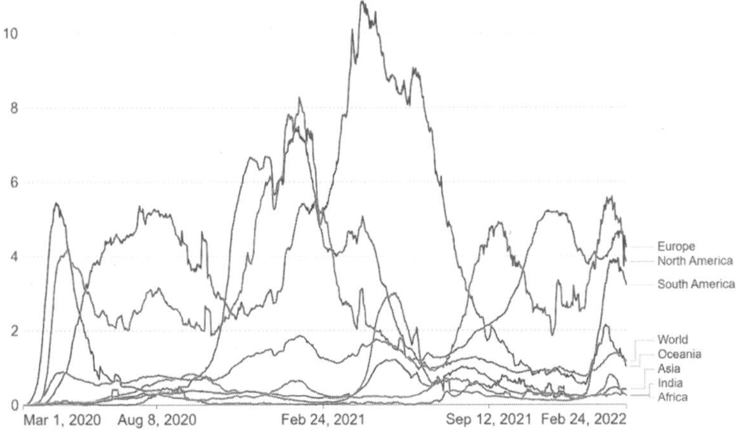

Source: *Our World in Data*, retrieved 25 February 2022.

There were very large differences in the manner in which the pandemic played out within regions as well. Some countries that had earlier been perceived as being better equipped to withstand pandemics because of supposedly superior health infrastructure, like the United States and the United Kingdom, were among the worst affected, both during the first wave and in subsequent waves driven by new variants of the virus. For most of the developing world, Covid-19 was still less lethal than the four other top killer diseases taken together (neo-natal conditions, lower respiratory infections, diarrhoeal diseases, and tuberculosis). However, the burden of these four diseases is overwhelmingly felt in the developing world, in poor or low-middle-income countries. In 2020, rich and upper-middle-income countries accounted for only 26 per cent of global mortality from these four diseases, but more than half the global mortality from Covid-19.[4]

This significance of Covid-19 for the developed world could provide a pointer to the global obsession with the disease and the urgency with which governments of rich countries sought to contain it, compared to much less enthusiasm for dealing with the other major killers. As Ray and Subramanian put it, this enables an 'Animal Farm' perspective on the pandemic: all communicable diseases are equal, but some are more equal than others.[5] The massive governmental support in the rich countries for rapid vaccine development, to deal with the Covid-19 pandemic, stands in stark contrast to the much weaker response to funding vaccines for previous epidemics like Ebola or SARS.

The active interest displayed in controlling the pandemic in the rich countries shaped their own national responses as well as global policy, generating another outcome that made this pandemic unusual. The widespread use of lockdowns, mobility restrictions, and emphasis on 'social distancing' (more accurately described as 'physical distancing', which is the term that will be used in this book) could well have been the most effective ways of addressing the problem, though there have been different views on this even from within the scientific/medical community.[6] However, the containment of the disease necessarily requires certain conditions to ensure success: the ability of people to implement physical distancing norms in a feasible way, given their living conditions, and without having to compromise on basic necessities for survival; and the provision of, at least, minimum subsistence needs to those who are instructed to follow lockdown guidelines and avoid economic

---

[4]S. Subramanian and Debraj Ray, 'Covid-19 and other diseases: An "Animal Farm" perspective', *Ideas for India*, 23 February 2021.

[5]Ibid.

[6]See, for example, K. Farsalinos et al., 'Improved strategies to counter the COVID-19 pandemic: Lockdowns vs. primary and community healthcare', *Toxicology Reports,* 2021, Vol. 8, pp. 1–9.

activity, for the entire period of such lockdowns. Such conditions simply did not exist in large parts of the developing world, and may not have been fulfilled even in some developed countries.

However, the economic impact was significantly worse for most developing countries (excepting China and a few other countries in East Asia). These differences went well beyond the projected changes in economic activity or GDP: they were particularly evident in changes in wage incomes and livelihoods across regions. Apart from the obvious mental and physical health implications of lockdowns, this strategy had major economic impacts that went well beyond the results of the disease per se. The lockdowns themselves had varying effects on the control of the disease in different locations, with suppression of the infection in some areas and continued rise in others. But, they had, undoubtedly, direct effects on economic processes, reflected within national economies as well as on global trade and investment. These impacts have been so severe that they have led many analysts to mark this pandemic as the inflection point for global economic integration, catalysing and accelerating the reversal of globalization that some see as having begun a few years earlier.

Consider, for example, the impact on the supply of smartphones, now more than just an icon of globalization, but almost a necessity for economic and civic participation in a world which is becoming increasingly digital. The global production of smartphones mostly takes place in coastal Asia, especially in China, which was first affected by the disease. The temporary disruptions witnessed in the production of smartphones highlighted the fragility of the supply chain: essential components like some metals and 'raw earth' minerals could not be easily accessed; the logistics of moving both components and manufactured phones became far more complicated, making it harder to produce and sell. So, just when more people across the world sought to use smartphones because of lockdowns and other pandemic restrictions, their supply was badly affected, falling by around 40 per cent in April 2020 compared to the previous year.[7] Production rose in the second half of the year only due to China's ability to control the pandemic and resume economic activity. But the fragility of many other supply chains became underlined, and more multinational firms opted to reduce these risks by bringing down the geographical spread of production of goods as much as possible.

The more rapid proliferation of the disease and higher mortality rates in the advanced countries led to widespread adoption of the 'Wuhan model' that was used to contain the spread of the virus in China. This essentially involved lockdowns, curbing most social and economic activities beyond that deemed to be 'essential', and placing severe restrictions on people's mobility. In China, this strategy was adopted only in the province of Wuhan, the origin and first epicentre of the pandemic, and was utilized sparingly and for limited periods in other regions when there was evidence of new waves of the disease. But, in most advanced countries which saw new infections arising out of subsequent mutations of the virus, this became the default strategy. However, lockdowns essentially delay the spread of the infection, and the idea is to use that delay to boost healthcare systems and infrastructure, so they are only effective if this is done. Obviously, total or even partial lockdowns cannot be sustained indefinitely. Comparative experiences suggest that the more successful and effective strategy to contain the spread of the disease is not lockdown per se, but widespread testing, isolating positive cases, tracing their contacts, and treating patients. This may seem to be more expensive immediately, but it is ultimately cheaper if it works in limiting the spread of

[7]Nina Goetzen, 'Mobile phone shipments are down worldwide amid Coronavirus-related supply chain disruptions', *Insider Intelligence*, 7 May 2020.

the disease and when the costs of lost economic activities with lockdowns are factored in.

A lockdown-based strategy can be viable for limited periods in countries that have relatively wide social safety nets, with largely formal work forces and the ability to provide social protection and compensatory income to those whose livelihoods would be affected by lockdowns and closures. But in much of the developing world, as shown in what follows, most workers are informal, social protection systems are less developed, and governments have less fiscal space to spend enough to provide minimally adequate compensation for the loss of incomes resulting from lockdowns. The fact that such measures became the international norm (even if they were applied with varying degrees of stringency in different countries) had major effects across the global economy and within national economies.

The Domination of Informal Work in the Developing World

The worst material impacts of the lockdowns and other restrictions were felt by informal workers. They faced a dismal spectrum of probabilities: simply losing their jobs, or getting only a fraction of former wages, or missing out on incomes if they were self-employed. Formal workers typically get some legal and social protection when circumstances dictate that they cannot go to work, like continued pay or at least furloughs that ensure some benefits. By contrast, informal workers are not so fortunate: remuneration is entirely work-based. Barring just a handful of countries, very few governments in developing countries declared strong measures to counter these negative effects.

Who exactly are informal workers? The International Labour Organization (ILO) considers a worker to be informal if s/he is a worker whose social security is not paid for by the employer; is not entitled to paid annual leave and paid sick leave; or works in a household; or owns and runs an informal enterprise, typically in the form of self-employment, but also in micro-enterprises. Essentially, being an informal worker means that a person does not have any legal or social protection that would put some responsibility on the employer. This can span across all sectors—agriculture, of course, but also manufacturing, construction, and services—from farm workers to petty traders to domestic workers to those working in small manufacturing units. People who work in informal, unregistered enterprises, or in households, or own their own small-scale enterprises, are generally informal workers. But even formal organizations can also employ informal workers, on casual, daily wage, or part-time basis—and across the world, the tendency to employ more workers on informal contracts has been growing.

According to the ILO, 61 per cent of all employment was informal in 2018 (Figure 1.3), and most of this was also in the informal-sector enterprises that rarely, if ever, get the benefits of government subsidies or protection, even in periods of crisis. But in developed countries, employment is still predominantly formal, with 80 per cent of all workers on formal contracts, with some protection. In the emerging and developing countries, by contrast, two out of every three workers are informal. Most agriculturalists are informal or self-employed workers, but even in non-agricultural activities, informal workers were 60 per cent of all workers in the Global South. These are workers who lack most rights at work, decent working conditions, and most forms of social protection—except whatever minimal amounts may be provided by the state. They and their families are clearly the most vulnerable to any economic downturn. When such a downturn comes in the wake of an unprecedented public health calamity, the concerns are obviously multiplied.

Consider just some examples of how the impact of the pandemic and resulting lockdowns played out in the lives of informal workers in the developing world: the pregnant garment worker in Bangladesh who lost her job in April 2020, thereby losing not just her wages but any maternity benefits she might have got from her employer;[8] the women workers who were pushed out of informal employment in Mexico and Colombia and faced starvation before some government handouts were provided;[9] the sanitation workers in India who developed Covid-19 because of exposure during work, but after losing their daily wages on account of being sick, had to pay for their own treatment in private hospitals;[10] the street food vendors in Uganda who were first not allowed to ply their wares, then had to face official harassment and exposure to the disease to somehow manage to get some sales;[11] the Ethiopian and Nigerian migrant domestic workers in Lebanon, who were left stranded on the streets by their employers, with no shelter or compensation and unable to return home.[12] Compare their situation to workers in similar occupations in advanced economies, who were more likely to be in formal employment and so would have received sick pay when ill, continued wages or furlough pay even when they were not allowed to work because of lockdowns, and other benefits through most of the pandemic.

---

[8]Esmé Berkhout, Nick Galasso, Max Lawson, et al., *The Inequality Virus: Bringing together a world torn apart by Coronavirus through a fair, just and sustainable economy*, Oxfam, January 2021.

[9]Nora Lustig, V. Martinez, F. Sanz, and S. Younger, 'The impact of COVID-19 Lockdowns and Expanded Social Assistance on Inequality, Poverty and Mobility in Argentina, Brazil, Colombia and Mexico', ECINEQ, Society for the Study of Economic Inequality, 2020.

[10]K. J. Siddharth, Sylvia Karpagam, and Alwyn Prakash D'Souza, *Working at the Margins: A Report on the Conditions of Invisibilized Frontline Workers*, Bengaluru: Ashirwad Centre for Social Concern, 2020.

[11]Christopher Busiinge, 'Uganda's hungry food vendors: counting the cost of COVID-19', International Institute for Environment and Development, 11 June 2020.

[12]Berkhout, Galasso, Lawson, et al., *The Inequality Virus*.

Figure 1.3

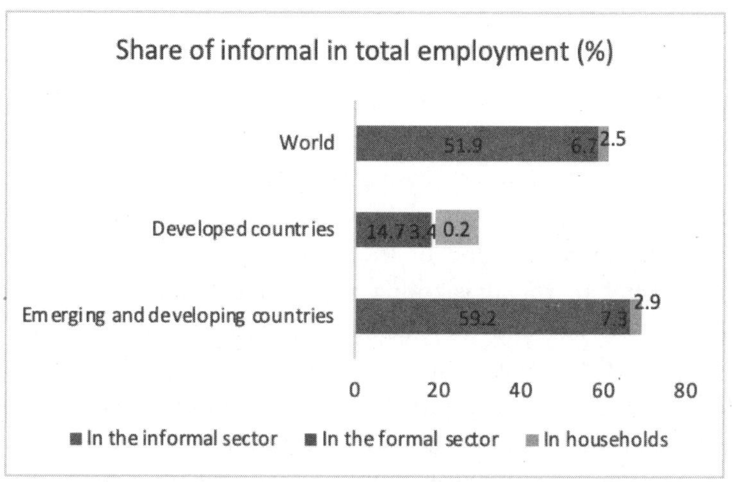

Source: Women and Men in the Informal Economy: A Statistical Picture, Geneva: ILO, 2018.

Figure 1.4: Informality across developing regions

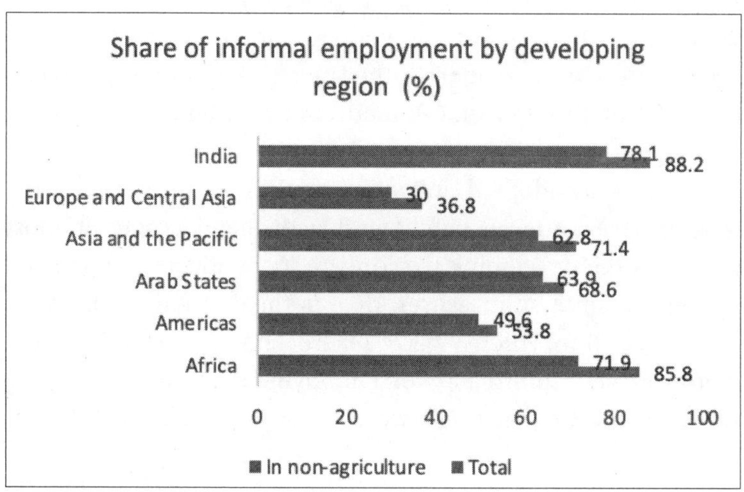

Source: Women and Men in the Informal Economy: A Statistical Picture, Geneva: ILO, 2018.

In the developing world, there are significant variations across regions, as Figure 1.4 indicates. Some of the countries imposing the most stringent lockdowns were the ones with high proportions of informal workers, who would not be protected against the loss of income during a lockdown. According to the ILO, many developing countries with extremely severe or moderately severe Covid-19 containment measures had disproportionately high shares of informal workers.[13] For example, India has one of the highest rates of employment informality in the developing world, much higher than the average of Asia and the Pacific or African countries—and it was also the country that implemented the most stringent lockdown in the early phase, with devastating consequences for employment and livelihoods of informal workers.

The purpose of the lockdowns was obviously to contain infections, build medical infrastructure, and ensure public health through this means. But that also required providing people with adequate nutrition and enabling workers and their families to follow rules that would minimize contagion. That is why income support and food provision for all, including informal workers, would have been essential, making sure that everyone had access to essential food and other necessities, whether directly provided or through time-bound cash transfers. But in many developing countries, these social protection measures were not universally adopted; in fact, except for a few countries, the measures were uneven, patchy, and inadequate. As a result, most people in the developing world were more adversely impacted by the containment measures, than in the developed countries.

In addition, there were macroeconomic consequences of the greater informality of employment in the developing world. It meant that there were fewer 'automatic stabilizers',

[13]International Labour Organisation 2020-2021, *ILO monitor: COVID-19 and the world of work*, Geneva: ILO, pp. 6–7.

like unemployment benefits or health insurance, which would prevent a complete collapse of workers' incomes. These would have mitigated the reduction of demand that results from lockdowns and similar closures, and there does seem to have been some positive effect of these in some advanced countries. But there was little or no such protection for most workers in the developing countries, so the restrictions on economic activity had more direct negative effects on aggregate demand, and therefore deeper and, likely, more prolonged declines in economic activity.

Inequalities in Fiscal Response

Lockdowns, closures, and restrictions on mobility meant a simultaneous attack on demand and supply. Previous regional and global economic and financial crises did not entail this near cessation of most economic activities. During lockdowns, many people (especially those without formal work contracts and in jobs that could not continue 'remotely') either lost their jobs or were deprived of incomes for a certain period. At the same time, production and distribution were restricted for all but essential commodities and services—and even for these, supply was affected in many cases because of the ways in which lockdowns were implemented and when policymakers did not pay attention to the supply chains and linkages that enabled production and distribution. These adverse effects were less marked in developed countries like the US and much of Europe, as well as in East Asia. In these countries, both fiscal and monetary policies were aggressively used to shore up incomes during the lockdown periods, and active efforts were made to ensure that the supply chains were maintained as far as possible. But in many other countries, especially in the developing world, supply chains were impacted; and in some cases, they were broken, while inadequate fiscal spending to ensure some income compensation and social protection meant that demand contracted and would take some time to recover.

In the wake of the pandemic, many developed countries put in place some of the biggest fiscal stimuli ever. Advanced economies as a group have provided significant *additional* funds during this period, both in terms of increased public spending and revenues foregone through tax concessions. They have also provided significant amounts through equity, loans, and guarantees of various kinds. Together these amounted to around 18 per cent of 2020 GDP, while the US spent a quarter of the first pandemic year's GDP![14] This level of fiscal increase has not been seen in capitalist economies outside war time, not even during the storied New Deal of President Roosevelt in the USA to combat the Great Depression.[15] Of the total global additional fiscal measures amounting to about $10.8 trillion, the ten advanced countries in G20 accounted for nearly 80 per cent, and the US alone accounted for almost half.[16]

In addition, monetary policy added to fiscal capacity at sub-national levels of government. From lower interest rates to central bank purchases of provincial and municipal bonds to new facilities for lending to different sectors and enterprises, the US Federal Reserve (the US central bank) sought to keep borrowing costs down and provide liquidity for public agencies. The 'exorbitant privilege' of the US as the holder of the world's favoured reserve currency obviously gave it the freedom to take these measures to prop up its own economy, and plan on doing even more. But other developed countries also put in place large fiscal packages. Japan's Emergency Economic Package was more

---

[14]IMF Fiscal Affairs Department, 'Fiscal Monitor Database of Country Fiscal Measures in Response to the COVID-19 Pandemic', IMF, April 2021.

[15]Bill Dupor, 'How Recent Fiscal Interventions Compare with the New Deal', *Regional Economist,* Federal Reserve Bank of St. Louis, 13 July 2021.

[16]IMF Fiscal Affairs Department, 'Fiscal Monitor Database of Country Fiscal Measures in Response to the COVID-19 Pandemic', IMF, October 2021.

than 21 per cent of GDP, Australia's increased spending was nearly 10 per cent, and Canada's was 8.4 per cent. In December 2020, the EU put in motion a 'recovery plan' worth $2.2 trillion, that would also provide a significant fiscal stimulus, and for the first time, allowed joint borrowing by the members of the EU and fiscal transfers between countries.[17] This meant that across Europe, governments would be spending significantly more.

As a result, the pandemic led developed country governments, that had advocated fiscal conservatism and promoted austerity, to drop that perspective quite rapidly. This also meant that economic declines in the advanced countries were less than had been originally projected because of the aggressive crisis response policies they adopted. By contrast, in most developing countries, the fiscal response was underwhelming at best. Emerging market economies devoted on average less than 6 per cent of GDP on additional public spending and revenues foregone, and 4.2 per cent of GDP on equity, loans, and guarantees. In low income countries, fiscal measures came to only 2.1 per cent of GDP. Most governments in the developing world remained hesitant to engage in significantly more public spending, and some (particularly India and Mexico) even pursued austerity during the crisis.

This was not because developing countries faced any less of an economic challenge: if anything, the lockdowns and global headwinds caused much greater macroeconomic disaster than in the advanced world. (One important exception to this is China, which is so much of an outlier that it is not even considered in this discussion of the relative impact of the pandemic on advanced and developing countries.) This fiscal reticence reflected the unwillingness or inability of governments in developing countries, especially the poorer ones, to extend

---

[17]'Recovery plan for Europe', European Commission, see https://ec.europa.eu/info/strategy/recovery-plan-europe_en.

themselves, even when faced with a crisis as severe as this. This was largely the result of the shift to a neoliberal development strategy, a core element of which is fiscal conservatism that reins in the government deficit. That shift, in turn, was partly due to conditions imposed by the International Monetary Fund (IMF) and World Bank when they provided loans to countries,[18] and partly due to voluntary action by developing country governments wishing to earn brownie points to attract foreign investors. However, in the face of the pandemic, the IMF changed its position, at least in terms of statements by its top leadership, and became more open to enhanced public spending. Unfortunately, there were still double standards for developing countries, as negotiations with countries facing severe debt problems (such as Ecuador, Argentina, and Nigeria) still saw the IMF requiring fiscal austerity and regressive taxation that would hit the incomes of ordinary people.

But even without IMF pressure, developing countries mostly did not respond to the crisis with significantly more stimulus spending. Why was this, even when they knew that advanced country governments were spending so much more? Much of this difference in fiscal response can be explained by other, more systemic inequalities in the global economy. Developing countries that do not issue internationally accepted reserve currencies (like US dollars, euro, yen, or now the Chinese RenMinBi) simply do not have the fiscal freedom available to those that do. First of all, any increased demand for imports that would come about from fiscal expansion would have to be paid with foreign exchange—which might require borrowing in these currencies. During the pandemic, this import dependence could have been worsened by domestic supply shocks resulting from partial or total lockdowns. Financing these increased imports

[18]'The Pandemic and the Public Sector: ActionAid Policy Brief', 13 October 2020.

became much more difficult because of the fall in export earnings and in remittances from workers abroad during the pandemic and global recession. So, much of the additional borrowing would have to be in foreign exchange—and this could eventually become exorbitant because of variable interest rates.

Second, as more developing countries liberalized their capital account transactions, they made themselves more vulnerable to capital flight even by residents—and since fiscal deficits are generally frowned upon by global finance, they feared that even announcing more government spending could trigger capital flight. This fear was reinforced by warnings from conservative economists, consultancy companies, and ratings by credit rating agencies, which are all hardwired to react negatively to bigger government deficits in developing countries, regardless of context. The fear of financial markets, thus, acts as a major constraint on even the most obvious and urgently required policies.

Fears about capital flight were confirmed by the experience of March–April 2020, when there were significant outflows from emerging markets and developing countries, simply with the news of the pandemic. There were more reasons to worry than before, because many developing countries had become reliant on external funding as they allowed more capital to come into domestic equity and debt markets. With growing reliance on private sources of external capital even in poor countries (as more low income economies have been discovered as 'frontier markets'), the share of private non-guaranteed debt and portfolio capital increased in total capital inflows to developing countries. Aside from foreign currency debt, more than a quarter of even local currency debt is held by foreigners, making them very vulnerable.[19] Meanwhile, liberalized exchange rules in most

[19]UNCTAD, 'From Global Pandemic to Prosperity for All: Avoiding Another Lost Decade', *Trade and Development Report*, Geneva: United Nations, 2020.

developing countries made it easier for domestic residents to shift their funds abroad.

For countries that did not face immediate external economic threats, there were concerns about domestic resource mobilization. Domestically, the pandemic and the lockdowns led to massive declines in tax collection and other public revenues, as economic activity slumped. Even if government spending simply remained at earlier levels, this decline in revenues would, on its own, generate an increase in the fiscal deficit. But more government spending was obviously required if only to deal with the pandemic. To pay for this, governments could borrow directly from the central bank, which involves a monetized deficit, or printing more money—something that most advanced countries have been doing, in spades, during this crisis. This is the cheapest and most obvious solution to finance the deficit. Yet, most developing country governments, with a few exceptions, have been remarkably hesitant to do so. Even countries that do not have immediate debt repayment concerns are showing less inclination to raise public spending to the levels necessary, just to stop the process of economic decline.

The usual reason why this is opposed is the fear of inflation: the idea is that printing more money will inevitably lead to price rises that will cut into people's real incomes. But if there is excess capacity and unemployment and people are so deprived of incomes that their demand is already very depressed, then new spending creates demand that causes production to increase in response. The threat of inflation only arises if there were supply bottlenecks in some areas—and if so, some of the government spending can be directed to remedy that. It is worth noting that the massive increases in money creation and larger public deficits financed by central banks in advanced countries in the 12 years after the Global Financial Crisis did not result in higher inflation. The increase in inflation rates from early 2021 essentially resulted from supply chain disruptions, made worse by geopolitical instability.

External debt concerns also loomed large in many developing countries. Many developing countries were already experiencing debt distress before the Covid-19 'black swan'. There was a massive accumulation of debt in both developed and developing countries since the 2008 global financial crisis (GFC). In developing countries, a growing part of this debt was held by private creditors and the burgeoning bond markets. Not all of this was sovereign debt issued by governments, but now governments know that when private liabilities cannot be met, they are likely to have to step in and bail out private borrowers. Well before the pandemic, it was evident that a minor event—some 'known unknown'—could have far-reaching destabilizing affects which could precipitate financial and debt crises.[20] But the long period of extraordinarily loose monetary policies in advanced economies after the GFC meant that asset prices in both advanced and emerging market economies kept rising, and this allowed investors and borrowers to underplay the concerns about mounting debt levels. Unfortunately, asset bubbles do not last forever, and when they burst, the value of the collateral underlying the debt shrinks. By contrast, debts do not deflate on their own, and then the problems of repayment become intense, so that, in extreme cases, they can only be resolved through state or central-bank intervention.

In 2018, the total debt (private, public, domestic, and external) across developing countries was equal to almost twice their combined GDP—the highest it has ever been.[21] There was a big build-up of private debt of non-financial corporations, which amounted to nearly three-quarters of

[20]UNCTAD, 'Power, Platforms and the Free Trade Delusion', *Trade and Development Report*, Geneva: United Nations, 2018.

[21]UNCTAD, 'The Coronavirus Shock: A Story of Another Global Crisis Foretold and What Policymakers Should Be Doing About It', *Trade and Development Report Update*, Geneva: United Nations, 9 March 2020.

total debt in developing countries (a much higher ratio than in advanced economies). According to UNCTAD, inherently volatile 'foreign shadow financial institutions' played a major role in fueling this accumulation. Around one-third of private non-financial corporate debt in developing countries (with the exception of China) was denominated in foreign currency and held by external creditors. Very large amounts of sovereign-debt repayments on short-maturity international bonds were becoming due. It was estimated by UNCTAD (2020) that as much as $1.62 trillion of external debt was due to be repaid by developing countries in 2020, with another $1.08 trillion due in 2021. Obviously, these numbers changed over the year, because the inability of many private and sovereign borrowers to repay meant that much of this debt was rescheduled, effectively kicking the (ever-growing) can down the road for a later reckoning. Debt repayment would have been a major struggle even earlier; the Covid-19 crisis made it impossible.

Prior to the pandemic, bond portfolio inflows into developing countries (including into the so called 'frontier' low-income economies) were significantly more than equity portfolio flows, with cumulative flows since 2005 of approximately $2.5 trillion of bond inflows (denominated in both foreign and local currency) compared to around $1 trillion for equity inflows.[22] But in the post-Covid economic context, the ability of many of these economies to meet their obligations was very much open to question. The half-hearted support of the advanced economies (for example, in the form of Debt Service Suspension Initiative or DSSI) was far too little. In fact, only forty-four of the seventy-three eligible countries opted for the DSSI. Others held back since a DSSI-recipient tag would reduce the sovereign credit rating of the country concerned and limit access to additional

---

[22]'Markets in the Time of COVID-19', *Global Financial Stability Report*, April 2020.

private credit. In the circumstances, fearing a balance of payments crisis that would necessitate even greater austerity, countries tended to curtail incremental government spending.

Credit rating agencies started declaring negative outlooks for several key emerging markets, such as Chile, Colombia, Mexico, Indonesia, and Malaysia.[23] Despite this, foreign-investor appetite for bonds issued in developing countries only grew in this period, with significant increases in borrowing by all emerging-market governments from international bond. Foreign investment in equities in emerging markets also surged, as the monetary expansion and low interest rates in advanced economies encouraged financial investors to search for higher yields using borrowed funds.[24] This was likely to be ephemeral, as even slightly higher interest returns in advanced economies, or any untoward shifts in any one emerging market, could easily lead to a reversal in the notoriously fickle international bond markets. Indeed, as it appeared more likely by late 2021 that the US Federal Reserve would move to monetary tightening and higher interest rates within a year rather than later, such concerns became more widespread.

It may not be surprising that countries with external debt concerns would be wary of adding to their debts. However, examples of self-imposed fiscal discipline proliferated even among countries that did not immediately face such concerns about sovereign debt, mainly because of the impression it might create among global investors. For example, in India, the Ministry of Finance chief economic adviser justified the pathetically low initial government response (of less than 1 per cent of GDP proposed additional spending) by explicitly linking the possibility of fiscal stimulus packages with the country's

---

[23]'Credit Conditions Emerging Markets: A Vaccine Won't Erase All Risks', S & P Global Ratings, 3 December 2020.

[24]Jonathan Wheatley, 'Foreign investors dash into emerging markets at swiftest pace since 2013', *Financial Times*, 18 December 2020.

sovereign ratings—even though it condemned the country to an economic collapse with hundreds of millions facing poverty and hunger.[25] In South Africa, the deputy finance minister was attacked for the perfectly reasonable suggestion that the central bank should buy government bonds directly, as was already common practice in much of the advanced world.[26] In this self-imposed neoliberal policy climate, fiscal expansion through increased public expenditure was automatically ruled out because of the possibility that it could result in capital flight. Of course, it would be possible to avoid this by instituting capital controls that would prevent extreme volatility of capital flows, but this was also seen in the same policymaking circles as an unacceptable measure because it was assumed to frighten away foreign investors. Indeed, most developing countries that have succumbed to international financial integration (for the dubious pleasure of being described as 'emerging markets') find that straying from this comes with immediate threats and costs imposed by international rating agencies, bond-market investors, and global creditors.

Such a position is absurd, not just because it prevents the government from meeting its obligations to the citizenry, but because it adds to future economic problems. Significantly increased public expenditure is absolutely essential for most developing economies to address their public health challenges and to even attempt economic revival. Fiscal austerity at this point would have the inevitable effect of further aggravating the downturn in economic activity, thereby also causing tax revenues to decline further. In any case, global finance is hardly likely to be attracted to devastated economies, other than for

---

[25]Gaurav Noronha and Deepshikha Sikarwar, 'Coronavirus: There's no free lunch, says CEA on demand for big-bang stimulus', *Economic Times*, 6 May 2020.

[26]Paul Richardson, 'South Africa's Masonda Backs Central Bank Bond Purchases', *Bloomberg*, 3 May 2020.

a few forays to buy up existing assets on the cheap. However, despite the counterproductive nature of such a strategy, it is the one that continues to be advocated by global finance. Even the IMF, which accepted and even proposed increases in public spending in developing countries during the pandemic, argued that it must be swiftly followed by retrenchment, as early as 2021. Most countries receiving emergency loans from the IMF had clauses in their agreements like this one for Ghana: 'The government (will) remain fully committed to maintaining macroeconomic stability and will pursue medium-term policies consistent with fiscal consolidation.'[27]

The expression of this particular global inequality was complex, but no less lethal for that. It prevented many, if not most, developing countries from increasing public spending at a time when failure to do so had devastating effects on the health of the people and the level of economic activity and employment. This could become an even more disastrous strategy as the existential threat of climate change becomes even more evident. In many developing and low-income countries, the pandemic driven disruptions in food supply only exacerbated their already severe problems with unfavourable climate events that damaged crops and triggered food shortages and price spikes.[28]

The Impact on the Global Trade and Finance

The global economic impact of this pandemic was already immense, dwarfing anything experienced in living memory. The shock to the global economy was certainly much bigger than that of the 2008 global financial crisis, and has been compared to

---

[27]Soren Ambrose, 'In the midst of the pandemic, why is the IMF still pushing austerity on the Global South?', *Open Democracy,* 13 October 2020.

[28]'Impacts of COVID-19 on food security and nutrition: developing effective policy responses to address the hunger and malnutrition pandemic', Rome: FAO, September 2020.

the Great Depression, although that lasted for nearly a decade. Even the two World Wars of the twentieth century, while they disrupted supply chains and devastated physical infrastructure and populations, did not involve the restrictions on mobility and economic activity that are still in place in many countries today in the wake of fears about public health.

The global economy was already decelerating in the previous year, with changes in world GDP, and trade volumes and prices significantly lower than the previous year. The Covid-19-driven economic crisis was evident almost everywhere except in China, which managed to contain the spread of the virus relatively early and therefore showed a sharp recovery from the second quarter of 2020, even though growth decelerated. However, in the first half of 2020, collapses in global trade affected all countries and hit certain sectors in particular (with the least affected being food items). Despite smaller shares of global trade, the decline in trade values and volumes was likely to have affected developing countries more. Because they do not have internationally accepted currencies, they have to receive foreign exchange through trade, remittance, or capital flows in order to import and make other payments such as on their external debt. During the first phase of national lockdowns across major economies, cross-border trade in goods—other than those deemed 'essential'—effectively ceased in many countries, and the subsequent revival was weak. While trade volumes and values declined across the board, the sharpest price declines were in primary commodities, which are of greater export importance for developing countries.

Within trade in services, global tourism and the travel sector, which include services such as hotels, restaurants, tour operators, and travel agencies, were probably the worst hit, since they were directly impacted by mobility restrictions, border closures, and reduced appetite of tourists for foreign travel because of increased health risks. Developing countries have also been more impacted by the decline in tourism and travel-related services than developed countries: such travel accounted for nearly one-third of the services exports of developing countries, and half for the Least Developed Countries.[29] Other cross-border services that could not be delivered electronically also contracted sharply. Developing countries are also, in general, much more dependent on remittances from migrant workers in other (typically advanced) countries and such transfers were also hard hit in the ongoing crisis.

These collapses in economic activity should have affected global finance, but financial markets proved to be remarkably resilient, with stock markets defying gravity and economic reality, and cross-border capital flows very volatile but still showing substantial risk appetite. As many economists have shown,[30] financial markets, rarely, if ever, function like textbook-perfect markets, because of the lack of information about the future, as well as the fact that some players in the market know things that others do not, and global capital markets are classic examples of this. That is why herd behaviour, contagion (when something that happens in one place or market spreads to other markets even without cause), and apparently 'inexplicable' movements of capital are quite common. However, there is no doubt that global finance was greatly assisted by the rapid and massive stimulus measures undertaken by advanced country governments.

In the immediate response to the pandemic, in March and April 2020, private finance responded with a 'flight to safety' out of developing countries to advanced economies, in particular, the US. There was a reversal of portfolio flows of over $100

---

[29]'Trade in Services in the Context of Covid-19', World Trade Organization, 28 May 2020.

[30]Joseph E. Stiglitz, 'Markets, Market Failures, and Development', *American Economic Review*, Vol. 79, No. 2, 1989, pp. 197–203; Jan A. Kregel, *Economic Development and Financial Instability: Selected Essays*, Rainer Kattel (ed.), London, New York, Melbourne: Anthem Press, 2014.

billion to these countries in the month of March alone.[31] But by summer, capital inflows were flowing back to the emerging markets and developing countries, and they continued to increase through the rest of the year. By late 2020, there was a significant recovery of net inflows into emerging markets.[32] This revival of capital-flows into emerging markets was surprising, because debt concerns were already looming large. Financial bets and contracts made in the pre-Covid-19 era had become unrealistic and could not be plausibly sustained beyond a point. Most debts, including those incurred in private bond markets, were effectively unpayable and there were also concerns about possible insurance claims that could wipe out some insurers. Despite this, there was apparently undiminished appetite of global investors for risky financial assets of emerging markets.

The renewed flows of capital to developing countries were most likely due to the extraordinarily expansive monetary policies that were introduced in the advanced economies. Central banks in the US and in other developed countries dramatically increased the flow of credit to banks and even non-bank lenders, and cut interest rates to near zero, zero, or even negative levels. As noted above, the US Federal Reserve not only bought debt of all kinds to ease the pressure on the debt markets within the US, it also effectively provided bailouts to banks and other financial institutions. These policies created incentives for investors to exploit interest rate differentials across countries, by borrowing cheap in advanced economies and investing in short-term assets in developing countries where the interest rates were higher. Various other emerging-market assets (such as in equity and bond markets) became lucrative even when they offered relatively low nominal rates of return,

[31] UNCTAD, 'From Global Pandemic to Prosperity for All: Avoiding Another Lost Decade'.

[32] 'Vaccine, U.S. election news drive record $76.5 billion inflow to EM: IIF', *Reuters,* 1 December 2020.

simply because access to finance became so very cheap for global investors. As monetary tightening in the rich countries became more likely from early 2022 onwards, the likelihood of more volatility in capital flows to emerging markets and other developing countries also increased.

So the outcome for developing countries was not really to be celebrated, since such capital inflows made them more vulnerable. They could, once again, experience large swings in capital flows that did not necessarily reflect changes in their own policies and prospects, but depended much more on policies and other changes in the advanced economies. Many developing countries had already experienced precisely this process, from the Latin American countries that got large inflows in the 1970s, only to see them reversed in the early 1980s when the Reagan administration raised interest rates in the US; to countries like Indonesia, Malaysia, the Philippines, and Thailand that were favoured by global investors in the 1990s because of their high exports, but then experienced rapid outflows that led to the Southeast Asian crisis in 1997–98.[33] These and many other experiences made developing countries realize that the selective targeting of particular emerging markets by global investors can be problematic, because the country chosen as the favoured destination may change. In the Covid-19 context, there were also new fears generated by the pandemic and the possibility that different rates of recovery across advanced economies and developing countries, or changes in macroeconomic policies in the US and Europe, could trigger more episodes of capital flight.

As a result, even as developing countries attempted to address

---

[33]Jayati Ghosh and C. P. Chandrasekhar, 'The costs of "coupling": the global crisis and the Indian economy', *Cambridge Journal of Economics*, Vol. 33, Issue 4, July 2009, pp. 725–39; 'The Indian economic reform process and the implications of the Southeast Asian crisis', *Employment and Training Papers*, Geneva: International Labour Office, 1999.

the real economy crisis they were engulfed in, they also had to deal with processes generated by the monetary policy response so widely favoured in the advanced economies, of injecting even more cheap money into the system. Without policies that would prevent a speculative surge in financial markets riding on that increased liquidity, such as capital controls, they were buffeted by these highly speculative movements of capital in a way that most advanced economies were not. This, in turn, generated financial fragility that could explode with even slight shifts in investor expectations.

Vaccine Apartheid

As if these processes of intensification of global inequality were not enough, a further push was given by the processes of developing and distributing the vaccine candidates that had emerged to control the pandemic by the end of the year. It would appear to be obvious that a pandemic can be overcome only when it is overcome everywhere, making an every-country-for-itself approach irrational. And yet, that is exactly what happened. The approval in the US and Europe of three major vaccine candidates (from Pfizer-BioNTech, Moderna, and AstraZeneca) provided hopes of some light at the end of the tunnel and the possibility of defeating the pandemic. However, instead of following some internationally accepted principles for equitable distribution, rich country governments scrambled to lay claim to vaccine doses, thereby confirming the bleak prediction that wealthy countries and individuals would monopolize early doses of any effective vaccine. As a result, even by the end of 2021, only ten per cent of the population of low income countries had been vaccinated, while in some advanced economies, third and even fourth shots were being offered to the population. In the rich countries, vaccination rates were only constrained by vaccine hesitancy among some groups, whereas in much of the developing world, absolute scarcity was the binding constraint.

Figure 1.5

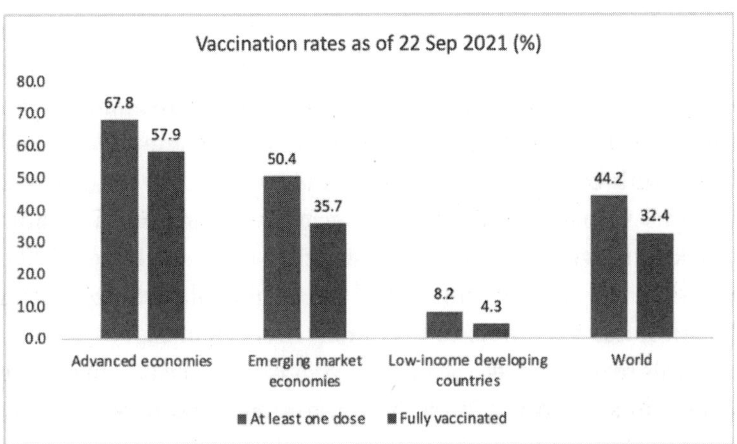

Source: Data from IMF World Economic Outlook, October 2021.

The Covid-19 Vaccines Global Access Facility (COVAX)—led by the World Health Organization, the Coalition for Epidemic Preparedness Innovations (CEPI), and Gavi (the Vaccine Alliance)—had supposedly been established precisely to prevent this outcome. The COVAX Facility aims to accelerate Covid-19 vaccine development, secure doses for all countries, and distribute those doses fairly, beginning with the highest risk groups. In other words, the facility was created partly to prevent hoarding by rich-country governments. By the end of 2020, more than 150 countries, representing nearly two-thirds of the world's population, had joined. The sixty-four higher-income countries, including twenty-nine in Europe, made commitments to provide both funds and vaccine doses to the facility and would also have access to the vaccines in the COVAX list, and pay for their doses individually. The ninety-two lower-income member countries would receive their doses free of charge.

The COVAX plan was to distribute vaccines in two phases. In the first phase, all participating countries would receive doses proportionate to their populations. It would begin with enough doses of the vaccine to immunize the 3 per cent of their population at highest risk, especially frontline workers in health and social care. Additional doses would then be delivered, until 20 per cent of each country's population—beginning with those most in danger from Covid-19, such as the elderly and those with comorbidities—is immunized. In the second phase, vaccines would be delivered to specific countries based on how quickly the virus is spreading; whether other pathogens (like measles) are also spreading; and how vulnerable the country's health infrastructure is to becoming overwhelmed.

This appeared to be a fair system, especially given the constraints on production. But the facility remained hugely underfunded and could not purchase the vaccines required for free distribution to poor countries, as planned. Worst of all, rich countries, including COVAX participants, competed to secure bilateral deals with pharmaceutical companies outside of COVAX. Within a month of the regulatory approval being granted to the first three vaccines (by Pfizer-BioNTech, Moderna, and AstraZeneca), advanced country governments accounting for only 14 per cent of the world's population moved to place orders for around 85 per cent of the estimated entire production for 2021.[34] This vaccine grab by rich countries—many of which preordered vaccines to the tune of several multiples of their own populations—meant that most of the world would get safe and approved vaccines only in late 2022, and in some cases not until 2023 or 2024.

In mid-January 2021, the head of the World Health Organization noted that while 39 million vaccine doses had

[34]Jayati Ghosh, 'Vaccine apartheid', *Project Syndicate,* 16 November 2020.

already been administered in the rich countries, in one poor country, only twenty-five doses had been given. He expressed his concern thus: 'I need to be blunt: the world is on the brink of a catastrophic moral failure—and the price of this failure will be paid with lives and livelihoods in the world's poorest countries.'[35] Over the course of the year, the inequalities in vaccine distribution did not reduce but grew even starker, as eighty high and middle income nations began to provide booster vaccine shots to their own population rather than providing even what they had committed to donate to COVAX. By late October 2021, the number of boosters administered around the world (nearly a million a day) was three times the number of first or second dose vaccines administered in low-income countries (about 330,000 doses a day),[36] such that governments in the rich countries provided more booster shots to their people than all the vaccines provided in poor countries.[37] It is true that other vaccines were being developed, in China, Russia, Cuba, and India, but questions were raised about inadequate testing and hasty regulatory approvals without completing the required trials and other processes. (The Indian experience is discussed in Chapter 3.)

The constraints on expanded production of the approved drugs were also hugely problematic. Because these companies had been granted patent rights that gave them a monopoly on production, supplies were limited to their own capacities and the licences they chose to issue. The companies had got these restrictive patents, known as intellectual property rights

---

[35]'WHO chief warns against "catastrophic moral failure" in COVID-19 vaccine access', *UN News*, 18 January 2021.

[36]WHO Chief Scientist Soumya Swaminathan at WHO press conference on 29 October 2021. See 'COVID-19 Virtual Press conference transcript - 28 October 2021', see https://www.who.int/publications.

[37]'Covid boosters in rich countries outnumber all jabs among poor nations', *Financial Times*, 19 December 2021.

(IPRs), even though they had mostly or entirely relied on public resources like prior public research and large subsidies from governments to develop these vaccines.[38] Advanced country governments repeatedly blocked attempts in the WTO by India, South Africa, and some other developing countries to suspend patents for Covid-19 vaccines and related treatment, even though such suspension would also benefit their own populations.[39] The WTO agreement on Trade-Related Intellectual Property Rights (TRIPS) specifically allows for compulsory licensing, and the Doha Declaration on TRIPS and Public Health explicitly mentions public health emergencies as adequate cause to issue compulsory licences that would allow other companies to produce essential drugs. It is difficult to imagine a more appropriate situation to trigger such a strategy, yet, even into early 2022, this was blocked by advanced country governments, presumably because of the lobbying power of multinational pharma companies.

This obviously had implications on dealing with the pandemic, since it raised concerns that mutations of the virus emerging in the non-inoculated populations could re-emerge to infect even those who had been vaccinated. It also adds to the economic inequality already described. The longer countries have to deal with the pandemic, the longer it will take for economies to recover and livelihoods to be restored, and the worse will be the internal and external economic constraints that developing countries have to face.

For these and other reasons, a post-pandemic global economic recovery is not likely with existing policies. The role of public spending and regulation will be pivotal in many ways, not only as a driver of demand and sustainer of employment,

---

[38]'Mariana Mazzucato, Jayati Ghosh, and Els Torreele on waiving covid patents', *The Economist,* 20 April 2021.

[39]Achal Prabhala, Arjun Jayadev, and Dean Baker, 'Want vaccines fast? Suspend intellectual property right', *New York Times*, 7 December 2020.

but also to enable redistribution, ensure financial stability, and contribute to future resilience. Yet, in the recent past, across the world, the public-sector roles in these were replaced by finance-led schemes and reliance on 'public–private partnerships' that moved ever further from these goals.[40] A fundamental re-orientation of economic policymaking would be required, with major changes in national strategies and in the international economic architecture.

[40]Nelson H. Barbosa-Filho and Alex Izurieta, 'The Risk of a Second Wave of Post-Crisis Frailty in the World Economy', *International Journal of Political Economy*, Vol. 49, No. 4, 21 January 2021, pp. 278–303.

chapter 2

INDIA BEFORE COVID-19

I. The Health of the Economy

In early 2020, India was politically an unsettled country. This was not really expected. The previous year, in May 2019, the Modi government had been re-elected to power with an even stronger mandate than before, which ensured a comfortable majority in parliament. It was suggested, especially by the ruling party, that the ensuing political stability would spill over into better economic performance as well. Yet from about the middle of 2019, there were growing public protests by different groups: farmers[1], students[2], workers[3]—all concerned with falling incomes,

[1]Puneet Kumar Sharma, 'Farmers from UP march towards Delhi to protest over agri crisis, heavy security deployed', *India Today*, 21 September 2019; 'Kisan long march: Thousands of farmers begin protest march from Nashik to Mumbai', *Scroll.in*, 21 February 2019.

[2]Some student protests were over fee hikes and denying students their rights, see 'Education for all? Universities across India fight fee hikes', *India Today*, 1 December 2019; others reflected student engagement with wider issues such as concerns over citizenship laws, such as Hannah Ellis-Petersen, 'India protests: students condemn "barbaric" police', *The Guardian*, 17 December 2019; still others resulted from open violent attacks on students and teachers that were not prevented and subsequently not properly investigated by the local police forces, such as 'Fresh student protests hit India over university attack', *DW*, 6 January 2020.

[3]Workers' protests erupted in many different locations, and also led up to one of the largest general strikes in India in early 2020, 'Strike by millions of workers hit businesses in India', *AP*, 8 January 2020; and Jamie Woodcock,

declining material prospects, more oppressive conditions and attempts by central and state governments to stifle their voices. The abrupt move on 5 August 2019 to dismember the state of Jammu and Kashmir into three Union Territories directly ruled by the Centre, and subsequent suppression of democratic rights in Kashmir,[4] including through curbs on mobility, freedom of speech, telecom and internet blackout, was a chilling taste of things that could come to the rest of India.[5]

In the last few months of 2019, more general peaceful public protests swept widely across the country, some (like the peaceful sit-in of women in Shaheen Bagh in Delhi)[6] capturing the imagination of people within India and across the world. These occurred as more and more people opposed a new Citizenship Amendment Act that had been hurriedly rushed through parliament, on the ground that it effectively discriminated by religion, rendering Muslims more prone to being 'denied' their basic citizenship. But the widespread nature of the protests, occurring across large metropoles and small towns and even villages, the huge crowds that they managed to attract and the growing involvement of young people, all pointed to more basic dissatisfaction with conditions in the country and its direction. This reflected not just political concerns but economic issues and social divides.

Indeed, the economic concerns were probably even greater than the political issues. Well before the impact of the

---

'India General Strike 2019', *Notes From Below,* 10 January 2019.

[4]'India: Abuses Persist in Jammu and Kashmir', Human Rights Watch, 4 August 2020.

[5]Ipsita Chakravarty, 'What exactly did the August 5 decisions achieve in Jammu and Kashmir?', *Scroll.in,* 5 August 2020.

[6]For more detailed considerations of the nature of this particular protest and its impact, see Seema Mustafa (ed.) *Shaheen Bagh and the Idea of India*, New Delhi: Speaking Tiger, 2020; Ziya us Salam and Uzma Ausaf, *Shaheen Bagh: From A Protest To A Movement*, New Delhi: Bloomsbury India, 2020.

pandemic was felt, the Indian economy was already quite sick. Every relevant indicator—output, employment, investment, consumption, real wages, sales of different goods and services—suggested slowdown or even decline. Some indicators had been deteriorating for several years, while others showed more recent but still significant declines particularly from 2017.

This was quite a change from the previous decade, when India was regarded (along with China) as one of the 'success stories' of globalization, likely to emerge into a giant economy and global economic power in the twenty-first century. The perception of a vibrant democracy on the move, especially in economic terms, was reinforced by a domestic economic boom that was relatively prolonged. An increasingly confident capitalist class started taking on the world through investment abroad; there was euphoria in the financial markets; and growing self-confidence among the elite, professional, and middle classes. That changed in the 2010s, as domestic and global investors began to recognize what should have been evident even during the boom phase: the fragility of the Indian balance of payments, lack of employment generation, poor infrastructure development, and growing inequality.

Despite this, there is a common but misleading narrative about the economic trajectory of the past two decades, which states that growth for at least two decades from the early 1990s was unleashed by globalization and liberalization, while the subsequent slowdown was because of 'policy paralysis' and lack of continuing market-oriented and privatizing reforms. This view misinterprets both phases. The boom of the 2000s was related to financial deregulation, which sparked a retail credit boom and combined with fiscal concessions to spur consumption among the richer sections of the population (around 100 million people). There was a substantial rise in profit shares in the economy, and the share of finance, insurance, and real estate activities in GDP went up from 12 per cent in 1990–91 to 16 per cent in 2010–11. The expansion of finance enabled a credit-financed consumption splurge among the rich and the middle classes, especially in urban areas. During the upswing, private investment rates rose, and debt-financed housing investment and private consumption of the elite and burgeoning middle classes became the principal stimulus for growth.[7] There were rapid increases in national income, but insufficient public spending, low employment generation, and persistent agrarian crisis meant that the majority of the population did not benefit much and mass consumption stayed low.

This was the result of an economic strategy that relied on big capital to deliver more investment, which was expected to create faster growth, higher productivity, and more formal sector jobs. At least, that was the goal. And in pursuit of this goal, large private companies were incentivized in every possible way: through relatively cheap credit (much of which was not repaid), subsidized inputs, cheap land, and natural resources—and, of course, cheap labour. Banks were encouraged to lend aggressively, which they did in the state of euphoria typical of a boom. In fact, state-owned commercial banks were actually pushed into risky lending for long-term investments, something that commercial banks are not really supposed to do.

This strategy actually worked during the boom of 2003 to 2012, when GDP grew rapidly and investment rates picked up. Even the global financial crisis caused only a temporary blip, creating a complacent belief that this trajectory could run for ever. But there were many adverse fallouts of this particular path: terrible environmental damage, growing bad loans with banks, rising inequality, and a proliferation of 'scams' that were the by-product of all these incentives being offered to big capitalists. Significantly, the boom did not generate the expected increase in good quality employment: formal jobs barely increased at

---

[7]Ghosh and Chandrasekhar, 'The costs of "coupling"'.

all, and even informal work grew at a measly rate of around 2 per cent per annum, while the potential labour force expanded much faster. Real wages did increase until 2011–12, but the share of wages in total national income fell.[8]

This process was similar to the speculative bubble-led progress in several other developed and developing countries; and it had the same problem of lack of sustainability. It is well-known now that debt-driven bubbles usually end in tears, whether in rich developed countries or in 'emerging markets'. In the Indian case, the lack of sustainability was accentuated by social and political problems that were driven by the unequal pattern of growth. Despite some reductions in income poverty, the growth process excluded the bulk of Indians from the benefits. There was persistence of widespread multidimensional poverty; stagnant formal employment; poor nutrition and food insecurity of a significant proportion of the population; the inability to ensure basic needs of housing, sanitation, and adequate healthcare to the population as a whole; very unequal access to education, and uneven quality of schooling. There were also problems caused by the very pattern of economic growth: aggravated regional imbalances; greater inequalities in the control over assets and in access to incomes; dispossession and displacement of people from land and livelihood without adequate compensation and rehabilitation; severe ecological stress arising from ruthless exploitation of nature and unsustainable patterns of production and consumption.

Some of these depressing features reflected the lack of structural change that is usually seen as a necessary part of the development process.[9] The labour force did not shift out of low productivity activities, especially in agriculture, to higher

---

[8]International Labour Organization, *India Wage Report: Wage policies for decent work and inclusive growth*, 2018.

[9]Jayati Ghosh, 'Growth, industrialisation and inequality in India', *Journal of the Asia Pacific Economy*, 2015, Vol. 20, No. 1, pp. 42–56.

productivity and better remunerated activities. Agriculture and related activities continue to account for just under half the work force even though its share of GDP fell to 15 per cent, and low-paid services accounted for a big share of employment. Agriculture became less viable, especially for small holders (with rising costs, volatile crop prices, and increasing indebtedness) but there were not enough employment opportunities elsewhere.

Recent Economic Policies

The Modi government came to power in 2014 on the promise of changing all this, by meeting the aspirations of many sections of society who felt unhappy with this state of affairs: farmers, young people, people in the working and middle classes who felt deprived of economic opportunities. But over the next seven years it turned out that the focus of the government was less on turning the economy around and more on extension of the BJP's political control and establishing the basis for Hindu majoritarian rule. Two specific policies of the government (the abrupt demonetization of November 2016 and the institution of the national Goods and Services Tax or GST) revealed both a penchant for 'shock and awe' centralization and poor policy design and implementation, which created large economic shocks.

The demonetization of supposedly 'high-value' notes (of ₹500 and ₹1,000) in India on 8 November 2016 was without doubt the most extreme of monetary experiments to have occurred anywhere in the world in recent history. More than 86 per cent of the value of currency in circulation was simply declared to be invalid, with only four hours' notice. Because hardly anyone even in government or the central bank had been consulted or even informed, administrative chaos ensued. It took nearly a year to replace 90 per cent of the value of the demonetized currency in circulation. This resulted in a severe liquidity crunch for many months, with a serious impact on economic activity.

The move was supposed to eliminate 'black money' and corruption, reduce the spread of counterfeit notes and their use in the financing of terrorist activities, and push people to move to digital transactions. It did not actually meet any of these goals.[10] But it did result in major disruption of the economy, loss of jobs and incomes, and considerable material distress.[11] Around 95 per cent of transactions were estimated to occur in cash before this move, so this measure effectively froze many markets, caused demand to fall, disrupted supply chains, and led to significant loss of livelihood and employment. It especially affected informal activities, small and micro enterprises, and casual labourers who either lost employment or had to work for much lower money wages. Inequality increased, as the rich escaped relatively unscathed through this process: they could switch to digital transactions and were able to exchange their earlier notes (including through a quickly developed black market) without too much loss. But the poor suffered disproportionately. Supply chains were broken, including some that linked formal and informal enterprises, and this eventually impacted the organized sector's production and exports. The initial decline in employment and incomes led to more prolonged adverse effects, as mass consumption declined. This caused further income losses along the chain, with repercussions on aggregate demand that persisted for several years. Inevitably,

---

[10]There were other, more political, goals that may have been served by this move: creating a narrative around and public impression of fighting corruption without undertaking some less dramatic but more effective measures; stealing a march on Opposition parties ahead of important regional elections such as those held in Uttar Pradesh in mid-2017; and so on.

[11]Jayati Ghosh, C. P. Chandrasekhar, and Prabhat Patnaik, *Demonetisation Decoded: A Critique of India's Monetary Experiment*, New Delhi: Routledge Taylor and Francis Publishers, 2017; C. Rammanohar Reddy, *Demonetisation and Black Money*, Hyderabad: Orient Blackswan, 2017; Meera H. Sanyal, *The Big Reverse: How Demonetisation Knocked India Out*, New Delhi: Harper Business, 2018.

these then had a dampening effect on private investment. Demonetization also affected the banking system and credit provision, as discussed later.

It might have been expected that after such a body blow that demonetization had delivered to informal activities, the government would provide some sort of a package to assist them and help them recover. That was unfortunately not forthcoming; instead, there was yet another shock in the pipeline for micro, small, and medium enterprises—the Goods and Services Tax (GST). This is essentially a hybrid version of the Value Added Tax (VAT), modified to suit the complexities of a federal system. VAT is meant to be paid on sales at each stage of a production process, with offsets for taxes paid on purchases, which are supposed to be shown through invoices from input suppliers. The idea was to make tax payments easier and simultaneously improve tax compliance, since suppliers would have to declare the prices and taxes on their sales of goods and services to enable upstream producers to claim their offsets. If companies then chose to deal only with other GST compliant companies, this would push the formalisation of enterprises.

The GST had been discussed for several years, but it required agreement of all state governments, which would have to give up their powers to impose sales taxes. The final agreement was reached only in early 2017, when the Centre agreed to a formula for compensating state governments that were worried about revenue losses.[12] Just as with demonetization, the move showed extreme haste, inadequate planning, poor preparation,

---

[12]The agreement was that total GST collections were projected to increase by 14 per cent every year, and states would be compensated by the Centre for any shortfall from that projected increase. As it happens, the Centre has been tardy in meeting this, and in recent years has more or less refused to pay the full compensation, citing its own poor fiscal collections. This has become a major bone of contention between the central and state governments, especially during the pandemic.

and subsequent confusion. It has taken most countries that have implemented GST several years to do this, even developed economies like Australia and Canada. They have also tended to introduce it gradually, allowing people and enterprises enough time to get used to the new regulations and processes. In India, the Modi government decided to do it in only three months, from the passage of the law in April 2017 to the formal announcement of its implementation from 1 July 2017.[13] This was a very short time, especially since infrastructure and compliance systems were not yet ready and there was relatively low literacy and numeracy among those who would have to follow the new system. The system created a centralized tax structure in place of the more federal system envisaged by the Constitution. But it was also very poorly conceived and designed, and even more poorly implemented. Instead of a simple uniform system, it was extremely complicated, with seven rates varying from zero to 28 per cent and changing classifications of goods. Compliance turned out to be both cumbersome and costly, requiring companies to file frequent returns in an unreliable and user-unfriendly online system.

The impact on small and informal enterprises was severe: many units with small margins had to close down or lived in constant fear of scrutiny and punishment because they could not comply. This also affected supply chains and markets. Somewhat surprisingly, GST also failed to increase revenues. It is a regressive tax that falls more on the poor and so adds to inequality, but it did not deliver the promised revenue increases. GST collections were consistently below targets.[14] Some of this was due to the economic slowdown, which naturally meant that less taxes would be collected on economic activity. But some

---

[13]'Goods and Services tax formally launched in Parliament by Prime Minister Narendra Modi and President Pranab Mukherjee', *The Hindu*, 1 July 2017.

[14]C. P. Chandrasekhar and Jayati Ghosh, 'Three years on, GST hasn't lived up to its billing', *Hindu BusinessLine*, 27 July 2020.

was also due to the fact that GST rates on many commodities were actually lower than the earlier central and state excise duties combined—although prices of goods and services faced by consumers did not come down.

The GST quickly became a flashpoint in centre–state relations. State governments effectively lost their revenue raising powers from sales taxes (other than duties on alcohol and petroleum products, which were exempted). To persuade all state governments to accept this, the central government had offered a major sop: a guarantee that states should expect revenue increases of 14 per cent every year, and any shortage of revenue receipts below that would be met and *fully compensated* by the central government for the next five years. It was really this promise, incorporated into the GST Act, that persuaded some holdout state governments to accept the new tax system. However, the central government reneged on this legal guarantee from the start. GST compensation payments from the centre to the states were well below the promised amounts in every year since its implementation,[15] creating huge difficulties for states whose own annual budgets were based on receiving these expected payments. Some state governments even threatened to approach the Supreme Court of India for relief,[16] especially during the pandemic when the non-payment of GST compensation dues became a major source of tension.

These policies served as body blows to informal economic

[15]See Nachiket Kelkar, 'GST: A story of missed targets and inconsistent performance', *The Week*, 30 January 2019. By September 2019, in what was seen as yet another indicator of economic downturn well before the pandemic, the GST collections dropped below the ₹100,000 crore level, to the lowest level of nineteen months. This was aggravated to the point that several states were considering legal action to ensure timely and complete payment of the GST compensation cess. See 'GST collection slips below ₹1 lakh crore mark to ₹91,916 crore in September', *Economic Times*, 1 October 2019.

[16]'GST compensation: State governments mulling legal remedy', *The Hindu*, 13 October 2020.

activity that dominates employment in India, causing major declines in livelihoods. At first, they did not affect formal enterprises so much, as they gained at the cost of informal ones. But the resulting loss in livelihoods and wage incomes eventually had an effect on demand for formal sector output as well, by reducing the market for and the profit expectations of formal enterprises. This became worse over time because there were no counterbalancing moves by the government. The government could have provided a fiscal stimulus through more public spending, especially in desperately needed areas of social services. This would have alleviated suffering and increased domestic demand. But it did not do so. Instead, it kept assuming or hoping that using largely optical measures, such as advertising the improvement of India's position in the World Bank's 'Doing Business' index (which was subsequently shown to be based on manipulated indicators[17]) and offering further incentives to foreign capital to attract more inflows, however volatile, would somehow attract more investment into the economy that would counteract all the negative impulses.

In mid-2019, as the economic slowdown became too marked to ignore, the government offered significant tax concessions to large corporations. It lowered the base corporate tax rate from 30 per cent to 22 per cent (25 per cent with surcharges) and from 25 per cent to only 15 per cent for new manufacturing companies. This was meant to create an incentive to invest, although it effectively benefited only the top 1 per cent of companies.[18] This led to a massive fiscal loss to the exchequer, with revenue losses on corporate taxes of more than ₹2 trillion

[17]Justin Sandefur and Divyanshi Wadhwa, 'A change in World Bank methodology (not reform) explains India's rise in Doing Business rankings', Centre for Global Development, 5 February 2018.

[18]PTI, 'Corporate tax cut to mostly benefit less than 1 pc of companies: Survey', *Economic Times*, 31 January 2020.

(around 1.4 per cent of GDP).[19] However, it did not have any impact on increasing corporate investment, which continued to decline.[20] Private investors simply kept demanding more fiscal and regulatory concessions, while they continued to sit on their investment plans and waited for demand conditions to improve.

The Fallout for the Economy

For these reasons, economic activity had been slowing down much before the pandemic disruption (Figure 2.1). In the January–March 2020 quarter, just before the lockdown had its impact, the economy grew by only 3.4 per cent compared to the previous year, the lowest rate in nearly two decades. Actual growth was probably even lower: there were many concerns that the new series of national accounts overestimated economic activity, especially industrial output.[21] Also, recent GDP estimates rely mainly on data from formal enterprises, but these policies harmed informal activity more, though that

---

[19]Budget estimates for corporate tax collection for 2019–20 were ₹7.66 trillion. The provisional estimated in the following year's budget were just ₹5.56 trillion, a shortfall of ₹2.09 trillion. See Roshan Kishore, 'Corporate tax cuts a bad gamble', *Hindustan Times*, 1 June 2020.

[20]Ashish Khetan, 'Why India needs to rethink its corporate tax cut', *Scroll.in*, 14 March 2020.

[21]Instead of using the Annual Survey of Industries (ASI) to measure industrial output as was done earlier, corporate financial data collected by the Ministry of Corporate Affairs (MCA) were used. This was done on the grounds that the ASI supposedly excluded activities outside the factory of an enterprise, although this claim was wrong (see Ravindra Dholakia, R. Nagaraj, and Manish Pandya, 'Manufacturing Output in New GDP Series: Some Methodological Issues', *Economic and Political Weekly*, Vol. LIII, No. 35, 1 September 2018). This change resulted in industry having a higher share in GDP and a faster growth rate, compared to the older series. The MCA database turned out to contain a large number of non-existent or shell companies, making the data even more unreliable (see R. Nagaraj, 'Seeds of Doubt on New GDP Numbers: Private Corporate Sector Overestimated?', *Economic & Political Weekly*, Vol. 50, No. 13, 2015, pp. 14–17.

was not fully captured. It is likely that actual GDP was both significantly lower and increasing more slowly.[22]

The massive impact that demonetization and GST had on smaller and informal units is exemplified by the story of Surat, the industrial hub of the Prime Minister Modi's home state of Gujarat. Famous for its diamond and textile industries, in 2017 it produced 40 per cent of all of India's synthetic fabrics, and specially dominated the polyester sari market.[23] First demonetization disrupted the supply chains and lowered demand for the final goods. Then the imposition of GST meant that small units that operated in clusters in a decentralized value chain (the bulk of the textile industry's employment in the city) were suddenly at a huge disadvantage, having to pay 20 per cent more tax than their vertically integrated counterparts. Their costs increased even as they had to compete with cheap Chinese imports, and many simply became unviable. It was predicted that the 10,000 companies operating power looms would dwindle to only 2,000 at most, with similar consolidation in other textile processing. The businessmen who managed to escape with some money chose to invest in the stock market rather than putting any more into their floundering enterprises. This pattern was repeated across the country: as more businesses chose that route, stock markets performed well even though the real economy declined.

---

[22]See, for example, Arvind Subramanian, 'India's GDP Mis-estimation: Likelihood, Magnitudes, Mechanisms, and Implications', CID Faculty Working Paper No. 354, Harvard University, 2019. He suggested that annual average GDP growth between 2011–12 and 2016–17 was not 7 per cent, but closer to about 4.5 per cent. Other economists also suggest that growth was slower over the decade, and that the more recent deceleration was even more drastic than suggested by the official figures.

[23]M. Rajshekhar, *Despite the State: Why India Lets Its People Down and How They Cope*, New Delhi: Context (Westland Books), 2020.

Figure 2.1: India's GDP by quarter, 2011–12 Q1 to 2020–21 Q1

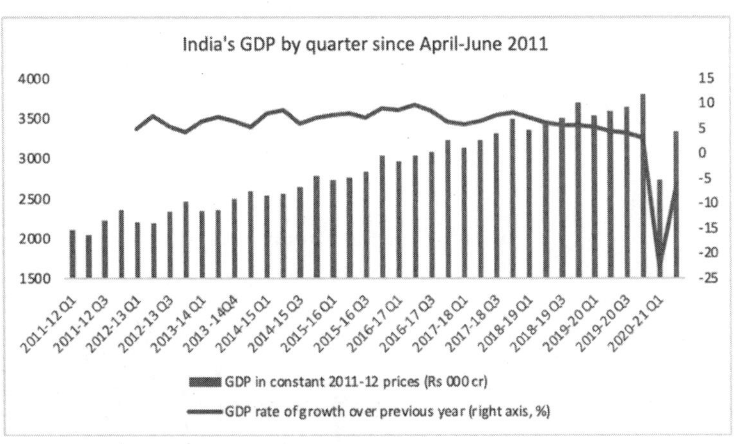

Source: RBI, rbi.org.in, accessed on 28 July 2020.

Despite the tax concessions, the investment rate continued to decline. Figure 2.2 shows that the share of gross fixed capital formation (or investment) to national income fell substantially from nearly 36 per cent of GDP in July–September 2011 to only around 29 per cent in October–December 2019—a decline of more than 6 percentage points. By January–March 2020, even absolute investment levels were lower than they had been three years earlier.

There were some obvious reasons for declining investment: companies faced credit constraints as rising bad loans made banks more cautious; more projects were held up or delayed because of environmental and legal concerns; and so on. But the most important reason was that the domestic market for mass consumption goods did not grow very much, since wage incomes were suppressed. It was ironic—but predictable—that the strategy to deliver more profits to corporates by suppressing wages ended up reducing total profits by shrinking the market.

The focus on large companies also left out the small and medium enterprises that provide the bulk of employment in the country, which also suffered the most due to demonetization and the GST imposition.

Figure 2.2: Investment in India by quarter, 2010–11 Q1 to 2019–20 Q4

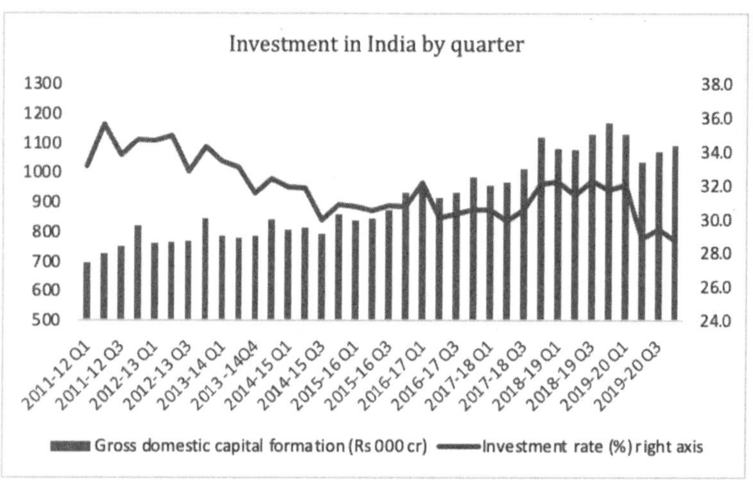

Source: MOSPI, mospi.nic.in, accessed on 14 July 2020.

The mess in the banking system clearly affected investment. There was a legacy of large 'non-performing loans' (which were unlikely to be ever repaid) that resulted from the euphoria of the boom period, when both public and private banks lent excessively, especially to crony borrowers with political connections. By the middle of the 2010s, the problem was significant enough for the then Governor of the Reserve Bank of India, Raghuram Rajan, to demand a clean-up and greater enforcement of loan recovery. This acted as a damper on some new investment, but it did not resolve the issue. In fact, the volume of bad loans in the banking system more than tripled between 2014 and 2019,[24] suggesting that the Modi government was not only unable to clean up the mess but also added to it significantly.

Problems also emerged with the non-bank lenders whose lending increased in the wake of demonetization. For several months after that disastrous move, commercial banks were in no position to provide credit, so firms faced serious problems in accessing even working capital to allow them to continue to function. To counter this credit famine, the government (or more correctly, the Reserve Bank of India) allowed, encouraged, and even nudged 'shadow banking' lenders[25] like the Infrastructure Leasing and Financial Services Ltd (IL&FS) and Dewan Housing Finance Ltd to lend freely and mostly without due diligence.[26] Anyone could have foreseen that this would end badly—and in fact it took less than two years for that sad denouement. The spectacular near collapse of IL&FS in September 2018 had to be dealt with through a major public bailout, and caused lending by other non-bank financial companies to freeze up as well. Cooperative banks also faced difficulties, and some well-publicized bank collapses tended to destroy or reduce the trust of depositors, so they also could lend out less. As both banks and non-bank lenders became increasingly unable or reluctant to lend, finance became scarce, especially for micro, small, and medium enterprises. Also, since some sectors like automobiles and housing depended on credit-driven demand, they were also affected.[27]

---

[24]Kumar Vikram, 'Gross bad loans up more than 3 times in NDA rule, says RBI data', *New Indian Express*, 11 January 2021.

[25]Shadow banks are financial intermediaries that provide services similar to banks like offering credit, but because they do not take deposits, but rely on 'investment' and their own borrowing to lend further; they are not subject to the same regulations as banks.

[26]C. P. Chandrasekhar, 'Towards a meltdown', *Frontline*, 5 July 2019.

[27]See C. P. Chandrasekhar, 'Liquidity conundrum', *Frontline*, 8 November 2019.

All these indicators pointed to one overwhelming reality: there was a genuine slump in aggregate demand in the country, driven by declining consumption. The consumption data provided as part of the Periodic Labour Force Survey of 2017–18 showed an alarming picture. For the first time since such data began to be collected, average consumption expenditure actually *declined* in real terms between 2014 and 2017–18, even though national income was supposedly growing.[28] In rural areas it declined from ₹1,587 per person per month in 2014 to ₹1,524, and in urban areas from ₹2,926 per person per month ₹2,909. Between 2015–16 and 2017–18, real per capita consumption spending declined at an annual rate of 4.4 per cent in rural areas and 4.8 per cent in urban areas.

The National Sample Survey Organisation also conducted a large survey of consumption expenditure in 2017–18, but the central government refused to release the report because of 'data quality issues', even though it had been approved by the statistical agency.[29] However, a version of the report that had already been prepared for publication was leaked to media.[30] It provided further evidence *of absolute declines* in total consumption (driven by falling rural consumption) in the six years between 2011–12 and 2017–18, a period when India's GDP increased by nearly 50 per cent according to national income data. In urban areas, consumption did not fall in real terms, although it did not increase much either, and definitely not enough to offset the rural decline.

---

[28]Himanshu, 'What happened to poverty during the first term of Modi?', *Live Mint,* 15 August 2019.

[29]ANI, 'Consumer expenditure report not to be released because of data quality issues', *Business Standard,* 15 November 2019.

[30]Somesh Jha, 'Consumer spend sees first fall in three decades due to weak rural demand: NSSO data', *Business Standard,* 15 November 2019.

Table 2.1: Indications of changes in rural consumption spending (All monetary values are ₹ in 2011–12 prices)

	2011–12	*2017–18*	*Change (per cent)*
Average consumption	1429.96	1304.07	-8.8
Average spending on food	756.45	711.78	-5.9
Average spending of poorest half of population	687.81	669.64	-2.6
Headcount poverty ratio	31.2%	35.1%	+12.7
Millions of poor people	270.43	322.21	+19.2

Source: S. Subramanian (2019, using data from the withheld but leaked NSSO report).[31]

Table 2.1 indicates the extent of the collapse in household consumption in rural areas. Average consumption declined in real terms by nearly 9 per cent, a remarkable outcome in what was supposedly one of the most dynamic economies in the world over that period. This decline was evident across all classes of the rural population, from the poorest to the richest, with some of the bigger declines occurring among the richer categories. Overall, this decline in consumption meant a significant increase in rural poverty, by nearly 13 per cent and almost 20 million people.

It is easy to see how this can become a downward spiral—which was evident by the first quarter of 2020. Low investment, employment declines, and real wage stagnation lowered consumption demand, which reduced capacity utilization and

[31]S. Subramaniam, 'Letting the Data Speak: Consumption Spending, Rural Distress, Urban Slow-Down, and Overall Stagnation', *The Hindu Centre*, 11 December 2019.

depressed profit expectations. As a result, investment fell further, as investors decided to wait and see or hold back until they could be sure that they would be able to sell their output. And all this occurred well before the economic disruptions created by the pandemic, so it was in an already bleak economic scenario that the novel Coronavirus struck.

Trends in investment and consumption inevitably had their impact on employment, as a result of which, between 2011–12 and 2017–18, both labour force participation and employment fell relative to working age population. Even open unemployment rates went up to as much as 6.1 per cent, the highest recorded level in more than four decades,[32] even though there are no unemployment benefits in India and most workers are forced to try and earn something, however meagre. Estimates of employment declines range from 6 to 11 million, although one outlier estimate argued that employment increased slightly.[33] (The numbers vary because of different population projections for 2017–18, since it is hard to estimate the actual population in that year without the results of the next decennial Census.) Table 2.2 presents one of the more plausible estimates. This suggests that total employment in the country had barely increased by 15 million (from 459 to 474 million) even during the period of peak expansion between 2004–05 and 2011–12; but in the subsequent period up to 2017–18,

[32]Somesh Jha, 'Unemployment rate at four-decade year high of 6.1% in 2017-18: NSSO Survey', *Business Standard*, 6 February 2019.

[33]The differences arise because the labour force survey provides only rates per population, and so total numbers will depend on the estimate of total population in 2017–18. Since the Registrar General of India has not yet released official population projections, the numbers can vary from 1.31 billion (the number that emerges from the official data on per capita GDP) to 1.33 billion (the World Bank's estimate) to 1.35 billion (the Census-projected population) to 1.36 billion (used by the PM's Economic Advisory Council). Using a larger population estimate obviously increases the estimate of total numbers of those employed. See Udit Misra, 'Employment falls first time—by 9 million in 6 years: Study', *Indian Express*, 1 November 2019.

it declined by 9 million. Both agriculture and manufacturing experienced declining employment, while construction (which had become a major and growing employer in the previous period) decelerated sharply. Paid jobs only increased in services, but most of these were low-paid precarious jobs or self-employment with poor working conditions.

Table 2.2: Sectoral employment trends (millions)

	2004–05	*2011–12*	*2017–18*
Agriculture	269	232	205
Manufacturing	54	60	56
Other industry (including construction)	29	55	59
Services	107	127	144
Total	459	474	465

Source: Santosh Mehrotra and Jajati Parida, 'India's Employment Crisis: Rising Education Levels and Falling Non-agricultural Job Growth', *CSE Working Paper 2019-04*, Hyderabad: Azim Premji University, 2019, Table 2, p. 6.

This meant that India's much anticipated 'demographic dividend', which was supposed to result from the population bulge of young people who would be available for productive employment, had already become a nightmare because of insufficient job creation in the economy. Greater 'skilling' did not help: a reporter visiting a village in Moradabad district of western Uttar Pradesh in January 2020 found a bunch of twenty young men—all graduates and postgraduates, mostly engineers and software specialists—playing cricket day after day in the village field, with no jobs or prospects of paid work.[34]

[34]Sanya Dhingra, 'Young, educated, jobless: These men in UP villages have nothing to do but play cricket', *The Print*, 23 January 2020.

Some had lost their jobs in private companies within a year or two after the 2016 demonetization; some who graduated after that never found jobs at all; most of them had travelled to cities to work or seek work, and had to return because of the economic slowdown. Across the country, graduates in engineering, computer science, commerce, and other fields that were supposed to be lucrative professions, found no employment. Women graduates were the worst off, with terrible job prospects after spending substantial amounts on expensive technical education, which their families had paid for by selling assets and taking on debt.[35]

Women's labour market participation, which had been falling from already low levels since 1993, experienced further very sharp declines. Labour force participation among women aged fifteen years or more effectively halved between 2004–05 and 2017–18, falling from 49.4 per cent in 2004–05 to 35.8 per cent in 2011–12 and finally only 24.6 per cent in 2017–18.[36] In urban areas, rates of labour force participation were already extremely low by international standards; but they fell further, from 24.4 per cent in 1994–94 to 20.4 per cent in 2017–18. Only some part of this phenomenon of women moving out of the labour market could be explained by greater involvement in education, especially for the age cohort fifteen to nineteen years. In fact, participation rates fell sharply for women across all age groups, so that even for women above thirty years, labour force participation fell from 41 per cent in 2011–12 to 30 per cent in 2017–18.[37] Clearly, there was a process in operation, which

---

[35]Reuters, 'India's jobs crisis for real: Unemployed youth narrate their stories', 4 March 2019.

[36]NSSO, *Annual Report on Periodic Labour Force Survey 2017–18*, New Delhi: Ministry of Statistics and Programme Implementation, 2019.

[37]Radhicka Kapoor, 'Understanding India's Jobs Challenge', *India Forum*, 10 September 2019.

has also been noted globally[38] of women being squeezed out of employment because of overall scarcity of paid work, which was probably why more and more women withdrew from the labour force, along with some men.

One of the difficulties with discussions on employment in India is the tendency to conflate employment and work. But employment covers only work that is remunerated, and in India a vast amount of work is actually unpaid and often not even socially recognized. This is especially true of women's work. The labour force surveys have categories that are described as 'not in the labour force', including people who 'attend to domestic duties' and who do other work like free collection of goods like vegetables, roots, firewood, cattle feed, water collection, sewing, tailoring, weaving, etc., for household use. Most women in India are involved in these activities, and if they are included as workers (using the ILO definition of work rather than paid employment) then in 2011–12, women's work participation was as high as 86 per cent, compared to 80 per cent for men. The decline in women's employment rates really reflects a shift of women from paid to unpaid work, mainly in domestic and allied work.

This was most marked for poor women, in the bottom 40 per cent of households according to consumption expenditure. A significant share of such unpaid women workers (40 per cent in rural areas and 22 per cent in urban areas in 2011–12) was dominantly involved in fetching water for household consumption, an activity that took longer than before. More than half of the poorest women had to do this, as well as to collect biofuels for cooking as they did not have access to or could not afford other fuel. This suggests that lack of basic amenities

[38]Stephanie Seguino and Elissa Braunstein, 'The Costs of Exclusion: Gender Job Segregation, Structural Change and the Labour Share of Income', *Development and Change*, 22 November 2018.

was an important factor driving the increase in unpaid work. A National Sample Survey Office (NSSO) survey in 2012 found that in rural areas, the average trip to the water source took twenty minutes, with an additional waiting time of fifteen minutes at the water source, and that several trips were required in order to meet the water needs for household consumption. In urban areas the time for travel to the source was fifteen minutes and the time spent waiting per trip was sixteen minutes.[39]

Similarly, significant time was spent by women on collecting fuelwood and fodder for animals. The Ujjwala scheme providing a free first cooking gas cylinder to women in households below the poverty line was successful in providing a first gas cylinder to many women, but it failed to overcome the problem, because most households found that they could not afford to buy the subsequent cylinders.[40] In addition to these extended domestic tasks, there are the various activities associated with the 'care economy': care of the young, the old, the sick, and the differently abled; cooking, cleaning, and generally looking after healthy adults—all of which are dominantly seen as the responsibility of women in the household. When these services are outsourced and provided commercially, the providers are seen as workers in India; but when they are performed by women within households, such women are classified as 'not in the labour force'.

A time use survey conducted over January to December 2019 by the NSSO revealed the enormous disparities in time use and in paid versus unpaid work performed by men and

---

[39]NSS Report No. 556 (69/1.2/1), *Drinking Water, Sanitation, Hygiene and Housing Condition in India*, New Delhi: Ministry of Statistics and Programme Implementation, 2014, available at http://mospi.nic.in/sites/default/files/publication_reports/nss_rep_556_14aug14.pdf.

[40]Sumant Sen, 'How effective has the Pradhan Mantri Ujjwala Yojana been?', *The Hindu*, 19 December 2019.

women.[41] This survey also confirmed that engagement in paid work among women aged fifteen to fifty-nine years across India came to only 20.6 per cent and the difference between rural and urban areas has continued to narrow as women's participation has continued to decline in the rural economy. This compares to paid work participation by nearly 70 per cent of men, pointing to a significant gender gap in access to monetary income. But the much bigger gap was in unpaid work of various kinds. 94 per cent of all women were forced to engage in unpaid activities, mostly involving household work and care of other family members, whereas only around one-fifth of men did so. Women also spent much more time on such activities: on average, more than two and a half times the minutes per day than men. In rural areas, women spent nearly six and a half hours every day in unpaid activities, and in urban areas slightly more than six hours. In urban areas, the difference between women's and men's unpaid work time was nearly three and a half times. Even within unpaid work, men spent 9 per cent of their daily time on production of goods for their own final use, whereas women spent only 5 per cent of their time on this. By contrast, when it came to working for others in unpaid ways, whether in the form of unpaid domestic services (cooking, cleaning, other processing for domestic use, fetching water and/or fuelwood, kitchen gardening, etc.) or unpaid caregiving services for other

[41]It should be borne in mind that this time use survey was based on the recall method, asking respondents about their activities for the previous twenty-four hours. This is known to be an inferior and more potentially misleading method, since recall is notoriously inaccurate, and people are often unable to remember and then aggregate the time involved in activities, especially when several activities are combined (as is the case with much home-based work). Also, for a significant proportion of respondents, this recalled information was not provided directly by the person concerned: for around half the males and one-third of the females, some other household members provided the responses, which could make them even less accurate and would be likely to understate the extent of unpaid work.

household members, men spend only 7 per cent of their daily time on this while women spend 17 per cent, or two and a half times more than men.

The unpaid–paid continuum of women's work serves to devalue both women and the work they do. Thus, when women do enter labour markets, their wages tend to be lower than those of men—not only because they are willing to work for lower wages but because so much of their work is available for free. India has one of the largest gender gaps in wages to be found anywhere in the world, with women's wages on average only around two-thirds that of men's wages. Occupations in which women dominate tend to be lower paid, and the wage penalty extends even to men doing similar work, such as in the low paid care sector. In India, not just private employers but even governments have used these gender-segmented labour markets to provide public services on the cheap, by employing frontline health workers (like Anganwadi workers and helpers and ASHAs) as 'volunteers' who are paid only a fraction of the official minimum wages.[42] Similarly, women are disproportionately employed by state governments as para-teachers and ANMs (auxiliary nurses and midwives) and paid far less than regular employees.

Real wages started decelerating 2015 onwards, and declined from 2017 onwards. The NSSO surveys indicate that real wages for all types of regular workers (whether rural or urban, male or female) declined between 2011–12 and 2017–18, by an average of 1.76 per cent, while those for casual workers increased only marginally by 2.26 per cent in this six-year period.[43] For an economy in which real per capita income supposedly increased

---

[42]Jayati Ghosh, *Never Done and Poorly Paid: Women's Work in Globalising India*, New Delhi: Women Unlimited, 2019.

[43]Ravi Srivastava and Balakrushna Padhi, 'Collapse in Wage/Salary Income Growth in India, 2011-12 to 2017-18', *CES Working Paper 01/2020*, New Delhi: Institute for Human Development, 2020.

by nearly 50 per cent over the same period, this was a strong reflection of the worsening conditions and substantially reduced bargaining power of the work force.

Low wages and poor working conditions reflect the extensive informality of the labour market: around 95 per cent of all workers do not have formal contracts that provide them with some legal and social protection from their employers; and around half are self-employed, which means that they have to bear all the risks and costs of production themselves.[44] Furthermore, simply ensuring that enterprises become 'formal', registered, or organized does not ensure that their workers will have formal contracts and receive associated benefits. Indeed, the NSSO surveys show that while informal employment predictably dominated in private unorganized activity, even within organized private enterprises, more than half of the workers had informal contracts. In the organized public sector, nearly a quarter of such workers were informal, including the (mostly women) frontline care workers.

Table 2.3 shows that most workers do not get even the most minimal conditions of formal employment, such as a written contract, paid leave, or any kind of social security provided by the employer. Women workers are even less likely than men to get paid leave—ironic, considering that most such women also face the double burden of household work and various family responsibilities. A marginally higher share of men workers had access to some form of social security, but this was mostly rudimentary, in the form of registered participation in a provident fund. Most forms of social security (such as access to health coverage or provident funds) typically provide minuscule amounts and do not serve to provide much protection especially in extreme situations, like the Covid-19 pandemic.

---

[44]NSSO, *Annual Report on Periodic Labour Force Survey 2017-18*, New Delhi: Ministry of Statistics and Programme Implementation, 2019.

Table 2.3: Conditions of employment in 2017–18 (per cent of workers)

	Rural men workers	*Rural women workers*	*Urban men workers*	*Urban women workers*
Without written contract	71.7	58.5	72.7	71.4
Not eligible for paid leave	58.1	47.9	53.1	51.8
Not eligible for any kind of social security	51.9	55.1	47	50.1

Source: NSSO Periodic Labour Force Survey, 2017–18.

In the pre-pandemic period, worsening conditions in agriculture meant that cultivators fared even worse than casual rural wage workers. Problems in agriculture were deep-rooted and systemic.[45] Per capita public investment in agriculture had been declining for three decades, affecting infrastructure for irrigation and transport. Financial liberalization measures reduced the availability of institutional credit for farmers and forced many cultivators, particularly smaller farmers, tenant farmers, and those without clear titles to land, to seek recourse from informal channels of credit like input dealers and traditional moneylenders. All this made farm investment and working capital for cultivation more expensive and more difficult, especially for smaller farmers. Inputs for cultivation became a particular concern, with the reduction in public research and extension services and reduced access to subsidized inputs. Trade liberalization meant that Indian agriculturalists were increasingly exposed to

[45]Himanshu, 'India's Farm Crisis: Decades Old and with Deep Roots', *The India Forum*, 29 April 2019.

global competition even as the protections they had in terms of support prices, input assistance, and public extension services were gradually being reduced or even withdrawn. Indian farmers had to operate in a highly uncertain and volatile international environment, effectively competing against highly subsidized large agribusinesses in the developed countries. This led to a peculiar combination of low prices and output volatility for cash crops. While output volatility increased especially with new seeds and other inputs, the prices of most non-foodgrain crops weakened, and in some cases plummeted. Further, farmers were squeezed as input costs kept rising, either because of reduced subsidies and rising input prices, or because of the need to use more and more inputs (such as seeds, fertilizer, and pesticides) to achieve the same levels of output.

All these forces led to a slowdown in agricultural growth and by the late 1990s, widespread distress in the countryside. The most extreme form of expression of such distress was in the spate of farmers' suicides, which occurred typically when heavily indebted farmers whose farms had lost viability could find no other recourse. By the mid-2000s, it was evident that the problems facing agriculture were severe and would require express policy attention. The Congress-led UPA government that came to power in 2004 had made the problems facing cultivation and rural distress generally a major plank of the electoral campaign, and they sought for some years to reverse the pattern of declining public spending, with increased public investment on irrigation and rural infrastructure, and more central government spending on agricultural research and extension, as well as increased credit to rural areas. These positives were very limited in extent, but they did partially reverse the trend of rural decline, aided by high and rising prices of agricultural goods in global trade.

The difficulties experienced by farmers led to the setting up of the National Commission on Farmers, better known as the

Swaminathan Commission, during the UPA regime. However, there was no real effort to implement its recommendations. In 2014, the BJP in 2014 promised to implement the Commission's recommendations, so much so that its electoral manifesto lifted large chunks from the Swaminathan Report and promised to double farmers' income in five years.[46] But in actual practice it did more or less *the opposite of what was promised*.[47] That is why 2018 and 2019 witnessed massive agitations by farmers across the country. These included a huge congregation of farmers marching to Parliament in November 2018, several other big marches in states like Maharashtra and protests in many other parts of the country. Well before the pandemic generated a wider collapse, farmers in India were demanding changed policies to ensure their economic viability: a loan waiver, reduction of electricity tariffs, higher procurement prices for their crops, immediate payment of the long overdue arrears for sugarcane sales, lower GST on agricultural machinery and implements, legal recognition of the land rights of so-called 'forest dwellers' whose families had cultivated their land for generations, and so on. The ongoing farmers' protests against new farm laws must be seen in that context.

Obviously, the general decline in economic dynamism was reflected in slowing industrial production, which declined over the year 2019–20, after increasing only at a very modest rate in the years before that (Figure 2.3), nowhere near as fast as could be expected in a dynamic economy. In fact, by the last quarter of 2019–20, industry was already in recession.[48]

---

[46]This five-year period then became a moving target, with periodic extensions, to 2022, and now seems to have been abandoned altogether; not mentioned anymore by the Prime Minister or his ministerial colleagues.

[47]Himanshu, 'India's Farm Crisis: Decades Old and with Deep Roots'.

[48]Surajit Mazumdar, 'The Coronavirus and India's Economic Crisis: Continuity and Change', MPRA Paper 104969, University Library of Munich, Germany, revised 20 Dec 2020.

Figure 2.3: Growth rates of industrial production

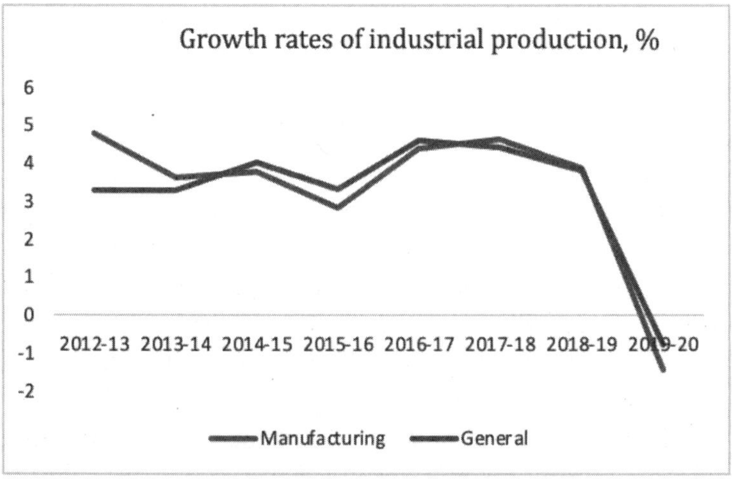

Source: MOSPI, mospi.nic.in, accessed on 16 July 2020.

Several analysts declared that the economic crisis in the country in 2019 was even worse than the situation in India after the Global Financial Crisis of 2008–09.[49] This was reflected in activity in different industrial sectors. The automobile industry, seen as a bellwether of activity in the post-liberalization years, faced major declines in sales and more than 350,000 workers were laid off by automakers, parts manufacturers, and dealers just between April and June.[50] Capacity utilization in all manufacturing was below 70 per cent on average, even as inventories piled up. Air traffic passenger numbers were down, and rail freight traffic—an

---

[49]For example, Goldman Sachs, the consultancy company, whose report on the Indian economy was quite dire. See, 'Present Indian Economic Crisis Bigger Than 2008, Says Goldman Sachs as Slump More Protracted Now', *News18*, 17 October 2019.

[50]Sudarshan Varadhan, Aditi Shah, and Aftab Ahmed, 'Exclusive: Tens of thousands losing jobs as India's auto crisis deepens–sources', *Reuters*, 6 August 2019.

indicator of total national sales—were below the past five years' average. The construction sector was in deep gloom, and the real estate business was stuck with more than seven years' stock of unsold buildings.

Lower sales of items consumed by the less well-off also indicated worsening material conditions. Sales in the fast-moving consumer goods (FMCG) sector showed the worst performance in seven years, led by declines in rural demand.[51] The collapse was across food and non-food items, with the biggest reductions in salty snacks and biscuits, spices, soaps, and packaged tea. These items are 'discretionary consumer spending' among the poor, the items more likely to be cut down when household budgets are under strain.

Clearly, therefore, the Covid-19 pandemic came at a time when the Indian economy was already very weak and all major indicators were stagnating or in decline. It could not have been a worse time for a public health crisis. The aggressive lockdown imposed without any compensating economic measures speedily transformed it into an economic calamity as well.

II. The Health of the People

Human development has been one of the major failures of India's development project. This is particularly evident in health indicators, which remained relatively poor for decades and did not improve as much as could have been expected even with higher economic growth. The country ranks a lowly 131 out of 189 countries in the UNDP's Human Development Index,[52] and its rank is even lower for the two non-income dimensions (health and education). As the Human Development Report

---

[51]'FMCG performance in rural India worst in 7 years: Nielsen', *Hindu BusinessLine*, 17 October 2019.

[52]UNDP, Human Development Reports, Latest Human Development Index Ranking, available at http://hdr.undp.org/en/countries/profiles.

2020 shows, India's health performance has been worse than other countries with similar or lower per capita incomes. Among the BRICS group (Brazil, Russia, India, China, South Africa), India has the poorest health indicators,[53] except for South Africa in some cases. India has underperformed even relative to South Asian neighbours, most of which have significantly lower per capita income, with two (Bangladesh and Nepal) still classified as Least Developed Countries.

Table 2.4 gives an idea of this. Sri Lanka has the best health indicators in South Asia, reflecting a long history of higher per capita public health spending. India does much worse in comparison, and even worse than Bangladesh on indicators like life expectancy at birth and child mortality. It is on par with Nepal and Pakistan for most indicators, despite much higher per capita income and supposed level of development.

Table 2.4: Some health indicators for South Asian countries

	Bangladesh	*India*	*Nepal*	*Pakistan*	*Sri Lanka*
Per capita GDP (US$ in 2019)	1,856	2,100	1,071	1,285	3,853
Current health spending per capita (US$ in 2016)	34	62	45	40	153
Out of pocket spending as % of current health spending (in 2016)	72	65	55	65	50

[53]World Health Organization, 'BRICS Health and WHO Country Presence Profile', available at https://apps.who.int/iris/bitstream/handle/10665/255800/WHO-CCU-17.05-eng.pdf;sequence=.

	Bangladesh	*India*	*Nepal*	*Pakistan*	*Sri Lanka*
Life expectancy at birth (years, in 2016)	72.7	68.8	70.2	66.5	75.3
Neonatal mortality rate (per 1000 live births, in 2017)	18	24	21	44	6
Under 5 mortality rate (per 1000 live births, in 2017)	32	39	34	75	9
Maternal mortality rate (per 100,000 live births, in 2015)	176	174	258	178	30
Child malnutrition (stunting % under 5)	36	38	36	38	17
Incidence of Tuberculosis (per 100,000 people)	221	204	152	267	1
Incidence of Malaria (per 1,000 people at risk)	2	7.7	0.5	4.5	1
UHC Service coverage index (0-100)*	46	56	46	40	62

Source: World Bank World Development Indicators, https://data.worldbank.org/indicator/NY.GDP.PCAP.CD, WHO World Health Statistics, 2018 and 2019, and UNDP Country Profiles, http://hdr.undp.org/en/countries/profiles.

Low public spending over decades has resulted in low levels of health infrastructure and numbers of health personnel. For every 10,000 people, India has less than 8 physicians, 21 nurses and midwives, and 7 hospital beds. This is well below the WHO threshold for meeting the SDGs, of 44.5 doctors, nurses, and midwives per 10,000 people,[54] and much lower than say, Norway, which has 46 physicians, 181 nurses, and 39 hospital beds per 10,000 population. There are large shortfalls in workers in the public health system, with very inadequate staffing of doctors, nurses, and other health workers in primary health centres, and big gaps in specialists like surgeons, obstetricians, and gynaecologists at community health centres. Low public health spending also means that communicable diseases like TB and malaria are rife and have been very hard to control, and others like dengue and encephalitis also appear seasonally with some force. As a result, India had a relatively low level of preparedness or apparent resilience when confronted with a major pandemic like Covid-19.

In the early decades, low public health spending tended to be explained by relatively low rates of per capita income growth. But even in the three decades leading up to 2020, when India was one of the fastest growing economies in the world, the fruits of economic growth were not utilized to invest more in public health or in the health infrastructure and personnel. Despite promises by successive governments to increase the share of government health spending to 3 per cent of GDP, it has remained at less than one third of that,

---

*The UHC Service coverage index tracks coverage of universal healthcare services, as an index from 0 to 100, computed as the geometric mean of 14 tracer indicators of health service coverage organized into 4 components: (1) Reproductive, maternal, newborn and child health (2) Infectious diseases (3) Non-communicable diseases (4) Service capacity and access.

[54]WHO, *Health Workforce Requirement for Universal Health Coverage and the Sustainable Development Goals,* available at https://apps.who.int/iris/bitstream/handle/10665/250330/9789241511407-eng.pdf.

at *less than 1 per cent of GDP*, one of the lowest such ratios in the world.[55] Central government spending on health is only one-third of that, at around 0.3 per cent of GDP. This is obviously completely inadequate to meet the needs for ensuring minimally reasonable health services accessible to the entire population. While India's total health spending per capita is higher than Bangladesh, Nepal, and Pakistan, nearly two-thirds is undertaken by private households and individuals, as out-of-pocket spending. Figure 2.4 shows that, as a result, India's total health spending in relation to GDP was the lowest among five South Asian nations.

This has meant high—and growing—inequality in access to healthcare. The rich are able to access super-speciality hospitals with luxury facilities and state-of-the-art treatment, which even attract medical tourists from abroad. But the bulk of the population has to cope with very inadequate and overcrowded public facilities and deal with often poorly trained local practitioners, and often cannot even afford the essential medicines required for treatment. The resulting reliance on private healthcare providers has other problems that are discussed below.

Nutrition plays a very important role in affecting health conditions; and both undernutrition and malnutrition in the form of overweight and obesity due to unhealthy diets can have adverse health effects. The prevalence of stunting among children has been linked to poor nutrition, not only from birth, but even in the womb because of lack of adequate nourishment of mothers. The continuing presence of large numbers of hungry people and those who cannot afford a balanced diet, is therefore a sign of relatively poor health conditions. The most recent National Family Health Survey 2019–20 (NFHS-5), revealed some alarming trends: overall, child nutrition indicators *did not improve at all* between 2015–16 and 2019–20

[55]WHO, *Global Spending on Health: Weathering the Storm*, Geneva, 2020.

in ten major states for which data were available in December 2020; in seven states the proportion of underweight children increased; and stunting increased in six states. This suggests that for India as a whole, progress in reducing undernutrition stalled after 2015 and more than one-third of children under the age of five years are likely to be underweight and stunted. The implications for future health and development are serious, and there is already evidence of slowdown, pauses, and reversals in infant mortality decline in large parts of India in 2017 and 2018 from other data sources.[56]

Figure 2.4: Government health spending

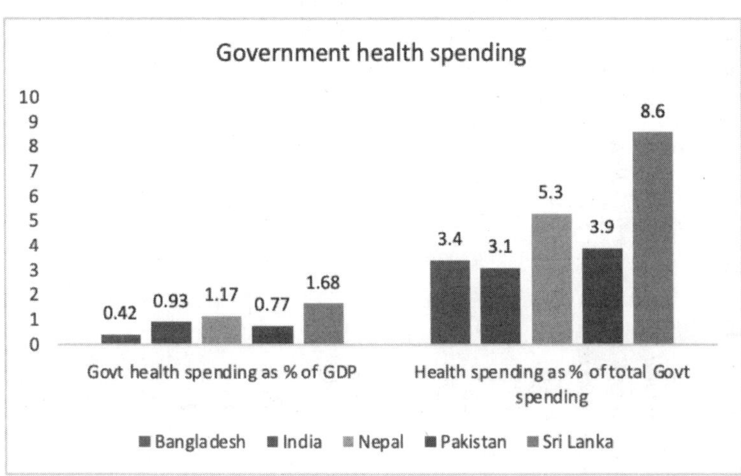

Source: WHO World Health Statistics 2018 and 2019.

[56]Jean Drèze, Aashish Gupta, Sai Ankit Parashar, and Kanika Sharma, 'Pauses and Reversals of Infant Mortality Decline in India in 2017 and 2018', SSRN, 8 November 2020.

Table 2.5: Some health indicators by state, most recent year

	Neonatal Mortality Rate (per 1000 live births)	*Under 5 Mortality Rate (per 1000 live births)*	*Sex ratio at birth (Girls per 1000 boys)*	*Full immunization rate (%)*	*Institutional delivery (%)*
Andhra Pradesh	23	37	913	100	86
Assam	23	52	896	83	72
Bihar	27	43	908	90	56
Chhattisgarh	26	49	963	87	76
Gujarat	21	33	848	92	92
Haryana	22	37	832	89	84
Himachal Pradesh	16	27	917	79	68
Jammu & Kashmir	18	26	906	100	85
Jharkhand	21	33	918	100	88
Karnataka	18	29	935	94	80
Kerala	6	11	959	100	91
Madhya Pradesh	32	55	922	78	62
Maharashtra	13	21	876	96	90

Odisha	32	50	948	60	71
Punjab	13	24	893	93	82
Rajasthan	28	45	857	82	75
Tamil Nadu	12	19	915	76	81
Telangana	21	34	901	90	92
Uttar Pradesh	30	47	882	85	51
Uttarakhand	30	41	850	95	67
West Bengal	17	27	937	96	81

Source: NITI Aayog, *Healthy States, Progressive India: Report on the Ranks of States and Union Territories*, p. 72.

India is a country of subcontinental dimensions with a federal political and governance structure, with health primarily a state subject under the Constitution. So it is not surprising that there are differences across states in both health facilities and health outcomes. Health and nutrition indicators vary so widely that some states have reached levels similar to advanced countries while others share characteristics with the least developed nations. Richer states typically have better health outcomes than poorer ones, but this is not inevitable: the state with the best health indicators among the large states (Kerala) is in the middle in terms of per capita income and had made significant achievements in health and education even when it was at lower levels of per capita income. Meanwhile, Gujarat—one of the richer states—shows relatively poor indicators, on par with much poorer states.

Differential performance on different health indicators can be explained by historical processes, institutional structures, social relations, and political economy factors that vary across regions and states. But they certainly reflect differences in the level, spread, and efficacy of public health services over decades. The states with the best (Kerala) and most improved (Tamil Nadu) health outcomes are those with much better availability of essential health infrastructure: health centres at various levels; ratios of doctors, nurses, and other health workers to population; and so on. Per capita public spending on health in Kerala and Tamil Nadu has been roughly double of that in Uttar Pradesh and Bihar for the past three decades. While state governments were constrained by the fiscal resources they could collect and what they receive as devolution from national taxes, how much of their total spending they put on health also depended on the traditions established in that state and the extent of public pressure. The scholar Dipa Sinha has suggested that women's status and public action influence each other and work together to affect health and other human development outcomes across states.[57] Public investment contributed to improving women's status, as in the push for female education by governments in Kerala and Tamil Nadu; better women's status then helped to determine the issues that became important for political parties, thereby affecting levels and distribution of public spending. The effectiveness of such spending also matters, and this is once again where political economy considerations, social structures, greater awareness of the citizenry, and some degree of public accountability all come into play. The extent to which reliable public health services actually reach the people depends on all of these.

This helps to understand the very substantial differences in health indicators across states before the pandemic—and partly explains the varying responses to the pandemic and the relative ability to control it. However, while states do differ a great deal, they are all affected directly by national health policies. These had even more impact on states in the past three decades, because of the growing role of some centrally sponsored schemes like the National Health Mission and the more recent Ayushman Bharat, and because low public spending led to much greater privatization of health services, with very unequal private health service delivery.

India may be one of the few countries in the world where essential government healthcare provision, which is part of normal government functions in most societies, is delivered primarily through special 'programmes', or 'missions'. Whenever the crises created by inadequate basic health services have become too extreme to ignore, the central government in India has responded by creating special 'schemes', 'programmes' or 'missions' that are supposed to fill the gaps created by decades of public underprovision. But this approach allows for many

---

[57]Dipa Sinha, *Women, Public Services and Health in India: Why are States Different?*, New Delhi: Routledge India, 2016.

anomalies in the treatment of health workers. For example, the government does not treat health workers engaged in 'schemes' as regular employees. Instead, they are supposedly 'volunteers', 'community workers' or 'friends' of particular schemes, with low to non-existent wages, no job security or other social security and poor working conditions. Many important schemes tend to be staffed and run by locally recruited women workers who, in most states, officially get a fraction of even unskilled legal minimum wages.[58]

This trend started in the 1990s, as both central and state governments reduced the numbers in permanent public employment and worsened the conditions of work for new recruits.[59] Many public services in India started relying increasingly on the unpaid or underpaid labour of women. For health, underfunded public provision was institutionalized through two programmes: the Integrated Child Development Scheme (ICDS) which provides essential nutrition and care services to pregnant and lactating mothers and infant children; and the National Health Mission (NHM), which aims to ensure universal access to quality health services. These schemes rely on underpaid frontline workers who are dominantly if not exclusively women, generating extreme inequalities both among public health workers and among those receiving health services.[60] Such workers (Anganwadi workers and helpers in the ICDS and Accredited Social Health Activists or ASHAs

---

[58]A few state governments, like that of Telangana, have sought to increase the remuneration provided to Anganwadi workers and ASHAs out of their own funds, but they still remain lower than wages paid to other government employees. See, 'Telangana Anganwadi Workers & Helpers Salaries Hiked', TeachersBadi.in.

[59]Jayati Ghosh, 'Public employment for public purpose', *India Exclusion Report 2019-20*, New Delhi: Centre for Equity Studies, 2020, pp. 243–60.

[60]Ravi Duggal, 'A New Health Policy for Health Sector Reforms', *Cehat*, Mumbai: Centre for Enquiry into Health and Allied Themes, 2007, available at www.cehat.org/cehat/uploads/files/a87.pdf.

in the NHM) are not treated on par with other government employees; instead, they are described as 'voluntary workers' who are not paid wages (which would require paying at least minimum wages) but only an 'honorarium' that is typically a fraction of the official minimum wage. The wages have been increased by some states, but in general they continue to receive less than the minimum wages.[61] Their work is described as 'part time', even though their required activities are very extensive,[62] and typically require at least seven or eight hours a day, and often longer.

---

[61]'Increase in Salary of Workers and Helpers', Press Information Bureau, Government of India, Ministry of Women and Child Development, 21 November 2019.

[62]Consider just some of the tasks listed for ASHAs: create awareness and provide information to the community on determinants of health such as nutrition, basic sanitation, and hygiene, healthy living and working conditions, information on existing health services, and the need for timely utilization of health and family welfare services; counsel women on birth preparedness, importance of safe delivery, breastfeeding, and complementary feeding, immunization, contraception, and prevention of common infections (including reproductive tract infections and sexually transmitted diseases), and care of young children; mobilize the community and facilitate local people's access to health and related services provided by the government at the local level, including immunization, antenatal, and post-natal check-ups, ICDS, sanitation, etc.; arrange to escort pregnant women and children requiring treatment and/ or admission to the nearest health facility; provide primary medical care for minor ailments such as diarrhoea, fevers, and first aid for minor injuries as well as short course treatment of tuberculosis; act as a depot holder for essential health provisions being made available to every habitation like Oral Rehydration Therapy, iron and folic acid tablets, chloroquine for treating malaria, Disposable Delivery Kits, oral contraceptive pills and condoms, etc.; manage and allocate to members of the community the contents of the Drug Kit supposedly provided to each ASHA; inform the health authorities at the primary health centre or sub-centre about the births and deaths in her village and any unusual health problems or outbreak of disease in the community; promote the construction of household toilets under the official sanitation campaigns; work with the local elected body to develop a comprehensive community health plan.

Such workers also tend to be loaded with additional tasks, simply because in most states they have been found to be among the most dedicated and committed of public servants who have grassroots contacts and are able to identify particular individuals and groups in any community easily. So they are increasingly engaged in a wide range of other public interventions, like mobilization and awareness campaigns, and even called upon to help in election duties. In the ongoing pandemic, they have been tasked to disseminate information about required behaviour to all households, track actual and potential cases, do the contact tracing, and ensure that quarantines are maintained.[63]

In many states, for want of better regular public health infrastructure and facilities, the NHM and ICDS effectively became the basic sources of public health delivery for the poor. But public spending on this was not only inadequate but even reduced over time. This left very significant gaps that private health service providers arose to fill, so out-of-pocket spending became even more important for households across the country.[64] Therefore private provision effectively became the major source of health services for most Indians.

This was an unfortunate outcome. There are good reasons why even the most ardent aficionados of market-based systems generally agree that there is an important role for *public* provision and regulation of health services. Health is one of those sectors (like finance and education) that is much more marked by what economists call information asymmetries: the idea that everyone involved in the market does not have access to the same

---

[63]See, for example, the guidelines issued to frontline workers by the Ministry of Health and Family Welfare, 'Role of frontline workers in prevention and management of Coronavirus', available at www.mohfw.gov.in/pdf/PreventionandManagementofCOVID19FLWEnglish.pdf.

[64]Unfortunately, since the NSSO consumption expenditure survey conducted in 2017–18 was not released by the Modi government, we do not have any recent data to assess this.

information and so cannot make decisions on the same footing. This goes beyond 'incomplete information' (the idea that final outcomes cannot be fully known to anyone) because one party to the transaction has information or knowledge that the other party does not. In the case of health, for example, patients usually do not know enough to judge whether a diagnostic procedure is required, whether a medicine has been correctly prescribed, whether a treatment is necessary or effective. Further, the incentives of the health providers (especially if they are commercially minded or profit-motivated) need not coincide with the interests of the patients. Many patients, especially those who are poor or less educated, may not be in a position to judge whether the doctor is adequately trained and qualified to treat them. There is the possibility that a doctor could prescribe an unnecessary or excessively expensive medical test or form of treatment, or misinform a patient about potential recovery. Private healthcare without proper regulation or monitoring leaves both rich and poor patients open to exploitation by private practitioners, who can recommend unnecessary and expensive diagnostic procedures or treatment, which they are not in a position to query or contest. This is why globally it has been found that health systems dominated by the public sector (such as in Canada or Italy) are generally both cheaper and more efficient, in terms of delivering better health outcomes, than those dominated by the private sector (such as in the US).

Within largely private health systems, there is the further problem that a lot of curative care can be very expensive and become a major drain on household finances, or can simply be unaffordable for poorer families who then just go without treatment. In India, it was estimated a decade ago that every year, around 40 million people fell into poverty because of these out-of-pocket health expenses.[65] The numbers are likely to have

[65]Y. Balarajan, S. Selvaraj, and S. V. Subramanian, 'Health care and equity in

increased significantly since then.

Some privately based systems are associated with insurance schemes that enable patients to draw upon resources based on premiums paid to insurance companies. In some models, governments pay for or subsidize the insurance premia to be paid by target groups, such as those defined as poor or otherwise vulnerable. This is seen to have two major benefits. First, it reduces the potential of catastrophic levels of health expenses to push families into poverty and would at least prevent extreme financial distress in the wake of a medical emergency or even prolonged treatment for long-term illnesses. Secondly, by enabling patients to seek out the health provider/hospital of their choice, it is supposed to further competition and encourage quality improvements among all health service providers, both public and private.

However, insurance-based health programmes come with their own, additional, set of problems. They add a further layer of commercial intermediary to the health delivery system; and insurance, just like health services, is also plagued by significant problems emerging from asymmetric information. When it is just private insurers dealing with patients and hospitals and clinics, insurers may be concerned that treatment is unnecessary or overly expensive; or that patients have withheld important information that could have increased the risk of particular illnesses, and so on. There are also possibilities of collusion between any two parties, since there are now three parties involved. If we throw the government into this mix, as in those situations where the government pays all or a part of the premium at least for some patients, the matter becomes even more complicated. Then, the incentives truly can conflict across the different parties: for example, the private health provider and patient could collude to result in more expensive treatment

---

India', *The Lancet*, 11 January 2011.

that would have to be paid for by the insurance company; or the insurance company could collect the premium and then refuse to pay the full cost of treatment citing particular conditions; or the patient could be denied the treatment or forced to pay because of collusion by the health provider and the insurance company; or the various private parties could collude to make the government pay when it is not warranted; and so on. There are all sorts of unfortunate possibilities. The example of the dysfunctional health system in the US suggests that these can be quite common in a health system that is based on private health delivery combining with private insurance companies and government support. As noted earlier, the US with its private and insurance-based system has the most expensive health system in the world,[66] yet it results in inferior health outcomes compared to countries spending much less and relying more on public provision.

Despite these clear dangers, the Modi government chose to reduce spending on public health and instead focus energies and resources on an insurance-based provision, relying on private participation, with some subsidies provided to some poor households. This scheme, Pradhan Mantri Jan Arogya Yojana (PM-JAY, also called 'Ayushman Bharat') was launched in 2018 and touted as 'the world's largest fully funded health insurance scheme'. It is supposed to provide cashless medical insurance cover of up to ₹5,00,000 per poor family per year for health expenses, for prevention, promotion, and ambulatory care at secondary and tertiary levels. Beneficiaries are those identified as 'poor' by the Socio-Economic Caste Census Survey of 2011,[67] approximately 107 million households. But this is a dated list, which was already questioned for its exclusions and in any

[66]See, for example, the World Health Organization data on this. Available at www.who.int/health_financing/documents/health-expenditure-report-2019.pdf.

[67]National Health Authority, 'How are the beneficiaries identified?'.

case does not take into account population increases over the subsequent decade. It has been plausibly argued that it excludes around 110 million poor people.[68]

The Ayushman Bharat insurance scheme is essentially a watered down and revised version of the US 'Medicare' system: a health insurance scheme that is publicly funded but privately managed through insurance companies and private medical service providers. This comes with all the acknowledged problems of moral hazard, conflict of interest, potentially inflated costs, and exclusion. Thus far, the main beneficiaries appear to have been insurance companies and private medical service providers rather than people. Many problems have been officially acknowledged,[69] such as difficulties in the identification of beneficiaries. Lack of 'portability' of the scheme across the country meant that patients had to travel back to their home state to get treated. There were many reports of fraud and abuse, including fraudulent claims (with ghost beneficiaries, impersonation, multiple packages); charging money from patients over the counter even though it is designed as a cashless scheme; and suspicious increases in a number of surgical procedures like hysterectomies, mostly in private hospitals.

In addition, the programme has been hugely underfunded even by official estimation of requirement. In the first year, the central government's budget allocation for the scheme was only ₹2,000 crore.[70] Even if the state governments had coughed

---

[68]Calculations by Jean Drèze, Reetika Khera, and Meghana Mungikar, reported in 'More than 100mn excluded from PDS as govt uses outdated Census 2011 data', *IndiaSpend*, 16 April 2020.

[69]'Lessons Learnt in One Year Implementation of PM-JAY 2018-19', New Delhi: National Health Authority.

[70]This was the budgetary allocation in addition to the allocation for a pre-existing health insurance scheme, the Rashtriya Swasthya Bima Yojana (RSBY – National Health Insurance Scheme). See 'Ayushman Bharat', Budget Brief, Vol. 11 Issue 5, New Delhi: Centre for Policy Research.

up their share of 40 per cent, that would mean only ₹3,300 crore—or just ₹330 per family for 100 million families. But the government's own estimates set a premium of ₹1,100 per family for an annual coverage of ₹500,000.[71] In 2019–20, the budget allocation was first increased to ₹6,400 crore, but then slashed to only ₹3,314 crore because of concerns over underutilization.[72]

Since the scheme is limited to diagnostic and treatment procedures that occur during hospitalization,[73] it shifted the focus of the government to tertiary care, and within that to hospitalization. Yet outpatient health services, and particularly drug purchases, make up around two-thirds of the out-of-pocket expenses of Indians. The lack of attention to primary care was also recognized by the government, when it announced new 'Health and Wellness Centres' to provide outpatient care, immunization, maternal and child health services, and treatment of non-communicable diseases at the primary level. These are simply the old primary health centres with a fancy new name: the difference is that these were earlier funded entirely by state governments out of their own budgets, and now the central government is also providing some funds for this. But the amounts allocated for this in the annual budgets for 2019–20 and 2020–21 were so small (₹1,350 crore for the whole country) that they were unlikely to have much impact.

For these and other reasons, the PM-JAY has not had much success in improving health access or reducing health-

---

[71]Indranil Mukhopadhaya and Dipa Sinha, 'Painting a picture of ill-health', in Rohit Azad et al. (eds.), *A Quantum Leap in the Wrong Direction?*, Hyderabad: Orient Blackswan, 2019, pp. 155–79.

[72]Himani Chandna, 'Sitharaman cuts budget for Modi's pet Ayushman Bharat scheme over fund "under-utilisation"', *The Print*, 1 February 2020.

[73]The PMJAY originally offered 1,393 treatment packages: 1,083 surgical procedures, 309 medical, and one unspecified. In April 2019, 554 packages were discontinued, the rates of fifty-seven packages were reduced, and 237 new packages were added. (See T. K. Rajalakshmi, 'Public funds for private benefit', *Frontline*, 8 November 2019.)

related financial insecurity of most Indians. Even people defined as 'beneficiaries' did not always benefit much. A study in Chhattisgarh found that enrolment under PM-JAY and similar publicly funded health insurance schemes did not increase utilization of hospital care or lead to decline in out-of-pocket health expenditure.[74] Only in states like Kerala that already had a relatively strong public health system, and used the scheme only for public hospitals, did this work reasonably well.

The PM-JAY scheme has added another layer of privatization and therefore potential exploitation of consumers into the Indian private health system, which is largely unregulated. Privatization has become a dominant force across all aspects of the health sector, from medical education to the production of medical equipment, pharmaceutical and therapeutic devices, to healthcare services—but attempts at regulation have been haphazard, limited, uneven, and largely ineffective.[75] These concerns became particularly important during the pandemic, when problems emerging from lack of regulation like excessive pricing by private providers have been evident almost from the start.

The health insurance system also left out the major element of health costs for Indians—medicines. Recent increases in prices of many essential medicines have made them unaffordable for a significant proportion of the population. This may seem surprising, because India was globally renowned for its low-cost

---

[74]S. Garg. K. K. Bebarta, and N. Tripathi, 'Performance of India's national publicly funded health insurance scheme, Pradhan Mantri Jan Arogya Yojana (PMJAY), in improving access and financial protection for hospital care: findings from household surveys in Chhattisgarh state', *BMC Public Health 2020*, Vol. 20. No. 949, 16 June 2020.

[75]See Rama V. Baru, *Private health care in India: Social characteristics and trends*, New Delhi: Sage Publications 1998; Leena V. Gangolli, Ravi Duggal, and Abhay Shukla, *Review of Healthcare in India*, Mumbai: Centre for Enquiry into Health and Allied Themes (Cehat), 2005.

generic drug industry, and many Indian producers are known to supply affordable drugs to countries across the world. Yet the Indian pharmaceutical market has been described as one in which there is poverty of supply of even essential drugs to the poor despite adequate drug production.[76] Only a tiny proportion of drug consumption in India occurs through the public sector, which caters mainly to some poor and middle-class sections who have access to government clinics where such drugs are provided. The overwhelming majority of drugs in India are purchased on the market.

This strong market dependence has generated several problems. First, most fixed dose combinations of drugs available in the Indian market are irrational, with only one drug being useful while the others are unnecessary additions. Second, despite substantial generic production, most drugs are marketed under their brand names, and the prices then depend on the marketing practices. Firms engage in 'intramolecular competition', claiming that certain combinations offer therapeutic advantages, to charge very different prices for what is effectively the same drug.[77] This problem has persisted for a while: for example, a study in 2002 found that for a particular drug for treating blood pressure (amlodipine) there were at least 40 formulations, with the highest priced version priced at 8.6 times that of the cheapest one.[78]

There have been varying policies over time on administrative control of drug prices, in the face of such evidence of profiteering by drug companies. Drug Price Control Orders (DPCO) have

---

[76]Malini Aisola, S. Srinivasan, and T. Srikrishna, 'Pharma Price Control Policy: Unrealistic and Unfair', *Economic & Political Weekly,* Vol. 49, No. 34, August 2014.
[77]Ravinder Jha, 'Prices of New Pharmaceuticals in India: A Cross Section Study', *Economic & Political Weekly,* Vol. 45, No. 10, 6 March 2010.
[78]Anurag Bhargava, 'Tremendous Variations in Drug Prices in the Indian Pharmaceutical Market', *Locost, Impoverishing the Poor: Pharmaceuticals and Drug Pricing in India,* Vadodara: Gujarat, 2004, pp. 37–45.

been periodically revised, with both the number of drugs under control and the price limits varying quite dramatically over time.[79] In theory, this should have made more essential drugs affordable, but the devil is in the detail: only 10 per cent of the market is effectively under price control, because fixed drug combinations are excluded. The current DPCO is based on an average of market prices rather than cost of production, and therefore is biased towards the market leaders—the large companies that charge higher prices for their branded products. As a result, the drugs that most patients typically need, especially for serious and debilitating diseases, may well be beyond what they can afford. Between 2013 and 2018, medicine prices rose more rapidly than the general price level,[80] and things have got worse since then. India's growing reliance on imports of Active Pharmaceutical Ingredients (API) that enter into final drugs means that costs of production are affected by these import prices and the exchange rate of the rupee. For example, the price of insulin used to treat diabetes increased by nearly 20 per cent between June 2018 and June 2019, not just because of increasing demand but because the rupee depreciated.[81] Cancer drugs are unaffordable even for the middle classes. The drugs for treating tuberculosis (TB), a communicable disease that dominantly affects the poor, are provided free at government health centres—but many patients do not have access to these, and some choose to be treated by private practitioners. The new drug-resistant TB strains have to be treated with new drugs that are prohibitively expensive, estimated to cost as

[79]The number of drugs covered by the DPCO fell from 347 in 1979 to 142 in 1987 to only 74 in 2004. Since then the range of control has increased again, to 680 in 2014 and 857 in 2019.

[80]Mukhopadhaya and Sinha, 'Painting a picture of ill-health'.

[81]Amir Ullah Khan, 'India's drug price fix is hurting healthcare', *Mint*, 29 October 2019.

much as ₹25 lakh over a two-year period[82]—nearly twenty times the estimated per capita income of the country in 2020–21. Therefore, a critical issue in India is the absence of public procurement and distribution of essential drugs, which could act as some kind of control on private profiteering and ensure that the poor get access to essential and life-saving drugs. This meant that the existing structures were not going to be adequate to deal with a major health shock.

In sum, just as the economy was already in a weak position that made it more vulnerable to a shock like the pandemic, India's public health system was also ill-equipped to deal with such a major challenge. How that played out is discussed in the next chapter.

[82]Malathy Iyer, 'MDR-TB treatment could cost up to 25L in Mumbai, says study', *Economic Times*, 3 October 2016.

chapter 3

THE COVID-19 OUTBREAK, LOCKDOWN, AND HEALTH FALLOUT

The first case of Covid-19 in India was reported in the state of Kerala on 30 January 2020, quickly followed by two more cases there and one in Delhi—all people with recent travel history to Wuhan, China. The subsequent early cases were also people returning from travel abroad, including from Europe, where the first phase of the pandemic was aleady raging. These cases remained confined to particular areas in the first weeks. It took until mid-March for the number of cases to cross 100.

In that early stage, it was argued (for example by the then Health Minister of Kerala K. K. Shailaja) that a rigorous system of checking those entering the country and isolating them and then following up with contact tracing, should be instituted, so as to limit the spread of the disease. However, this was done only to a very limited extent: there was somewhat lackadaisical thermal screening at airports of passengers arriving from abroad, but no serious attempt to identify those who were infected and contain the numbers. At first, it appeared that only the state government of Kerala took the matter seriously, probably due to its past experience with managing the Nipah virus epidemic in 2018, and Kerala's strong pattern of cross-border migration that rendered it more vulnerable.

Globally, the numbers of those infected had begun to rise by mid-March, and some states in India—those that had higher numbers of travellers from outside the country, including Delhi, Kerala, Maharashtra, Telangana, Andhra Pradesh, and Karnataka—began to bring in local measures restricting some travel and large gatherings. Prime Minister Narendra Modi spoke to the nation requesting a 'voluntary' fourteen-hour public curfew on 22 March, when according to the Union Health Ministry, there were just 315 confirmed cases in the entire country. As part of this supposedly voluntary 'Janta Curfew', public services like metros, railways, and markets and shops (except for those providing 'essential goods') were shut down.[1]

At that point, effective testing and contact tracing in those areas where early infections had been identified, along with tracking of new entries into those regions, could have worked to control the spread of the disease, as in several other Asian countries. Since the incidence of the disease was limited to a few cities and states, this could have been a feasible strategy that would not involve too much disruption in the entire country. Some states had already imposed local lockdowns, so restricting movement to and from those could also have helped. However, this was not attempted; instead, a nationwide lockdown was suddenly announced with only a few hours notice and imposed from 25 March.

This surprise announcement was typical of the 'shock and awe' strategic preferences of Prime Minister Modi, which had already been evident in previous actions like his sudden announcement of demonetization with only four hours' notice on 8 November 2016. The lockdown was presented as a limited 'war' of twenty-one days against the Coronavirus, which would be only slightly longer than the eighteen-day Kurukshetra war of the epic Mahabharata.[2] In his speech, Prime Minister Modi also referred to another Hindu epic, the Ramayana, exhorting people to forget what it is to step outside for twenty-one days: 'Draw a Laxman Rekha outside your door and remember that

---

[1]Aparna Banerjea, 'India observes "Janta Curfew" as Covid-19 cases rise above 300', *Mint*, 22 March 2020.

[2]'Covid-19: "Mahabharata was won in 18 days, war against Coronavirus will take 21 days," says PM Modi', *Scroll.in*, 25 March 2020.

even a step outside of it will bring Coronavirus into your house.'[3]

This was an excessive reaction given the inevitably widespread dislocation that would result, and it was also over optimistic about the time it would take to control the virus. At the time, many argued that this was a valid and even responsible reaction given the threat posed by the virus (which had not yet been declared as a pandemic). However, even those who supported the decision probably expected that there would be substantial measures taken by the government to provide social protection for the loss of livelihoods and other fallout of the lockdown. This expectation was belied.

The Lockdown

The Indian lockdown, which formally began on 25 March 2020, was recognized as the most stringent lockdown in the world, scoring 100 out of 100 on the Oxford Blavatnik School Stringency Index, based on eighteen different indicators.[4] It was adopted very abruptly and imposed across the nation, with only a few hours' notice given to the population. Even the state governments that had to implement it and deal with the fallout were not consulted or given prior warning. It covered even distant and relatively isolated locations where there was no sign of the infection. It involved oppressive controls on almost all activities and movement, with complete cessation of all public transport. It was enforced brutally, along the lines of a military curfew, which is what the local-level administrators understood to be the requirement. Those 'breaking the curfew' were often

---

[3]Nistula Hebbar, 'Coronavirus | PM's address to the nation updates: lockdown extended to entire country for next 21 days, says Modi', *The Hindu*, 24 March 2020.

[4]Oxford COVID-19 Government Response Tracker, available at https://covidtracker.bsg.ox.ac.uk/stringency-scatter.

severely punished, with several instances of police brutality, even leading to death.[5]

The initial lockdown, which was originally declared to last for twenty-one days, was extended to nearly two months until 17 May, when some measures were relaxed—though a majority of restrictions remained in place, with the stringency index at 80/100. Thereafter 'unlocking' proceeded in phases on the part of the central government, with statewise variations, as different states identified 'hotspots' and retained controls or put in their own restrictions periodically.[6]

The lockdown did not slow down the spread of the disease—although it could be argued (and has been claimed) that the disease would have spread even more rapidly in the initial phases without the lockdown.[7] Just before the national lockdown on 25 March 2020, the country had only 657 confirmed cases (mostly confined to large cities in a few regions and mostly among travellers returning from abroad) and twelve deaths from

---

[5]In many of these cases, despite the victims being beaten, the deaths were registered as 'accidental' or due to cardiac arrest or some other cause, by the police involved in the incidents. See Mural Krishnan, 'Police excesses for lockdown violation led to 12 deaths: Study', *Hindustan Times*, 26 May 2020.

[6]On 30 May 2020, phased reopening continued throughout the country. (Ministry of Home Affairs, Government of India Order dated 30 May 2020, available at https://www.mha.gov.in/sites/default/files/MHAOrderDt_30052020.pdf. From 8 June, places of worship, shopping malls, hotels, and restaurants were allowed to open, and restrictions on inter- and intra-state travel were also lifted (Neeraj Chauhan, 'After Covid-19 lockdown, plan to unlock India in phases', *Hindustan Times*, 31 May 2020). State governments were empowered to identify containment zones and could impose their own restrictions. While some states eased restrictions, others like Delhi, Maharashtra, Andhra Pradesh, Uttarakhand, Odisha, and Telangana continued with many of them ('Covid-19 lockdown: Check which states have extended or relaxed curbs from today', *Mint*, 1 June 2021).

[7]Sanjana Krishnan, Sahil Deo, and Shardul Manurkar, '50 Days of Lockdown: Measuring India's Success in Arresting COVID-19', ORF Special Report No. 107, May 2020, Observer Research Foundation.

Covid-19, in a population of more than 1.3 billion. By 18 May, after more than seven weeks of this severe lockdown, India had 100,328 cases and 3,156 registered deaths resulting from the Coronavirus.[8] Along with the Covid-19 deaths that continued to increase, there were many unnecessary additional deaths that resulted directly or indirectly from the lockdown, with at least 600 such deaths reported by late May (Figure 4.1). These include at least twelve reported deaths resulting from policy brutality on those deemed to have violated lockdown restrictions—there were several cases of police firing on people who were breaking the lockdown restrictions, even when they were simply out to buy essential groceries or medicines. There were even more deaths of migrant workers, who were denied wages and were facing penury and starvation, who tried to get to their homes in very difficult circumstances, many of whom walked hundreds of kilometres in the attempt to reach their homes when all public transport had been stopped.[9]

Even these lockdown death numbers are likely to be serious underestimates, as they do not include those who died while travelling in trains attempting to get home, or those killed on railway tracks. The Indian Railways has admitted that more 8,700 people died on railway tracks during the lockdown, many of them migrants attempting to get home to their villages.[10] There were others who died after reaching their destinations, often because they had become infected en route.

---

[8]*Our World in Data.*

[9]Shoaib Daniyal, 'Not China, not Italy: India's Coronavirus lockdown is the harshest in the world', *Scroll.in*, 29 March 2020.

[10]PTI, 'Over 8,700 people died on tracks during lockdown-many of them were migrants', *Indian Express*, 2 June 2021.

Figure 3.1: Deaths from Covid-19 and from distress related to containment policies (15 March to 18 May 2020)

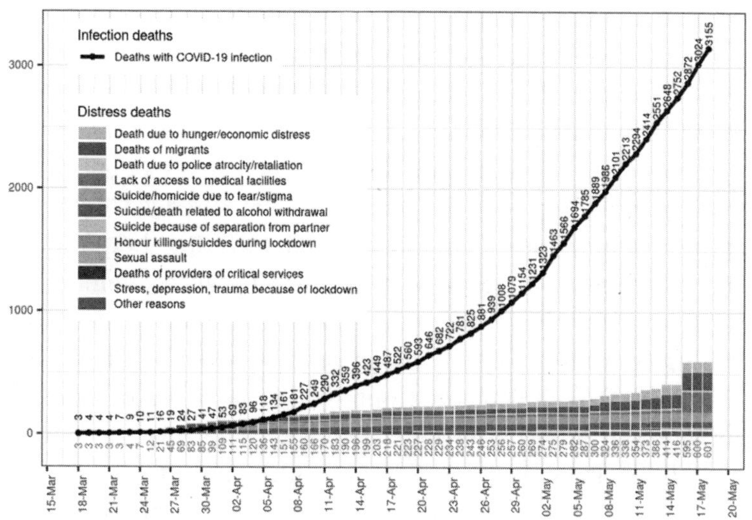

Source: Impact of Covid-19 Policies in India, coronapolicyimpact.org, last accessed on 27 May 2020.

While the need for the lockdown was presented in terms of the choice between lives and livelihoods, the reality was more complex. For the many millions who are at the very margin of subsistence, with little savings, and receiving no compensation and negligible or non-existent social protection, loss of livelihood can even lead to loss of life because of the debilitating effects of declining food intake and inability to deal with other health concerns. Poorly fed people became more vulnerable to various diseases,. even as other health services were hugely restricted and many just stopped during and after the lockdown. There was massive economic disruption and loss of livelihood for ordinary people, so the economic impact of the pandemic was felt across the country well before the onset of the disease in most parts of the country. It affected supply chains and reduced both wage employment and self-employed incomes. This is why the poorly planned and brutal lockdown in India created conditions for very significant spread of infection, especially once restrictions were eased. In an ironic twist, the material desperation that forced migrant workers to move back to their homes despite the constraints they faced was probably responsible for spreading the virus across the country and particularly among the poor.

From the start, despite the limited spread of infection when it was first imposed, the lockdown extended over the entire country, across all states and covering both urban and rural areas, stopping all transport and all economic and social activity other than some defined essential services. This was more severe than any other country: even in China, the lockdown was implemented only in the province of Wuhan, and public transport was not stopped but simply had to comply with distancing guidelines. Eliminating all public transport was especially cruel in a country where the vast majority of people do not have their own means of transport. The most extreme weapon that could be used against the pandemic was used first, with no strategy in reserve in case the virus continued to spread. Eventually, when such an aggressive lockdown became unsustainable because of the impact on the economy and livelihoods, the government was forced to lift restrictions precisely when it had become more dangerous to do so, because the disease had spread more and there were therefore greater chances of infection.

As in most other countries, the lockdown dealt a massive blow to both demand and supply—but with even greater effects on employment. Around 120 million jobs were lost in April 2020 alone.[11] The greater part of the non-agricultural work

[11]Govindraj Ethiraj, '"100-120 million jobs lost due to COVID-19 lockdown"', *IndiaSpend*, 20 April 2020.

force simply had no livelihood for at least two months, with no choice but to fall back on existing savings or borrowing for survival. The worst affected were migrant workers working in urban and rural locations different from their homes (estimated to be around 100–150 million in number). There was a slight revival in employment from June 2020, as lockdown restrictions were progressively eased, but wage incomes did not recover, as workers faced reduced days of employment and lower remuneration.

Around 95 per cent of all workers in India are informal, with no legal protection vis-à-vis their employers and also little or no social protection. Publicly provided ('universal') social protection like health insurance and unemployment benefit is also very limited and usually very niggardly in amount. Around half of all workers are self-employed, usually in informal micro-enterprises. All such workers were sharply affected by the lockdown, which deprived them of paid employment without warning. Since many of these workers already operated at the margin of subsistence, this generated severe economic distress, made worse by the fact that there was very little public assistance to prevent growing destitution and hunger.

For example, a tea seller who worked—and slept—in his roadside tea shop in Kolkata, said that earlier 'I worked well and lived with dignity.' But lack of customers because of the lockdown meant that he had to give up his shop and make a temporary home on the floor of the railway station. His savings were used up in the first few days; then he had to sell his mobile phone to buy food. When even that money ran out, he had to resort to begging. 'Suddenly I have turned homeless and been made a beggar.'[12] But even as the number of beggars increased,

[12]Hannah Ellis-Peterson and Shaikh Azizur Rahman, '"I just want to go home": the desperate millions hit by Modi's brutal lockdown', *The Guardian*, 4 April 2020.

those who earlier survived by begging were in more dire straits, facing absolute starvation. Temples and community kitchens in places of worship were closed and starving beggars were chased off the streets in the heart of New Delhi by over-zealous police.[13]

Despite this very severe lockdown, infections and deaths continued to increase, because the strategy failed to take into account the specific conditions of life and work for most Indians. At least one-third of the urban population and around a quarter of villagers in India live in extremely crowded and congested conditions, in very small dwellings with five or more people confined to one room.[14] 'Stay-at-home' policies in such contexts are unreasonable, oppressive, and even counterproductive when physical distancing norms cannot practically be followed. With limited access to clean water, hands cannot be washed frequently and repeatedly with soap and water. A survey of 1,594 households in 79 slums in Jaipur and Bhopal in 2015 had found that 40 per cent of households did not have domestic water taps. To get water, people had to congregate at public taps and truck-fed tanks, waiting in long queues to collect water for their daily needs.[15] So, even during the lockdown, women and girls living in congested slums without piped water and access to sanitation facilities within their homes had no choice but to come out and queue for hours in narrow lanes with no possibility of physical distancing, exposing themselves to the disease. As always, the poor were worst off in this. One study found that only 6 per cent of the poorest quintile (20 per cent) of households had access to non-shared sanitation, compared

---

[13]ANI, 'Woes of beggars outside Delhi's Hanuman Temple increase amid lockdown', *Business Standard*, 31 March 2020.

[14]NSS Report No. 556 (69/1.2/1), *Drinking Water, Sanitation, Hygiene and Housing Condition in India*.

[15]Adam Michael Auerbach, Tariq Thachil, 'How does Covid-19 affect urban slums? Evidence from settlement leaders in India', *World Development*, Vol. 140, April 2021.

to 93 per cent of the richest quintile.[16] The official guidelines also completely ignored the sizeable begging and homeless population,[17] who did not even have homes where they could confine themselves, much less 'balconies' from where they could clap for health workers.

These and other features that made the official guidelines impractical and counterproductive were quickly pointed out by many observers[18] but these concerns were ignored. This showed the extent of official insensitivity to the lived reality of a significant proportion of Indians, especially the poor. Essentially, official health instructions simply did not consider whether the poor could realistically comply with them.

These features could help explain why in the four months from March 2020, the rate of increase of Covid-19 infections in India was similar to neighbouring countries like Pakistan and Bangladesh that did not have such severe lockdowns, and much higher than in Sri Lanka. While the rate of transmission was reduced to some extent by these extreme restrictions on mobility and activity, as soon as they were eased, the virus spread even more rapidly. India overtook the average rate of new Covid-19 cases per million people in the world as a whole by late July. (Figure 4.2) In the first wave of the pandemic, the daily average number of new cases per million people peaked in late September at 67, which was significantly above the global average at the time. By then, the disease had spread across the country, including to relatively distant rural areas, as migrant

---

[16]Oxfam India, *Inequality Report 2021: India's Unequal Healthcare Story*, New Delhi, available at www.oxfamindia.org/knowledgehub/workingpaper/inequality-report-2021-indias-unequal-healthcare-story.

[17]Sabina Yasmin Rahman, '"Social distancing" during COVID-19: The metaphors and politics of pandemic response in India', *Health Sociology Review*, 28 June 2020.

[18]For a clear exposition, see D. Ray and S. Subramanian, 'Is There a Reasonable Alternative to a Comprehensive Lockdown?', *Ideas for India*, 28 March 2020.

workers in different urban areas across the country sought to return home to their villages in the wake of the livelihood collapse brought on by the lockdown. This is probably why the increase of recorded disease was so much more dramatic and far surpassed the global rate in the second wave of March–June 2021. Of course, all such comparisons are subject to an important caveat: the massive under-reporting of actual Covid-19 infections due to inadequate testing and official unwillingness to reveal the full extent of the spread.

Figure 3.2

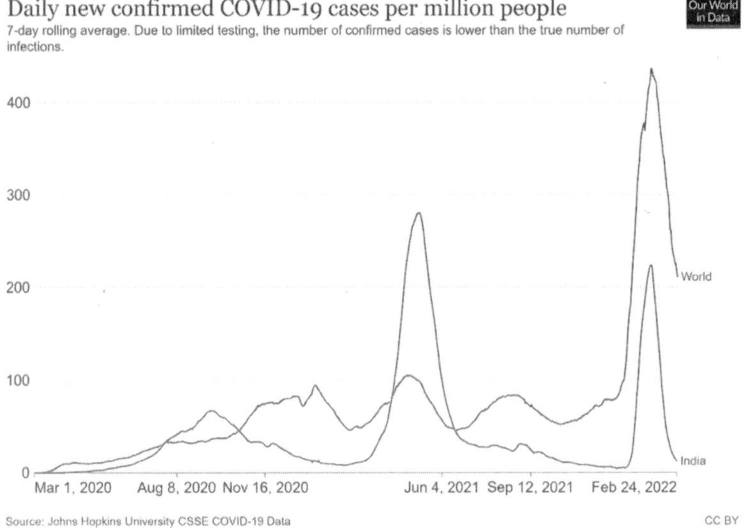

Source: *Our World in Data*, accessed on 25 February 2022.

Figure 3.3

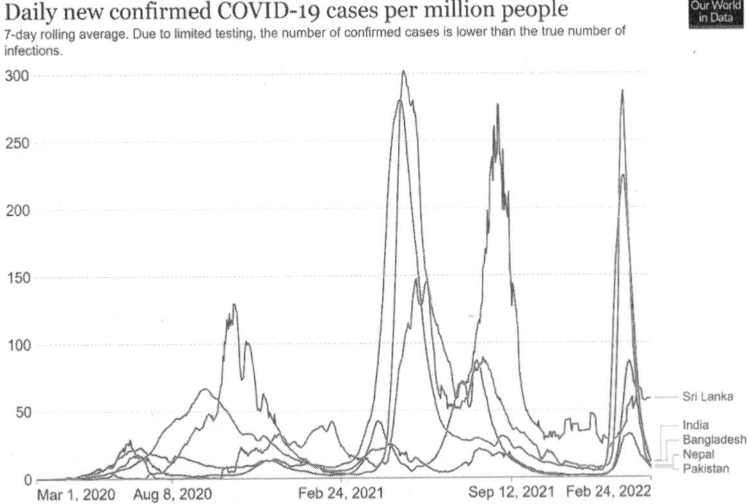

Source: *Our World in Data*, accessed on 25 February 2021.

The purpose of a lockdown can never be to completely suppress or eradicate the virus, which it obviously cannot do on its own. Essentially, a lockdown buys time: by delaying the spread of the virus, it allows the government to prepare and put in place infrastructure and arrangements to deal more effectively with the pandemic once the lockdown is lifted. This was repeatedly emphasized by the World Health Organization and by public health experts in India. The preparations required include expanding, training, and deploying the public health force; ramping up testing capacity and availability; developing a clear plan to trace and quarantine contacts; and ensuring key facilities (like hospital beds and intensive care units, ventilators and other machines, and personal protective equipment for healthcare workers) to treat and isolate patients.

The central government's actions on these fronts were limited and inadequate. In some cases, it even thwarted or made the efforts of state governments more difficult. Hardly any additional funds were allocated for public health expenditure to deal with the pandemic—only ₹15,000 crore, amounting to only 0.07 per cent of GDP in 2019–20; and that too, to be spent over four years. Eventually, less than half of that was actually distributed among states, and the distribution seemed to be quite arbitrary. State governments had to manage all the important issues arising in the pandemic, within their very limited resources. Only a handful of states (like Kerala) used the lockdown period to increase testing and contact tracing.[19] Testing increased very slowly: on 3 May the national testing rate (758 per million) was not even double the rate just before the lockdown. By late June the testing rate had increased to 5,371 per million, but was still low relative to most comparator countries, with high prices of tests deterring many.

More importantly, testing was not linked with effective contact tracing and isolating of positive cases, which is necessary for control of the disease. Even in big cities like Delhi and Mumbai, rigorous contact tracing seemed to have been nearly abandoned, despite (or perhaps because of?) surging cases.[20] The government introduced an Aarogya Setu app to enable contact tracing, but this had very limited success, since it typically failed to get relevant information either to health providers or to the people concerned, and even this was mostly not followed up with adequate physical contact tracing on the ground by June–July 2020.[21] In addition, supplies of basic equipment like protective equipment for health workers were not organized in

---

[19]Anuja Venkatachalam, 'Is India doing enough contact tracing in its battle against COVID-19?', *Health Analytics Asia*,18 September 2020.

[20]Arunabh Saikia, 'Covid-19: As cases surge in India, most states abandon contact tracing', *Scroll.in*, 13 July 2020.

[21]Aarefa Johari, 'Aarogya Setu: Has the world's most downloaded contact-tracing app actually been effective?', *Scroll.in*, 17 November 2020.

a timely manner, and shortages in these emerged quickly as the disease spread.[22] Other facilities like hospital beds, ventilators, etc., also remained well below the need. While the performance was uneven across state governments, much of this was related to fund shortages, because the central government provided so little in terms of additional resources to the states.

The centralization of power by the union government during the pandemic was rapid. Natural disasters are generally left for state governments to deal with, and health is also seen as fundamentally a state government responsibility. However, the Disaster Management Act, 2005 allows the central government and the National Disaster Management Authority to override any other law in force and issue directions to any authority in India, and requires that all such directions must be followed. This is supposed to enable the centre to evolve a common national strategy to deal with any disaster that requires continuous co-rdination across different states and regions, as well as different branches of government. This law was used to invoke and enforce the lockdown, without consultation with state governments, and even without informing them beforehand or giving them time to prepare.

The assumption implicit in the law that this central power would generate a national strategy to deal with the pandemic, in co-rdination with state governments, turned out not to be valid. Instead, in the first phase of the pandemic, top-down decisions imposed on states created confusion, avoidable delays, and gaps in responses at sub-national levels. For example, in the first few months, state governments that were sourcing Covid-19 testing kits from within and outside the country were told to desist

---

[22]An online survey conducted by a team of independent public health researchers revealed an inadequate supply of personal protective equipment (PPE) for healthcare workers in India. See Joel P. Joseph, 'COVID-19 India: Online Survey Shows Not All Is Well on PPE Availability Front', *The Wire*, 5 July 2020.

and wait for the centrally-approved kits, to be imported from China. When some of these Chinese kits were then found to give inaccurate results, the states were asked to stop using them and return the unused testing kits.[23] This meant that testing rates were even lower than would have been possible otherwise. Lack of coordination affected other conditions of life more directly. There was great confusion about interstate mobility, creating much inconvenience and even suffering among people. There was lack of clarity about interstate bus movements, even as rail services were largely suspended, resulting in chaos at state borders, unnecessary detours, and long delays when bus services were eventually started in some places. Air travel was suddenly opened up by the central government one week before the national lockdown ended, again without consulting the states. But some states with rising cases continued to insist on quarantine requirements that the centre had lifted on its own without checking with them, so there were flight cancellations and diversions as airports in some states refused flights from other states the permission to land.

Fiscal centralization—discussed in more detail in the next chapter—had even worse consequences. While the centre had unilaterally imposed the national lockdown, state governments continued to be responsible for essential public health measures even though they were strapped for cash. Having announced the severe and extremely destabilizing lockdown, the Modi government then seemed to wash its hands of the practical issues around implementation and dealing with the fallout, and more or less left the state governments to handle everything. It did not even provide a regular forum for them to coordinate their efforts, although institutional structures like the inter-state council supposedly exist precisely for this purpose. Prime

---

[23]Teena Thacker, 'Centre decides to withdraw faulty Covid 19 antibody test kits, cancels import orders from China', *Economic Times*, 27 April 2020.

Minister Modi refused to take any press conferences or answer any unscripted questions from the media, just as he had refused over the previous six years of his tenure;[24] and most central ministers also interacted with the media only rarely and briefly, thereby allowing confusions about policy decisions to multiply. (This was in sharp contrast to some states like Kerala, where the chief minister and health minister held joint daily briefings in the early months, in which they answered questions from the media and the public.) Instead, Modi used his few announcements on national media to encourage token symbolic gestures rather than effective action, such as exhorting people to come out on their balconies to bang vessels or light candles in support of the healthcare workers he called 'Corona warriors', while doing little to ensure that they were actually protected or even paid their wages on time.

Traditionally, public responses to calamities in India have been funded directly by the central governments as well as through the Prime Minister's National Relief Fund, which collects voluntary contributions from the public and is transparent and publicly audited. Instead of relying on this, on 27 March 2020 an entirely new fund was set up: the Prime Minister's Citizen Assistance and Relief in Emergency Situations (PM CARES) Fund. The prime minister called on people from all walks of life and companies to contribute to this fund, which was ostensibly to be used for containment and relief efforts against the Coronavirus outbreak and similar pandemic-like situations in the future. In April 2020, an ordinance promulgated by the central government made contributions to this fund tax-deductible, and companies were allowed to donate as part of their Corporate Social Responsibility (CSR) allocations (an advantage not shared by the Chief Ministers' Relief Funds in

---

[24]Ashok Upadhyay, 'No record available: PMO on RTI seeking details of PM Modi's media interaction', *India Today*, 15 January 2020.

the states).[25] Many public sector organizations (including the armed forces, departments of the government, banks, public sectors enterprises, and even public universities) deducted from their employees' salaries to make contributions, often without their consent; many private companies also contributed from their CSR funds; and individuals also donated to this rather than the PM's Relief Fund as they would have in the past. Donations estimated to be worth several thousand crores of rupees poured in, although exact amounts received are not known for reasons described below.

Despite having the prime minister and other central ministers as trustees, and being managed by a joint secretary of the government, it turned out that this fund would not be accountable to the public and no details would be revealed about its collections or spending! The website of the PM CARES fund says it is a 'public charitable trust', with the prime minister as ex-officio chairperson and the ministers of defence, home affairs, and finance of the central government as ex-officio members.[26] But it is not audited by the Comptroller and Auditor General of India, like all other public spending. Instead, a private company led by a person said to have close ties with the ruling BJP was appointed as auditor.[27] The trust deed of the fund explicitly declares that the trust 'is neither intended to be nor is in fact owned, controlled or substantially financed by the Government or any instrumentality of the Government.'[28] An attempt to have the fund legally transferred to the PM Relief Fund where it could be subject to public scrutiny and audit was rejected by

[25]The Epidemic Diseases (Amendment) Ordinance 2020, Government of India, *Gazette of India*, No. 25, 22 April 2020.

[26]'Donation Faqs', PM CARES, available at www.pmcares.gov.in/en/web/page/faq.

[27]Achis Mohan, 'Trustees of PM CARES appoint SARC & Associates as auditor of fund', *Business Standard*, 13 June 2020.

[28]Available at www.pmcares.gov.in/assets/donation/pdf/Trust_Deed.pdf.

the Supreme Court.[29] In a December 2020 response to a Right to Information query, the central government declared that the PM CARES is a body 'owned and established' by the government, but does not come under the RTI Act because it receives funds from private sources.[30] However, in September 2021, the Prime Minister's Office informed the Delhi High Court that PM CARES is not a fund of the Government of India.[31]

This is not only legally confusing, but was and remains an unusual, even unprecedented arrangement, not just in India but in any country. Quite apart from concerns about transparency and accountability, this also mattered during the pandemic because of the meagre relief and health spending by the central government. In such a situation, the funds collected under PM CARES could have been an important additional source of finance: indeed, state governments had demanded that money collected by this fund should be distributed to them for their use. The Indian people still do not know how much money has been collected by this fund or what it has been used for. One known use—the much-advertised purchase of ventilators for some states for a relatively small amount—also became controversial, as it became evident that there were large differences in prices charged by different suppliers, and the poor quality of purchased ventilators meant that many could not be used.[32]

The central government provided some additional funds for more public health spending by state governments, but this

---

[29]Prabhash K. Datta, 'PM Cares vs PMNRF: What is the fuss about?', *India Today*, 19 August 2020.

[30]'PM-CARES "controlled by government", but doesn't come under RTI Act, says Centre in new response', *Scroll.in,* 25 December 2020.

[31]Sofi Ahsan, 'PM-CARES Fund not a fund of Government of India, Delhi HC told', *Indian Express*, 23 September 2021.

[32]Priscilla Jebraj, 'Ventilators from firms funded by PM CARES fail trials', *The Hindu*, 21 August 2020; Arunabh Saikia, 'Modi government spent ₹2,250 crore on buying ventilators. Why aren't they working?', *Scroll.in*, 3 June 2021.

amounted to less than half of one per cent of GDP, to be spread over two years, which was trivial compared to the scale of the need. Even such disbursals were less than promised and delayed, as described in Chapter 4. Spending on social protection was also minuscule and this proved to be especially damaging for informal workers, especially migrant workers in different parts of the country, many of whom were stranded without income and faced destitution and hunger as their meagre savings ran out. (Their situation is described in more detail in Chapter 5.) In the initial phase, all movement of people was prohibited, so they could not return to their homes, and often were attacked and punished for even attempting to do so. In any case, all public transport—trains, buses, everything—was stopped for nearly two months and then only haltingly and inadequately provided, so it was difficult if not impossible for many people to try and move back. When material distress became particularly severe, after a month or more of the lockdown without any income or official relief, migrant workers were forced to travel by foot over long distances for want of any alternative. The central government took a month to allow interstate movement of migrants in buses, and even those were to be arranged and paid for not by the Centre but by the state governments, several of which took full fares from the desperate returnees. Special train services (Shramik Express) for migrants were started even later and required travellers to pay full fares even though most were already greatly impoverished because of the lockdown.[33] The overcrowding at train and bus stations, and then within the trains, without proper arrangements for physical distancing, meant that more workers were exposed and then arrived in their rural homes that often lacked proper medical facilities. Such delays in providing adequate and accessible transport facilities

---

[33]Sudiep Shrivastava, 'Far from subsidising Shramik trains, Modi government is actually charging extra for them', *Scroll.in*, 12 June 2020.

added to distress and led to wider transmission of the virus. The millions of migrant workers who were forced to congregate in stations to try and find their way home or had to walk hundreds of kilometres, arrived enervated and exhausted, with greater chances of exposure to the virus and likelihood of spreading infection at their destinations.

The spread of the disease across the country, to even remote locations with no evidence of the disease before migrants returned, and with poor medical facilities and almost no health infrastructure, was effectively created by this policy failure. There was a fatalistic tone to such journeys, exemplified by the story of two brothers, migrant workers from Ganjam district of Odisha who waited until early May at their place of work in the textile factories of Surat, Gujarat, before realising that there would be no work and no wages. Their savings were exhausted and so there was no option but to return home or face starvation.[34] 'If we're going to die, we should die at home,' said Rabindra Behera. With his brother Prafulla, he paid what was left of their meagre savings to travel over 1,000 miles from Mumbai to their home district of Ganjam, Odisha in a packed train. They travelled on the crowded trains, packed with other workers, in the height of the summer heat, making the journey of more than twenty-seven hours in terrible conditions without food or water. During the journey Prafulla got ill, and by the time they reached Ganjam—a district which at the time had no Coronavirus cases—he had a high fever. The brothers were quarantined in a makeshift facility with other returning migrants, but Prafulla died soon, without being able to see his wife and young daughters. Six of the seven men who had travelled with them tested positive for Covid-19, and cases began to proliferate

[34]Jeffrey Gettleman, Suhasini Raj, Sameer Yasir, and Karan Deep Singh, 'The virus trains: How lockdown chaos spread Covid-19 across India', *New York Times,* 15 December 2020.

across the district, with the hospital that had been converted into a Covid-19 facility quickly filling all its sixty intensive care beds and patients forced to lie on the floor. But the Shramik Special trains kept coming, sometimes as many as sixteen a day, each carrying 2,000 migrant workers, many of them already infected before or during the journey. Quarantine centres were overcrowded and unable to cope, so the district authorities reduced the required quarantine period from twenty-one days to seven days, allowing workers to go back to their homes even when they could be carriers of the disease. Indeed, workers at the quarantine centres in Ganjam were among the first to get infected, and then their families, so the infections spread rapidly among the rural population without adequate testing facilities, so both cases and deaths from the disease are unlikely to have been properly recorded.

The inexplicable delay in distributing foodgrain from the public distribution system to the hungry caused particular harm. Before the lockdown, the central government (through the Food Corporation of India or FCI) held around 77 million tonnes of foodgrain, more than three times the buffer stock requirement. There was some free distribution of free foodgrain (5 kg per person per month) to those covered by the National Food Security Act, but even a month later only 2.2 million tonnes of this had been distributed to states, which covered only a fraction of the entitled population, while an estimated 120 million deserving people were excluded because they did not have ration cards. Even many of those who had ration cards did not get their food entitlement: the government's own figures in June 2020 showed that more than 144 million people who were eligible did not get their entitlement for the month of May, while nearly 64 million were still waiting to receive their due rations for the month of June.[35] At the same time, the government

[35]Kabir Aggarwal, 'PM Garib Kalyan: 144 Million Ration Card Holders Not

sold some stocks in the open market, at a loss.[36] Since more wheat was being procured from farmers just after the harvest, the public stocks increased to more than 100 million tonnes by the beginning of June, which meant that some of the stock effectively rotted in the storage facilities.

All this added significantly to economic distress, most of which could not be ascribed to the disease per se, but were rather the result of the lockdown and the insufficiency of compensatory measures that would have mitigated the distress.

Communalizing the Virus and Suppressing Dissent

In the early phase of the pandemic, panic spread among the population, along with some overtly discriminatory examples of prejudice. India may be the only country in the world where accusations of spreading the virus were given an explicitly religious colour—and not just by fringe groups but by the ruling party and mainstream media, and even government officials. Some of the most unfortunate and aggressively discriminatory features of Indian society came to the fore at the start of the pandemic. In the early stages of the spread, there was widespread blaming of 'Chinese people' because of the origin of the disease in Wuhan, China, and irresponsible social media encouraged racist attacks on Indians from the Northeastern states who were living in other parts of the country. Various forms of discrimination and hate crimes were perpetrated against 'Mongoloid-looking people' in different cities, from being called 'Corona' and being spat upon, forcibly quarantined by local authorities despite showing no Covid-19 symptoms, denied entry into or threatened with eviction from housing complexes, to being forced to leave

---

Provided Grain in May', *The Wire*, 4 June 2020.

[36]Vikas Rawal, Manish Kumar, Ankur Verma, and Jesim Pais, 'COVID-19 Lockdown: Impact on Agriculture and Rural Economy', *Society for Social and Economic Research*, Vol. 13, No. 2, 2020.

restaurants and public transport because of the 'discomfort' of others.[37]

However, these early examples of unacceptable behaviour by both the public and officialdom paled in comparison with the treatment meted out to Muslims, when the entire community was sought to be tarred nationally because of one single episode of a religious gathering in one city, in which several Covid-19 positive travellers from abroad (who were unaware of their infected status) participated. The Tablighi Jamaat is a non-political Muslim missionary movement, which held a large international gathering of around 2,500 Muslim preachers in its 'markaz' in New Delhi over 13–15 March 2020, at a time when restrictions on such large gatherings had not yet been instituted. The organization had received permission to hold this event, which the authorities were fully aware of. Several of the attendees then travelled to different parts of India, and some of them were then found to be Covid-19 positive. Instead of pointing to inadequate testing at the arrival points into the country (when in fact there was no monitoring at the airports other than thermal screening) both state and central government officials instead chose to blame the organizers of the Tablighi Jamaat gathering.

The scapegoating of Muslims as 'super-spreaders' of the disease began with this incident. Throughout the rest of March, and the month of April, the spokesperson of the Union Health Ministry repeatedly referred to the 'fact' (subsequently shown to be false) that nearly one-third of all Covid-19 infected people in India had some connection to the Tablighi Jamaat congregation.[38] Government officials harped on the trouble and expense required to track all the participants in the congregation

---

[37]Suhas Chakma, 'Coronavirus Pandemic: India's Mongoloid Looking People Face Upsurge of Racism', Rights and Risk Analysis Group, 26 March 2020.

[38]'Tablighi Jamaat HQ is India's biggest Covid-19 hotspot, linked to 1,000 cases in India', *Hindustan Times,* 4 April 2020.

and the threat to the population at large from their 'irresponsible' behaviour[39]—ignoring the various other large meetings and events being organized by others associated with the ruling party even after that period, such as rituals organized at Ayodhya to celebrate the planned construction of a temple.[40] Right-wing media channels and other mainstream media quickly got on the bandwagon, constantly referring only to this incident as the basic reason for the spread of the disease in India and calling for bans on the organization. Some claimed that members of the Tablighi Jamaat had conspired to spread the Coronavirus in India, while social media spread vile and completely false rumours about supposed behaviour of Jamaati members in actively spreading the virus.[41] There were many completely unnecessary arrests made across the country, and it took several months before many of the hapless visitors could be freed through court interventions. Eventually, all of them were acquitted, with some courts noting that there was a 'smell of malice' in the government's actions taken against the Tablighi Jamaat and other Muslims.[42]

This was used to spread anti-Muslim sentiment and target Muslims in public places across the country, with Muslims being prevented from using public toilets and entering shops, calls for the boycott of Muslim businesses, and even cases of hospitals refusing to take in Muslim patients. Such egregious incitement fanned more open communal violence in different parts of the country, especially in states where elections would be held in

---

[39]Seema Chishti, 'The Nightmare: The Modi government's persecution of the Tablighi Jamaat',*The Caravan*, 30 January 2021.

[40]'In pictures: Ayodhya Ram Mandir Bhoomi Pujan', *Hindustan Times*, 5 August 2020.

[41]Ayan Sharma and Chahak Gupta, 'Audit of bigotry: How Indian media vilified Tablighi Jamaat over Coronavirus outbreak', *Newslaundry*, 27 April 2020.

[42]Aurangabad bench of the Mumbai High Court, quoted in Chishti, 'The Nightmare: The Modi government's persecution of the Tablighi Jamaat'.

the near future and religious polarization was seen to be of advantage to some political parties. For example, in mid-May, the small town of Telinipara in West Bengal witnessed three days of arson and rioting, in which Muslim homes, shops, and mosques were vandalised and destroyed, because of instigation by some local leaders based on presenting Muslims as carriers of the disease.[43] All this obviously contributed to communal disharmony, social tension, and much greater insecurity among minority groups—but it also distracted and diverted from the fight against the virus, and perversely contributed to its spread.

Just before the lockdown, there were many peaceful protests across the country, against the attempt to pass a new citizenship law that for the first time discriminated between potential citizens on the basis of religion. There were fears that this legislation would provide the basis for effectively giving lower status to Muslims within the country. Some of these peaceful protests, many involving prolonged sit-ins in public places by women, had been met with violence on the part of police and armed supporters of the ruling party even before the pandemic struck. The central government used the opportunity presented by the lockdown not just to prohibit any kind of public protest but to arrest several of those who had participated in peaceful protests, while protecting supporters of the ruling party.[44] The crackdown on dissent affected students, lawyers, human rights activists, journalists, and academics, many of whom were forced into prisons where Covid-19 infections were spreading.[45] Since the narrative about such prisoners (even clearly political

---

[43]Hannah Ellis-Petersen and Sheikh Azizur Rahman, 'How lives were destroyed under cover of lockdown in a small Indian town', *The Guardian,* 8 June 2020.

[44]'India: Arrests of Activists Politically Motivated', Human Rights Watch, 16 September 2020.

[45]Aditya Sharma, 'COVID: Political prisoners in India suffer under squalid conditions', *DW,* 16 June 2021; 'One-fourth jails in India report Covid-19 cases, many "highly" congested': Report', *Hindustan Times,* 16 September 2020.

prisoners) being a threat to society was sought to be maintained, the focus was on continued incarceration rather than releasing them, as was done in many other countries.[46] For example, the much-respected octogenarian priest and human rights activist Father Stan Swamy, who had spent decades working for realizing the rights of tribal people in Jharkhand and suffered from Parkinson's disease, was imprisoned on charges of 'terrorism' and even denied warm clothes for winter and a straw to help him drink, until court orders. He contracted Covid-19 in prison and eventually died, but the resulting national and international condemnation[47] was ignored by the government and did not result in any change in strategy towards such prisoners. The purpose of such continued repression during a period of national calamity could have been used to teach a lesson to those who had interrogated the government's intentions and actions; and to intimidate others from doing so. Unfortunately, such an atmosphere of repression also meant that the government's own ability to create a widespread social consensus and atmosphere of trust in which to combat the pandemic was correspondingly reduced.

Meanwhile it became apparent that the government would use the lockdown not only to crack down on protestors and increase its surveillance of all actual and potential dissenters, but also to suppress the existing institutional checks and balances on its own functioning. Covid-19 was used as the excuse to truncate the Budget and Monsoon sessions of both houses of Parliament, which had historically the lowest number of sittings in 2020—only thirty-three days for the entire year![48] Demands

---

[46]Vijay Raghavan, 'Prisons and the pandemic: the panopticon plays out', *Journal of Social and Economic Development*, 7 December 2020.

[47]'India: Death in custody of priest Stan Swamy is devastating – UN expert', United Nations Human Rights, 15 July 2021.

[48]Anuja Gyan Verma, 'Parliament may see historically low number of sittings this year', *Mint*, 25 November 2020.

by Opposition parties to convene virtual sessions of Parliament, or at least allow online meetings of the various Parliamentary panels that were supposed to monitor the executive and consider legislation, were ignored or outright refused.[49] The refusal to convene Parliament was particularly egregious as the central government progressively eased lockdown restrictions through the course of the year, forcing people to put themselves at risk at a time of high spread of the disease, because of the need to earn their livelihood; but elected representatives were not enabled or required to attend Parliament even with appropriate restrictions and distancing norms put in place. These truncated sessions were used to rush through controversial legislation like the farm bills and labour codes, without any consultation, discussion or consideration by the Parliamentary committees that usually vet any new legislation before it is put to vote.[50] Not surprisingly, these moves generated massive public protests subsequently; but the limited number of Parliamentary sessions made it easier for the government to ignore those.

The Second Wave

The first wave of the pandemic peaked in September 2020 in India. From late September, the number of new infections per million people fell continuously, to less than ten by the end of January 2021, even though the disease was spreading across the country by then. The Indian trajectory of decline was significant compared to the global average, though it was similar to most of Asia. Even within South Asia, India continued to have the highest rate of infection until late September, when it was overtaken by Nepal—and even in January 2021, Pakistan and Bangladesh

[49]'No winter session due to Covid-19; Opposition objects', *Hindustan Times*, 16 December 2020.

[50]S. N. Sahu, 'The Way Farm Bills Passed in Rajya Sabha Shows Decline in Culture of Legislative Scrutiny', *The Wire*, 21 September 2020.

showed lower daily rates of new infections. Nevertheless, the decline in reported Covid-19 cases made it appear—especially to the ruling government at the Centre—that the pandemic was waning in India by early 2021.

This created a sense of complacency, even hubris, to the point that in late January 2021 Prime Minister Modi was telling world leaders at the Davos World Economic Forum that 'India has been successful in saving so many lives, we saved the entire humanity from a big tragedy.... We fulfilled our responsibility towards the global community by sending vaccines and training people'.[51] Yet already by then, the incidence of Covid-19 cases had started rising once again in some states, and by February it was clear that the country could be facing the start of a second wave of infections. This was downplayed by the leadership, and it has even been suggested that senior government officials forced scientists at elite institutions to alter their predictive models to reduce the likely threat.[52] Central government leaders as well as those in some states lowered their guard and forgot about implementing the restrictions that were still in place. They seemed to be so self-confident in their own rhetoric that, despite officially approving two vaccines by December, the government had not even ordered more than 30 million doses of vaccines from the two concerned companies before March 2021. Not only were most lockdown restrictions eased or removed (other than in some states with rising cases), but in early 2021 the prime minister and other central government ministers actively encouraged massive public gatherings in the run-up to the state assembly elections in West Bengal and some other states. The

[51]'"India's success will help the entire world": PM Modi at WEF's Davos Dialogue', *Hindustan Times*, 28 January 2021; full speech available at www.weforum.org/videos/davos-2021-special-address-by-narendra-modi-prime-minister-of-india-english.

[52]Karan Deep Singh, 'As India's lethal second wave neared, politics, overrode science', *New York Times*, 14 September 2021.

prime minister even declared his satisfaction at seeing the huge crowds that had amassed at one of his many election rallies in West Bengal.[53] In a remarkably obtuse move, the huge religious festival, the Maha Kumbh Mela, held every twelve years on the banks of the Ganga River was actually brought forward by a full year, apparently on astrological advice, rather than being delayed because of the pandemic.[54] This festival had more than 9 million attendees over the month of April 2021, all concentrated in the relatively small town of Haridwar, despite the ongoing Covid-19 surge,[55] thereby creating a potent super-spreader event that allowed the disease to proliferate across rural and urban areas of large parts of north and central India. To some extent, therefore, the second wave was not inevitable but actually created by policy mismanagement.

In the event, the second wave was both more infectious and more lethal, associated with the emergence of mutant variants such as Delta and Delta Plus that then spread to other countries. Health systems throughout India completely collapsed in this onslaught, with major shortages of hospital beds, emergency facilities, oxygen, and therapeutic drugs—all of which added to the severity and fatality of the disease, and created much greater and more widespread social and economic devastation. The official death toll was significantly higher in the second wave, which extended in its greater force from March to June 2021. A study of some private hospitals found 40 per cent higher mortality in the second wave, even among those hospitalized—resulting from factors like late admission because of shortage of

---

[53]Monideepa Banerjie, '"Have Witnessed Such A Rally For The First Time...": PM Modi In Bengal', *NDTV.com*, 18 April 2021.

[54]There has been some speculation that even this could have been determined by political calculations, hoping for rewards from the religious faithful in the Uttar Pradesh Assembly elections due in 2022.

[55]Sandeep Rawat, '9.1 million thronged Mahakumbh despite Covid-19 surge: Govt data', *Hindustan Times*, 30 April 2021.

hospital beds, inadequate ICU beds, insufficient oxygen supplies, and the nature of the Delta variant.[56] At the peak of the second wave, in early May 2021, the official average seven-day rate of new infections, at 283 per million per day, was nearly three times the global and Asian averages.[57]

Further, this second wave of the pandemic hit a health system that was more strained than ever before. State governments had exhausted their capacity for additional spending. The population had been hugely debilitated by declining incomes and livelihood, eroded savings and increased household debt taken on for sheer survival, inability to access basic needs like food, and coping with other illness and health concerns (especially reproductive health) that had largely been ignored for a year. At the same time, the second wave saw even less in terms of relief measures than the first wave. Most of the so-called 'relief measures' were designed to enable the poor to take on more debt (by providing government benefits to banks for the issue of such loans), which they would clearly be unable to repay, while minimum compensation, such as enhanced free food rations, remained limited, and cash transfers were not even considered. Therefore, while there was no national lockdown destroying livelihoods in this period, the second wave was more brutal, not just in the extent and severity of the spread of the disease, but because it impacted upon an already weakened population.

The official estimate of total Covid-19 cases in India by the end of September 2021 was more than 33.7 million, with 448,062 deaths resulting from it.[58] Thereafter, from December 2021 there was a fresh wave of the disease with the more infectious Omicron variant of the Coronavirus, but this proved to be less lethal than the second wave. According to the official numbers, India has

[56]Kalyan Ray, '40% higher mortality in second Covid wave', *Deccan Herald,* 28 June 2021.

[57]*Our World in Data.*

[58]MyGov, www.mygov.in/covid-19.

the second highest number of cases, after the USA, and has also lost many more people to the disease than any other country in Asia. Overall, Covid-19 eclipsed all other communicable diseases within the country taken together in terms of both morbidity and mortality.

However, these official statistics are now generally recognized to be massive underestimates. While testing rates varied widely across different states, they were generally insufficient, certainly by international standards. Seroprevalence surveys (which capture antibodies resulting from past infection) that were conducted even before the peak of the second wave suggested that more than one-third of Indians had been infected with Covid-19.[59] Thereafter, in some cities, seroprevalence surveys found much higher rates of infection, in the range of 60-75 per cent in some congested urban settlements: a survey of five slums in Mumbai in October 2020 found that 75 per cent of those surveyed had antibodies.[60]

Testing was initially hampered across the country simply because of the lack of available testing kits; even thereafter, the performance with regard to testing was very varied across states, with some states able to ramp up testing and others simply unable to cope, largely because of lack of financial resources, health infrastructure, and personnel. There were also concerns about the quality of the tests themselves, as different tests have different degrees of reliability. The Rapid Antigen Tests are cheaper, easier to administer, and provide results quickly, but they are significantly less reliable, with false negatives (that is, failing to capture an infection that is actually present) which can

---

[59]Soumik Purkayastha, Ritoban Kundu, Ritwik Bhaduri, et al., 'Estimating the wave 1 and wave 2 infection fatality rates from SARS-CoV-2 in India', *BMC Res Notes*, Vol. 14, No. 262, 2021.

[60]Mustafa Sheikh, 'Serosurvey finds 75% test positive for Covid-19 antibodies in Mumbai slums', *India Today*, 30 November 2020.

be as high as 40–50 per cent.[61] The more reliable RT-PCR tests take longer to deliver results and are more expensive. Also, as the disease continued to spread to remote rural areas with very poor medical and other infrastructure, it was more and more likely that more people across the country were getting infected without getting tested or even showing symptoms. Even going by official estimates, by the end of 2021, every single state and Union Territory in the country had been affected, even in far-flung regions. In one startling case in November 2020, all but one of the villagers in an extremely remote Himalayan village in the Lahaul-Spiti district of Himachal Pradesh were found to be infected with Covid-19.[62]

Some states consistently showed higher rates of infection: Maharashtra, Kerala, Karnataka, Tamil Nadu, and Andhra Pradesh. These are all states with high rates of migration and greater exposure to travellers from abroad, and three of them contain large metropoles with congested urban slums, where the requirements of physical distancing simply could not be feasibly met. Other states that showed big increases in the second wave were Uttar Pradesh and West Bengal. But overall testing rates still varied hugely across the country: the states with the highest prevalence also had wider and more frequent testing, and some poorer states relied more heavily on the less reliable Rapid Antigen Tests. In the state of Bihar, for example, testing rates were ramped up by mid-August after being exceptionally low, but these increasingly relied on the cheaper, less effective Rapid Antigen Tests that accounted for 92 per cent of Bihar's Covid-19 testing over 2020. The likelihood of greater spread of the disease than officially recorded was underlined by the evidence of increased infections, overcrowding and strains

[61]'Interim Guidance for Rapid Antigen Testing for SARS-CoV-2', CDC, 9 September 2021.

[62]'41 of HP village's 42 residents test positive; MLA suspects tourist influx', *Indian Express,* 21 November 2020.

on existing medical facilities—such as the dramatic incident of the infected senior Bihar government bureaucrat who was forced to spend the night on the pavement of the All India Institute of Medical Sciences hospital in Patna because it had no beds to spare, and who subsequently succumbed to the disease.[63]

Further, in addition to the sheer absence of required medical facilities in many rural areas, even where such facilities did exist, the majority of the people could not afford the care. As a result, many cases have probably gone undetected because the majority of Indians did not have access to adequate public and affordable medical facilities and simply could not afford the high charges imposed by private medical providers. A study conducted by the Public Health Foundation of India found that the costs of contracting Covid-19 that required hospitalization (between April 2020 and March 2021) were simply unaffordable for the vast majority of people. Even testing was expensive: while Covid-19 testing has been free in public facilities, these were not always available, and in private labs they cost an average of ₹2,229 per test. A ten-day episode of hospital isolation in a private facility cost an average of ₹67,470 (with a range from ₹2,700 to ₹12,600), and admission to an intensive care unit cost anywhere from ₹82,500 to ₹200,000. Even for the middle classes, this was close to unaffordable. Comparing with wage incomes revealed in the Periodic Labour Force Survey of 2018–19, the study concluded that 'An Indian in regular employment needs to spend the equivalent of 124 days' wages to afford Covid hospital isolation. ICU treatment in hospital would cost self-employed workers and regular employees 318 days and 232 days of work respectively.'[64]

[63]Arunabh Saikia, 'Covid-19 seems under control in Bihar. But is that deceptive?', *Scroll.in*, 28 October 2020.

[64]Sakthivel Selvaraj et al., 'Costs and Affordability of COVID-19 Testing and Treatment in India', *Research Square*, 14 July 2021.

Even as late as September 2021, it was evident that accurate data on Covid-19 incidence was simply not being collected or not being made available in the required detail.[65] For example, the central government platform that currently provides the most Covid-19 data (MyGov) does not provide information disaggregated by districts, age, gender, or comorbidity. Data collection and availability varied widely across states: Nagaland, Kerala, and Odisha provide good Covid-19 reporting, but Delhi, Goa, and Manipur provide no granular data and states like Uttar Pradesh and Bihar do not even provide official websites to disseminate Covid-19 data. This makes it difficult if not impossible to do meaningful interstate comparisons.

Will We Ever Know How Many People Died of Covid-19 in India?

One of the major problems with describing the trajectory of the Covid-19 pandemic in India is the absence of reliable data on actual cases and deaths from the disease. It is true that even by the end of 2020, before the more devastating second wave, India's official death rate from Covid-19 was actually higher than most other countries in the Asian region, even those with lower per capita income and less health infrastructure, such as Nepal, Bangladesh, Pakistan, and Afghanistan.[66] It is possible that there was under-reporting of such deaths in these countries, but this was also true of India, especially for some states. So even with the disputed official figures, while India's Covid-19 death rate was lower than in other large countries that have shown rapid spread of the virus, it was still among the highest in Asia.

---

[65]S. Rukmini, '20 Months In, Gaps Persist In India's Official Covid-19 Data', *IndiaSpend*, 5 September 2021.

[66]Johns Hopkins University, national public health agencies and UN population data, updated on 25 November 2020, quoted in BBC.com, 'Delta variant: Which Asian countries are seeing rising cases?'.

Indeed, under-reporting of Covid-19 deaths has been a problem across the world. Some of this results from the unwillingness of authorities to record deaths as Covid-19 deaths or of relatives not reporting these due to fear of stigma. Some is simply because of lack of certainty as to the cause, especially with patients with comorbidities, whose deaths are often assigned to those, or because of 'false negatives' of the Covid-19 tests, which are known to be quite high. Even deaths that are medically certified could be underestimating Covid-19 deaths, since it is often the case that such deaths are not recorded as such because of the required procedures and conditions to be met before such certification. Advisory guidelines from the Indian Council of Medical Research (ICMR) say that people with suspected or probably Covid-19 should be included in the related mortality data, but most state and local governments have not implemented this. Sometimes—especially in the early months of the pandemic—it resulted from the shortage of testing kits, which were sought to be reserved for the living: a doctor in a Mumbai government hospital noted in mid-April 2020 noted that in a single day six patients with acute respiratory distress syndrome were brought to his hospital dead, and none were tested for Covid-19 because of a shortage of kits.[67]

In other cases, operational difficulties combined with bureaucratic requirements to reduce the numbers recorded as dying from the virus. For example, twenty-seven-year-old Manish was admitted into a hospital in Bhopal with a ruptured liver abscess. When he developed fluid in his lungs and showed other respiratory symptoms of Covid-19, he had tubes inserted in his windpipe and nasal channel to help him breathe and eat. But this meant that swabs could not be taken to test him for the disease. When he died, doctors were sure that the cause

[67]Murad Banaji, 'The Tricky Issue With Knowing How Many Are Dying From COVID-19 in India', *The Wire,* 15 May 2020.

was Covid-19 because of indirect evidence from the CT scans, but they could not record it as such because they were not allowed to record any deaths from Covid-19 unless they were confirmed by the RT-PCR test. Manish's death was therefore recorded as due to other causes. There are other cases of those who died in hospital with Covid-19 symptoms, whose tests came back negative; even though doctors believe these are part of the 'false negatives' that often require repeated testing, which is not possible for the dead, and they are not recorded as Covid-19 deaths.[68]

There was widespread incidence of deaths being recorded as due to the pre-existing conditions or comorbidities of the patients, rather than due to the virus. In extreme cases, as in Murshidabad in West Bengal, there was even evidence of orders to doctors at the local medical college hospital prohibiting such recording: 'In case of Covid positive - No mention of Covid in death certificate,' was the official directive![69] There were many reports across the country of different state governments attempting to suppress the number of Covid-19 cases and deaths through various means, even if not so blatant. The problem was compounded by the spread of the disease to more rural and remote areas, where both health facilities and official registration of deaths is less developed, and where it is likely that more cases have gone undetected or unrecorded.

These limitations are widely recognized, which is why several countries have moved to considering the number of 'excess deaths', that is number of all deaths per population in the period, beyond what could be statistically expected in 'normal conditions'. This has been used to suggest that actual deaths

---

[68]Examples quoted in Priyanka Pulla, 'India Is Undercounting Its COVID-19 Deaths. This Is How', *The Wire*, 4 August 2020.

[69]Joe Wallen, Ben Farmer, Ashfaq Yusufzai, and Vivashwan Singh, 'Asia's hidden deaths: Coronavirus fatalities are being covered up and undercounted', *The Telegraph*, 22 May 2020.

from the pandemic could be as much as 50–60 per cent higher than those reported.[70]

In India, recent estimates of excess mortality during the period of the pandemic have come up with even more stark and startling numbers. As it happens, even the excess death figures are underestimates in India, because official mortality numbers are themselves suspect, with not all deaths registered, and less than half of the registered deaths being medically certified.[71] Around 86 per cent of deaths are estimated to be registered even in urban areas. In 2018, only 21 per cent of registered deaths were medically certified as to cause.[72] Even in the national capital of Delhi, less than two-thirds of deaths get a medical 'cause of death' certification. The problem is much more acute in rural and remote areas. Despite this, attempts to assess the extent of excess mortality during the Covid-19 pandemic show death rates that would make India the worst affected country in the world. One academic study[73] used three different indicators to estimate excess death from the start of the pandemic to June 2021, when the official death toll from Covid-19 was at 400,000. Extrapolating the state-level civil registration of death data from seven states yielded 3.4 million excess deaths. Applying international age-specific infection fatality rates to Indian

---

[70]*Our World in Data*, https://ourworldindata.org/excess-mortality-covid, accessed on 16 November 2020.

[71]The Sample Registration Survey (which is based on all identifiable deaths being reported by a local frontline health worker and reviewed by a doctor) is another source of information which could provide a more accurate indication of actual mortality, but such data refer only to the sampled areas and are available only after several years—and therefore provide no assistance in estimating the loss of life that could be attributed to this pandemic.

[72]Ananth Krishnan, 'The many challenges in estimating deaths', *The Hindu*, 7 September 2020.

[73]Abhishek Anand, Justin Sandefur, and Arvind Subramanian, 'Three New Estimates of India's All Cause Excess Mortality during the COVID-19 Pandemic', Center for Global Development, Working Paper 589, July 2021.

seroprevalence data suggested 4 million deaths. Finally, using data from a private longitudinal panel survey of households by the CMIE pointed to as many as 4.9 million excess deaths. The lowest estimate pointed to more than 3 million excess deaths probably resulting from the pandemic.[74] Another, more conservative, scientific study by a team led from the University of Michigan, USA,[75] found a high degree of 'covert infections', with estimated under-reporting of infections by a factor of 11.11 and of deaths by 3.56. Combining both first and second waves until 15 May 2021, the estimated number of infections was 491 million (36 per cent of the population) and deaths 1.21 million. The study also noted the very considerable variation across states, making interstate comparison on the basis of official numbers effectively meaningless. A third academic study arrived at numbers somewhere in between these: using death registration data from seventeen states (excluding Uttar Pradesh among major states because of severe data concerns) found that between 1.8 and 2.63 million people may have died due to the Covid-19 pandemic up to the end of June 2021.[76] Another estimate examined all-cause mortality data from civil registration from twelve states during the period April 2020–May 2021 and compared it to expectations from 2019, and found 28 per cent increase in mortality.[77] Applied nationally, this suggests more than 2.8 million excess deaths. More limited data from June 2021 suggest excess deaths of 3.8 million. Depending

[74]Karan Deep Singh, 'India's true pandemic death toll is likely to be well over 3 million, a new study finds', *New York Times,* 20 July 2021.

[75]Soumik Purkayastha, Ritoban Kundu, Ritwik Bhaduri, et al., 'Estimating the wave 1 and wave 2 infection fatality rates from SARS-CoV-2 in India', *BMC Research Notes*, Vol. 14, No. 262, 2021

[76]Christopher T. Leffler, Joseph D. Lykins V, and Edward Yang, 'Preliminary Analysis of Excess Mortality in India During the Covid-19 Pandemic (update august 4, 2021)', *MedRxiv,* 2021.

[77]Murad Banaji and Aashish Gupta, 'Estimates of pandemic excess mortality in India based on civil registration data', *MedRxiv*, 1 October 2021.

on the assumptions used, this study suggests that excess deaths during this period until mid-2021 would credibly have been in the range 2.8–5.2 million, that is between six times and nearly twelve times the official numbers of dead.

Beyond these scholarly attempts to uncover the extent of mortality by combining large-scale survey data with information on registered deaths, there have been attempts by reporters to estimate 'excess deaths' in particular locations, based on data from hospitals, morgues, and cremation rounds. For example, one attempt used data obtained from the Brihanmumbai Municipal Corporation on deaths (which have not been officially released) to find that Mumbai recorded 13,058 *more* deaths between March 1 and July 31, 2020, relative to the same period in 2019. This amounts to 6,663 additional deaths over and above the 6,395 Covid-19 deaths reported during this period—in other words suggesting that excess deaths were more than double the recorded Covid-19 deaths.[78] Many factors could have influenced this number: people with other diseases (like cancer or TB) could have been denied treatment due to the lockdown; or people from outside Mumbai may have come to the city to get treated and then died; even as deaths from traffic accidents came down; and so on.

The extent of under-reporting varied widely across states. One attempt to compare excess deaths across eight states found that while overall the number of dead exceeded the official Covid-19 death toll by 8.22 times, the difference was relatively small in the state of Kerala (with 42 per cent more deaths) and massive, nearly twenty-four times more, in the state of Madhya Pradesh.[79]

The scholarly and other estimates of excess mortality during the pandemic point to death rates that are likely to have been

---

[78]Murad Banaji, 'Mumbai Had 13k "Excess" Deaths in March-July. How Does Its COVID Story Change?', *The Wire*, 10 September 2020.

[79]'Data | India's excess deaths could be highest among nations with the most recorded COVID-19 fatalities', *The Hindu*, 30 July 2021.

among the highest in the world, similar if not significantly greater than worst affected countries like the US and Brazil. Of course, not all of these excess deaths would have resulted from Covid-19 alone; but many of them would have been caused by related factors such as the neglect of other diseases like cancer and TB and inadequate nutrition due to the significant increase in income poverty and reduced access to food among those deprived of livelihood.

Vaccine Politics

India has been one of the world's leading producers of vaccines (although it has not really been a developer of new vaccines) and there was significant expectation that as Covid-19 vaccines were developed, tested, and got regulatory approval, vaccine production in India would be ramped up to enable rapid inoculation in India. Of course, there were several constraints to this, including the advanced countries, continued support of intellectual property rights of multinational pharma companies and their immediate attempts to grab the initial production of approved vaccines for their own populations, as discussed in Chapter 1. Nevertheless, there were reasons to be optimistic about access because of domestic supply. India is home to the world's largest vaccine producing company (Serum Institute of India) which relatively quickly established a production deal with Astra Zeneca to produce its Covid-19 vaccine (called Covishield in India). The government also put its hopes on a completely indigenous vaccine candidate, developed in collaboration with the public sector Indian Council of Medical Research and the National Institute of Virology, produced by the Bengaluru-based company Bharat Biotech.

Both vaccines were given regulatory approval in January 2021, even though at that point the Phase II trials of Covaxin were not complete. Originally, it was stated that the Covaxin vaccine would only be 'for emergency use' in the event of a major spike,[80] but subsequently the centre announced that the rollout scheduled from 16 January 2021 would involve both vaccines,[81] even as the Phase II trials of Covaxin were still in progress, with some concerns about such trials taking place among poor people without their informed consent.[82] However, such opacity in the regulatory process without proper testing became counterproductive, not only because of potential safety and efficacy concerns, but because they raised doubts in the public mind. This turned something presumably technical and science-based into a political issue, rather than providing answers to the legitimate questions being raised.[83] Indeed, the relevant data for Covaxin were not in the public domain and the vaccine did not receive the requested regulatory approval from the World Health Organization until November 2021, after several requests for more data. The fear was that this hasty imposition of one particular vaccine without going through the necessary procedures would affect public trust in all vaccinations and thereby could endanger subsequent vaccination drives as well. This would be unfortunate because the Indian population had in the past been very receptive to inoculation in general.

What was worse, however, was the Modi government's extraordinary approach to vaccine production and distribution, which was unlike any other government in the world responding to a pandemic, because it did not enable wider domestic production and did not make the vaccine free to all the public

---

[80]Vasudevan Mukunth, '10 Questions the DCGI Needs To Answer About the Two Vaccine Candidates Approved', *The Wire*, 3 January 2021.

[81]Nidhi Sharma and Anandita Singh Mankotia, 'Centre to begin Covid vaccination with both SII, Bharat Bio jabs', *Economic Times*, 11 January 2021.

[82]Anoo Bhuyan (anoobhu), Tweet, 9 January 2021, available at https://twitter.com/AnooBhu/status/1347799296540741632?s=20.

[83]PTI, 'Targeting Opposition, BJP says political row over indigenous vaccine helping "foreign forces"', *Economic Times*, 4 January 2021.

for several months. Even though the Covaxin vaccine had been produced under the aegis of the public institution, the Indian Council of Medical Research, Covaxin was allowed to hold the patent and have sole production rights. Licences for its production could easily have been issued compulsorily to other companies, but they were not—not even to several public sector enterprises with acknowledged vaccine production capacity. This was surprising also because the government of India, along with South Africa, had sponsored a motion in the World Trade Organisation to waive intellectual property rights under the TRIPS agreement for all Covid-19 related vaccines, drugs, and therapeutic treatments—yet it chose to allow private companies to hold their patents within India.

The central government initially promised to provide vaccines only for the initial rollout to health and frontline workers, covering 30 million people, and then for those aged above fifty-five years. It did not even order additional vaccines from the two Indian producers until March 2021. Despite formally allocating nearly ₹3.5 trillion ($5 billion) for vaccination in the Union Budget of 2021–22, very little of that announced money was actually spent, even when it was most urgently needed.

Instead, in March 2021 the central government announced that state governments could purchase vaccines at their own cost, forcing them to compete in a hugely supply-constrained global market. Private healthcare providers were then allowed to procure and provide vaccine doses for people aged eighteen to forty-five years, to be paid for by the recipients! The domestic vaccine producers started charging much higher rates to private agents and to state governments, coming to as much as $20 per dose for individuals. Meanwhile, global producers simply refused to supply the vaccines without a legal indemnity for the emergency use of their vaccines that other governments were providing. In India, state governments cannot provide such indemnity, only the central government can, but it did not do so.

No other country adopted such a blatantly 'free market' policy because it simply makes no sense in a public health crisis like a pandemic, when immunization becomes a public good and an urgent necessity. The absurdity—and fruitlessness—of differential markets and separate 'private' commercial sales for vaccines to deal with a pandemic seemed to be lost on both the Indian government and the pharma companies. Such a contradictory policy had to be abandoned relatively quickly, but only after creating avoidable confusion and inexcusable delays in vaccine distribution. Moreover, the government's insistence on the use of an online CoWin platform for accessing vaccines, in a country with huge digital disparities and major connectivity problems, further restricted access. As a result, the one area that was thought to be promising for India—the possibility of rapid and large-scale Covid-19 vaccine production and distribution—also emerged as being riddled with problems.

The Pandemic and Other Health Conditions

As was observed in Chapter 2, the health conditions of the bulk of Indians left much to be desired even before the pandemic struck. The lockdown as well as the diversion of medical attention and health infrastructure to dealing with the Covid-19 infections affected the already fragile health system's ability to deal with other important health requirements like immunization and reproductive health. In addition, other diseases and their treatment were ignored or given less attention. Prior to the pandemic, tuberculosis (TB) was the most significant killer among infectious diseases in India, causing more than 200,000 deaths every year. According to the World Health Organization, India topped the list of likely undercounted TB cases, accounting for 41 per cent of such cases globally.[84] Only 1 million children

[84]Kalyan Ray, 'India tops world in unreported tuberculosis cases', *Deccan*

received the BCG vaccine (which prevents severe TB) in April, half the number in pre-pandemic January. During the pandemic, many tuberculosis patients did not receive their required treatment, either because of the lockdown or because health providers were overburdened.

Critical care services were severely reduced during the lockdown, with predictable results. There are very few studies of excess mortality during this period, but the few that have been done show that patients with other illnesses or medical emergencies were less likely to receive the necessary treatment. One study looking at dialysis patients across Rajasthan found 64 per cent increase in mortality between March and May 2020 and an estimated 22–25 per cent total excess mortality between April and July 2020. Deaths were more likely among women and disadvantaged groups and transportation difficulties and disruptions in hospital services were identified as the main causes.[85]

This was not just due to overcrowding of hospital facilities because of Covid-19; rather it resulted from the poorly designed lockdown policies that prevented women from being able to access such facilities. It took a whole month after announcing the lockdown for the central government to issue guidelines on reproductive health access, which created confusion and caused many hospitals to turn women away. When the guidelines were finally issued, they scarcely helped: to enter a hospital a pregnant woman had to show a recent Covid-negative test result, but since such results typically take at least a day to come, it was not possible for a woman who had started her labour. This effectively denied many women access to institutional deliveries. It has been estimated that as many as 15 per cent of the 6 million pregnant

---

Herald, 18 October 2021.

[85]Pascaline Dupas and Radhika Jain, 'The Effects of India's Covid-19 Lockdown on Critical Non-Covid Health Care and Outcomes', Abdul Latif Jameel Poverty Action Lab (J-PAL).

women who needed critical care in the three months since the lockdown was imposed either could not receive such care or had to face huge difficulties in accessing it. There were some particularly horrific cases publicized even in the major metros, like the pregnant woman who lived in a 'containment zone', who was turned away from at least six hospitals and clinics in the capital city of Delhi and ultimately had to give birth on the road outside the premier All India Institute of Medical Sciences; or the anaemic pregnant woman in Telangana who died after being refused admittance by six hospitals; or the woman about to give birth who died in an ambulance after vainly trying to get admitted into several hospitals in Noida.[86] Many similar cases are likely to have gone unreported, especially in places with even fewer available medical services.

The unfortunate tendency of Indian officialdom to be insensitive to gender concerns was on show from the very announcement of the national lockdown. Lack of access to hygienic products to deal with menstrual periods has long been a major issue for girls and women in India, compounded by high costs of menstrual pads. In recent years, there have been attempts to improve on this, by removing taxes on these pads and making them available to girls in schools, for free or at subsidized rates, so that around two-thirds of women and girls now use hygienic products to manage their periods. But when the list of essential commodities exempt from national lockdown restrictions was first put out in late March, it excluded sanitary pads and similar hygienic products, creating confusion and leading to shortages.[87] Some states like Karnataka and Telangana issued their notifications to include sanitary pads in essential commodities, but the lack of clarity from the central

---

[86]Jasodhara Dasgupta, 'Maternal health matters', *The Hindu*, 18 June 2020.

[87]PTI, 'Due process must to declare sanitary pads as essential items', *Times of India*, 1 July 2020.

government affected production and supplies.[88] The closure of schools similarly affected distribution, and made it impossible for girls from poor families who could not afford to purchase these at higher prices in the market to access them. As late as July 2020, more than three months after imposition of the lockdown that had already shown the effects of such shortages, the central Ministry of Health and Family Welfare patronizingly informed the High Court of Maharashtra that the decision to bring sanitary napkins under essential commodities could be taken 'only after following due procedure, which includes understanding market scenario and keeping in mind quality, costing, and preferences of the beneficiaries.'[89]

Outpatient health services were severely affected, with the number of outpatients declining by half in April and May 2020 compared to January—and these included patients dealing with severe conditions like heart disease and cancer, which require constant medical monitoring. These adverse conditions persisted even after the national lockdown ended; indeed reduced access to other health services was a defining feature in many states even a year later. There were many reports of cancer patients and those requiring dialysis suffering neglect; while important operations were indefinitely postponed for large numbers of people. The closure of, or more limited services provided by, ICDS Anganwadi centres affected both nutrition and healthcare for infants and small children, pregnant women, and lactating mothers. This was particularly troubling as it would affect current and future nutrition and the health of mothers and children, with severe medium term effects. Overall, decline in access to food for much of the population also would have serious health consequences.

---

[88]'Coronavirus sparks a sanitary pad crisis in India', *BBC*, 22 May 2020.

[89]Omkar Gokhale, 'Willing to make sanitary napkins "essential commodity" but not without consulting all stakeholders: Centre to Bombay HC', *Indian Express*, 2 July 2020.

Reproductive health was a special concern, with both girls and young women, including mothers, suffering in various ways because of inadequate medical attention. There were 40 per cent fewer institutional deliveries of babies during the lockdown than in the same period of the previous year, with states like Uttar Pradesh, Bihar, West Bengal, Jharkhand, Odisha, and Chhattisgarh particularly badly affected.[90] The increase in institutional births had been seen as one of the major factors in the improvement of infant mortality and maternal mortality rates in India; this reversal led to a significant reversal of this trend. Even routine checks and tests essential for the health of mother and child were missed, and the number of beneficiaries of the Janani Swasthya Suraksha Yojana,[91] designed to assist in childbirth expenses, also declined in April 2020 to under half of its January level. The costs of childbirth also went up for other reasons, as for many months ambulance services were suspended for any non Covid-19 cases, which meant that money had to be spent for hiring taxis for hospital visits, paying for various items like gloves needed for obstetrician check-ups, and other pregnancy and delivery costs.[92]

Immunization for other diseases, for which India had an effective public programme, was also a major casualty. By mid-July 2020, the World Health Organization and UNICEF issued a joint statement warning of an 'alarming decline' in the number of children receiving life-saving vaccines in many developing countries, with India being named among them.[93] A

---

[90]Ruchir Kumar, Ritesh Mishra, and Rajesh Kumar Singh, 'During Covid-19 lockdown, births at clinics plummet by 40%', *Hindustan Times,* 30 May 2020.

[91]Roughly translated as Mother's Health Protection Programme. S. Rukmini, 'Covid-19 disrupted India's routine health services', *IndiaSpend,* 27 August 2020.

[92]SEWA Bharat, *Gendered precarity in the lockdown*, All India Federation of Self Employed Women's Association, May 2020.

[93]'WHO and UNICEF warn of a decline in vaccinations during COVID-19',

study by WHO and UNICEF estimated that nearly 3.5 million children missed their DPT vaccination in 2020—the largest such number in the world.[94] Coverage of other vaccinations like those designed to prevent measles also fell sharply.

These health concerns were made even more severe because of the poor treatment meted out to frontline workers dealing with public health, dominantly underpaid women operating not as regular public employees, but under 'schemes' through which they are paid 'honoraria' rather than wages, which, in fact, mostly fall well below the minimum wages. They do not receive any of the usual benefits associated with government employment such as security of tenure, minimum wages, social security, and so on. Often, they do not even have proper written contracts. The most glaring examples come from the Integrated Child Development Scheme (ICDS) and the National Health Mission (NHM), whose lakhs of workers—predominantly women—are not classified as workers and not paid even the legal minimum wages. Currently, there are estimated to be as many as 12.9 lakh Anganwadi Workers (AWWs) and 11.6 Anganwadi helpers under the ICDS alone, so they total a number that comes to more than 60 per cent of the official central government positions. Therefore, 'informal' public workers without the status or benefits of regular government employees actually form the majority in public employment. This has serious implications for the rights of such workers, but also for both the quantity and quality of public services.

The pandemic should have underscored the extreme importance of a public healthcare system and the folly of privatization of essential services. Instead, in addition to being understaffed, overworked, underpaid, and undervalued by

---

World Health Organization, 15 July 2020.

[94]Kalyan Ray, 'WHO asks India, others, to step up child immunisation programme', *Deccan Herald*, 8 September 2021.

society, these frontline health workers now faced additional risks in terms of health and physical safety hazards. They had to deal with shortages of PPE, longer working hours because of inadequate personnel, increased risk of infection, violence against healthcare workers, and stigma, ostracization, and ill treatment by other members of society. The treatment of workers involved in hospital waste management and dead body disposal, and municipal solid waste management and disposal, who were central to the control of the pandemic as well as other health system functioning, is instructive. A study of work chains in these two activities in Bengaluru[95] showed how these workers were effectively invisible to both the public and policymakers, and were denied the most basic protections during the pandemic, even as they remain overworked and underpaid and without minimal social security. They got no training about the additional occupational hazards because of the pandemic, and mostly were not provided even the most essential protective equipment. They did not get regular medical check-ups, life insurance cover, or free treatment for even the illnesses contracted at work, including Covid-19. Instead, most of them had to go to private hospitals when they got ill and had to pay from their own pockets. Meanwhile their employment was often very insecure. Contract workers and daily wage workers did not get pay for the days they were unable to work for whatever reason (even for an illness contracted because of the job), and those with regular work had only limited days of medical leave. The caste dimension may be significant in explaining how both state and society disdain such essential workers: these activities are typically performed by Dalit workers, and upper caste attitudes towards 'polluting activities' of dealing with human

---

[95] K. J. Siddharth, Sylvia Karpagam, and Alwyn Prakash D'Souza, *Working at the Margins: A Report on the Conditions of Invisibilized Frontline Workers*, Bengaluru: Ashirwad Centre for Social Concern, 2020.

waste in various forms and those who perform them still persist in determining how such workers are treated and remunerated. But it is also clear that such ill-treatment of essential workers also affects the quality of the work they are able to perform and the overall level of public health, which would continue to be a problem after the pandemic is over.

The trajectory of the Covid-19 outbreak in India thus suggests that it will leave lasting scars well after the pandemic is finally over. These are going to affect the health of the people both directly and indirectly, as well as conditions of life and livelihood that have been badly battered and will continue to be so for some time into the future. The impact on the economy and employment is explored in the next chapter, and how these in turn have affected material and social conditions of the people is discussed in Chapter 5.

chapter 4

THE ECONOMIC FALLOUT

It was only to be expected that something as drastic as the national lockdown would impact the economy severely. And the Indian economy was already weak, with many 'comorbidities', as described in Chapter 2. Inevitably, in the initial phase of extreme lockdown, both supply and demand were affected: supply and distribution chains were disrupted; informal workers found themselves without income and were forced to reduce consumption; many activities like construction and some services simply stopped; and investments were halted. In the April–June 2020 quarter, when the effects of the lockdown were evident, the Indian economy was among the worst performing in the world: official estimates of real GDP declined by 24.4 per cent compared to the same period of the previous year, and by 30 per cent compared to the previous quarter.[1] As the lockdown restrictions were eased in the following quarter, there was some recovery, but even so economic activity remained at least 7 per cent below the level of the previous year.

For the financial year 2020–21 as a whole, official figures suggest that GDP in constant prices declined by 8.9 per cent compared to the previous year (that is, taking account of inflation) and by 5.4 per cent in current prices.[2] This was

[1]MOSPI, Press Release, 31 May 2021, available at www.mospi.nic.in/sites/default/files/press_release/Press%20Note_31-05-2021.pdf.

[2]Government of India, 'Economic Survey 2020-21', Ministry of Finance, Statistical Appendix, available at www.indiabudget.gov.in/economicsurvey/doc/Statistical-Appendix-in-English.pdf.

the worst annual decline in national income in India since Independence. Per capita income in 2020–21 was lower than even four years earlier, and just barely above the level of five years before, undermining the growth of the intervening period.[3] In July–September 2021, GDP was still 7 per cent below the level of January–March 2020, the last pre-pandemic quarter.

More worryingly, the decline and inadequate recovery in incomes was spread across sectors. Agriculture provided the only ray of hope for the Indian economy in 2020–21, as a good monsoon enabled agricultural output to rise dramatically even as other sectors were in decline. But thereafter, the value added in agriculture declined continuously.[4] In July–September 2021, agricultural value added was 34 per cent lower than the peak of October–December 2020, and even lower (by 9 per cent) than the level in April–June 2019. Similarly, manufacturing was supposed to have swung back into higher activity. But despite a temporary jump in January–March 2021, by July–September 2021 the sector's value added was still lower than in the pre-pandemic quarter January–March 2020. Even construction, which showed a big jump in January–March 2021, fell thereafter, so that by July–September it was 13 per cent lower than the level reached just before the pandemic. The recovery in the services was also extremely uneven. The only consistent increases after the lockdown slump were in public administration, defence, and other services—largely as state governments stepped up their spending to deal at least partially with the massive humanitarian crisis that was unfolding. But trade, transport communication, and other services that are closely related to material economic

---

[3]See C. P. Chandrasekhar and Jayati Ghosh, 'National income during the pandemic', 22 Feb 2022, available at www.networkideas.org/featured-articles/2022/02/national-income-during-the-pandemic/.

[4]Data in this paragraph are based on CSO's First Advance Estimates of National Income, January 2022, https://pib.gov.in/PressReleasePage.aspx?PRID=1788380.

activity did not recover in the same way: in July–September 2021 the value added was 21 per cent lower than in the pre-pandemic quarter. By late 2021, finance, real estate, and professional services were on the rise, but since this seemed unmoored to the real economy, it could reflect a speculative bubble rather than a sustainable trajectory.

However, even these projections of economic activity were on the higher side; many independent economists consider the decline in GDP to have been even more severe. This is because the national accounts data are heavily biased in favour of formal sector trends and therefore underestimate the impact of declining informal economic activity. The Central Statistical Organization uses a survey conducted more than fifteen years earlier, in 2004–05, to estimate the relative sizes of formal and informal sectors and assumes that the two grow at similar rates, though that is clearly not the case. Just as with demonetization and the GST (discussed in Chapter 2), informal activities were much more affected by the lockdown and the consequent shrinking of mass consumption. More realistic calculations point to more substantial declines in economic activity: for example, it was estimated that GDP had declined by at least 12.5 per cent in the fiscal year 2020–21.[5] But even such estimates did not factor in the possibility of a very low or even negative fiscal stimulus from the central government. When all the dust has settled and more reliable assessments of economic activity are finally available (which is likely to be several years from now) it is likely to be found that the decline was much more severe than the official projections of this period.

Further, since all the evidence points to greater inequality of income and assets in this period (as discussed below), it is not surprising that private consumption, which was already sluggish

[5]Pronab Sen, 'The Covid-19 shock: Learnings from the past, addressing the present - III', *Ideas for India*, 7 June 2020.

before the pandemic, collapsed in April–June 2020 and then showed very uncertain recovery. In July–September 2021, it still remained 7.5 per cent below the pre-pandemic level, suggesting a real curtailment of domestic effective demand. In such a context, it was not surprising that investment did not really recover, with investment in July–September 2021 still 5 per cent below the pre-pandemic level. This reflected the fundamental macroeconomic problem of the Indian economy: a contraction of domestic demand because of falling employment, and wages and incomes of the self-employed, as the informal economy and small and micro enterprises continued to bear the brunt of the economic difficulties. Growing inequalities could create more consumption by the super-rich, but that was clearly not enough to dig the economy out of its hole.

Employment was inevitably very badly affected, with estimates of at least 50 million job losses over the year, even after some revival of informal work after the lockdown was lifted.[6] Open unemployment rates, which calculate the ratio of those actively seeking work to the total labour force (all those who are working and seeking work together) are generally very low in India because most workers are informal and do not have access to any kind of unemployment insurance or benefit. So they are forced to try to keep doing something, no matter how low paying it is. But during this pandemic, rates of open unemployment surged despite that. Even after the economy was allowed to open again, there was only partial recovery in employment, and these were typically associated with lower wages, so that purchasing power of the masses remained very weak. By the end of the year, the negative effects on employment (discussed in more detail in Chapter 5) were even being felt among formal

[6]'Economy to Shrink 12.5%, 50 Million to Lose Jobs: Former Chief Statistician', Karan Thapar interview with Pronab Sen, *The Wire*, 11 June 2020, available at www.youtube.com/watch?v=_wmeDzSWdSs.

jobs that had earlier been spared the worst of the layoffs.

Throughout the first year of the pandemic, India was among the worst performers among emerging markets by most indicators, falling to bottom place in the months of June and November 2020.[7] An index based on seven high-frequency indicators, including those describing real economic activity, such as GDP growth and the manufacturing purchasing managers' index (PMI), rates of inflation, and financial indicators like exchange rate movements and changes in stock market capitalization, showed that in general other emerging market economies performed better than India. Meanwhile, railways' passenger revenue declined by 87 per cent to just ₹4,600 crore in 2020 compared with ₹53,000 crore the previous year, even though freight volumes and revenues increased slightly because of greater movement of items like foodgrains.[8]

What explains why the Indian economy was so much worse hit than other developing countries, and even worse off than other South Asian economies? The severe nature of the lockdown certainly had an impact, especially since the overwhelming majority of India's workers are informal or self-employed and had no automatic social protection that could have provided some assistance during the lockdown. But what made matters much worse was the extreme parsimony of the government's fiscal response, which was among the stingiest in the world in terms of very little additional expenditure during the pandemic, and despite the extreme lockdown creating much greater material distress among the people. This was a major factor in the very poor performance of the economy, since the impact of the lockdown and pandemic were not counterbalanced by big fiscal increases. This had immediate effects on suppressing

---

[7]Tauseef Shahidi, 'India slips to bottom of EM rungs for the second time in six months', *Mint*, 24 December 2020.

[8]PTI,'Indian Railways earnings on track', *The Telegraph*, 30 December 2020.

domestic demand, and also impacted the future path of the economy, reducing its investment and growth potential.

The Government's Relief Packages

The limited central government was first and foremost felt in the small size of the relief packages, as described below. Despite sharp declines in wage incomes and self-employed livelihoods because of the lockdown, official relief was minuscule. A wide range of feasible policy suggestions were made immediately after the lockdown[9] that could be speedily implemented within the existing institutional framework. These included, for example, significant increases in social protection in the form of greatly enlarged and universal access to the public food distribution system, compensatory income transfers of around ₹7,000 per month for at least three months to all who were not in formal employment, and significantly increased health expenditure. These were indeed similar to measures undertaken by most governments across the world over this period, even in lower income countries. But none of these was really considered seriously in official circles. Instead, the central government exhibited extreme parsimony. This had serious—sometimes even fatal—implications for people, but it also spelt macroeconomic disaster, as the lack of government spending contributed to the overall economic collapse.

The first relief package announced after the lockdown, the Pradhan Mantri Garib Kalyan Yojana—roughly translated as the Prime Minister's Poor Welfare Scheme—was announced by the finance minister on 26 March, in the midst of the economic chaos created by the sudden national lockdown. The total package was

---

[9]For a summary of different proposals, see Debraj Ray and S. Subramanian, 'India's Response to Covid-19 is a Humanitarian Disaster', *Boston Review*, 16 July 2020.

declared to amount to ₹1.7 lakh crore (around 1.2 per cent of the then estimated GDP) but since it actually included many items that were already budgeted for and committed public spending, the proposed additional expenditure amounted to only around 0.5 per cent of GDP.[10] The main elements of this were some free food rations to those holding ration cards, very limited cash transfers to women holding Jan Dhan bank accounts (meant for the poor), an insurance scheme for public health workers for the period of the pandemic, some liquidity support to organized workers covered under the Employees' Provident Fund, and some underwriting of bank loans to specified target groups through official provision of collateral.

Those who were already accessing foodgrains from the public distribution system under the National Food Security Act were offered 5 kilograms of wheat or rice and one kilogram of pulses free for three months (later extended until March 2022). This was the most significant element of the relief package, but it was still much less than what could easily have been provided given the huge excess food stocks being held by the central government. It excluded all those who did not have ration cards, which meant that at least 100 million deserving people were deprived of this benefit precisely when it was most required, while migrant workers whose cards were based in their homes also could not benefit. In the event, even these limited amounts did not reach all the intended beneficiaries, because the government did not take steps to improve the distribution system and was tardy in delivering grain to the states.[11]

The cash transfers that were provided as part of the relief

---

[10] *Numbers on the Edge: Assessing India's fiscal response to Covid-19*, New Delhi: Centre for Budget and Governance Accountability, 29 May 2020.

[11] Abhijit Sen and Vikas Rawal, 'The Covid-19 pandemic impact on Indian agriculture', in Vikas Rawal, Jayati Ghosh, and C. P. Chandrasekhar (eds.), *When Governments Fail: A Pandemic and Its Aftermath*, Tulika Books and Columbia University Press, 2021.

package were so small and limited in coverage as to be almost embarrassing. 30 million people receiving public pensions (widows and elderly people who were categorized as falling below the poverty line and people with disabilities) were to receive only ₹1,000 each, and that too in two instalments spread over three months. Women holders of Jan Dhan bank accounts (designed to be for poor households without collateral, but actually covering a range of other households) who were estimated to number around 300 million, were to receive a one-time transfer of ₹500. Households that had received gas cylinders for cooking under the Ujjwala scheme would receive three free cylinders. Health workers, including frontline and sanitation workers, were to be covered by a special insurance scheme—but only for the period of the pandemic. The frontline health workers (ASHAs) who were given many additional duties during the pandemic were also to be offered additional cash incentives of ₹1000 per month for six months. Other elements of the relief package simply involved frontloading payments that had already been announced and budgeted for (such as a transfer of ₹2000 to farmers under the existing PM-KISAN scheme). Even the normal annual increase in wage rates paid to workers under the rural employment programme was included in this 'relief' package!

It soon became evident that this package was completely inadequate to deal with the scale of the economic disaster that had befallen the country because of the brutal manner in which the lockdown had destroyed livelihoods, and that it did not provide meaningful social protection. The calls for another, much bigger relief package that would also include a significant fiscal stimulus became stronger, and even representatives of big business began to demand more substantial public spending to reverse the downturn. Six weeks into the lockdown, on 20 May, the Prime Minister announced another package, the Atmanirbhar Bharat Abhiyan (roughly translated as Self-Reliant

India Campaign). This was supposedly much larger, at ₹20 lakh crore, equivalent to 10 per cent of GDP. But this turned out to be yet another smoke and mirrors exercise. Clearly, the ground had not been prepared with the administration, in particular the Ministry of Finance, that was charged with implementing it. This is probably why the details of what this package actually entailed were revealed in piecemeal fashion in six separate news conferences of the finance minister over several weeks. Eventually, it became clear that there would be very little new spending by the central government in this 'new' package, since much of it involved shifting existing spending across budgetary heads and renaming or revamping existing schemes to reach the total magic number announced by the prime minister.[12]

Some of the measures were only oriented to providing liquidity for businesses, and therefore did not require the government to spend. Rather, banks had to act, either through moratoria on repayment or expanding loan facilities to farmers and micro, small, and medium enterprises (MSMEs) at slightly reduced interest rates. Contributions to the Employee Provident Fund (largely for formal workers) were subsidized for three months, and those workers who were enrolled in the fund were allowed to make some early withdrawals. State governments were allowed to borrow beyond their defined limits, from 3 per cent to 5 per cent of their domestic product. This reinforced the pattern of the central government limiting its own spending, and instead passing on the future debt burden to the states, who (unlike the central government) no longer had any revenue raising powers beyond petrol and alcohol sales taxes. This is likely to create future fiscal problems for state governments, who could be forced to cut back on future spending to repay

[12]'Analysis of the Aatma Nirbhar Bharat Abhiyaan', PRS Legislative Research; Udit Misra, 'ExplainSpeaking: Why Atmanirbhar Bharat Abhiyan economic package is being criticised', *Indian Express*, 21 May 2020.

these enhanced loans required to cover immediate pandemic-related spending.

Ultimately, much of this stimulus package was in the form of credit guarantees and other liquidity provision that did not require additional fiscal outlay—and it turned out that even these liquidity measures were never fully extended. Total additional public spending by the central government promised by these relief measures amounted to only around 1 per cent of GDP. Ultimately even these announced allocations were not spent: in the period of greatest need, the seven months to December 2020, less than 10 per cent of the promised ₹10 trillion had actually been spent.[13]

Even compared to other developing countries, the Government of India provided very little social protection during the course of the pandemic. Less than a quarter of the Indian population was covered by additional social protection, significantly lower than other countries at similar levels of per capita income.[14] And the amounts provided to those who were covered were very small, not enough to compensate even a fraction of the loss of income; sometimes enabling workers to draw on their own savings in their provident funds.[15] The major source of relief for informal workers was the rural employment guarantee programme (on the basis of a law enacted in 2005, which promises 100 days of work per rural household at a national wage). This programme is countercyclical in its very design, as it is supposed to provide 100 days of employment

[13]'₹20 lakh cr stimulus package: Less than 10% disbursed in 7 months under govt's Atmanirbhar Abhiyaan', *Financial Express*, 13 December 2020.

[14]Liliana Marcos Barba, Hilde van Regenmortel, and Ellen Ehmke, *Shelter from the Storm: The Global Need for Universal Social Protection in Times of COVID-19*, Oxfam International, December 2020.

[15]Ugo Gentilini, Mohamed Almenfi, Ian Orton, and Pamela Dale, *Social Protection and Jobs Responses to COVID-19: A Real-Time Review of Country Measures*, Washington D. C.: World Bank, 2020.

to any households that ask for it, and more people ask for it when other sources of livelihood decline. Demand for such work definitely went up, as migrant workers returned from urban areas to their rural homes. But in April 2020, employment in this programme fell by 83 per cent relative to the previous year, partly because of confusion among state governments about the lockdown, and partly because money was not immediately released from the centre to the states to enable an increase in the programme.[16] Subsequently, the central government increased the budgetary allocation from ₹68,000 crore to ₹105,000 crore but this simply brought it to levels required to meet the pre-pandemic demand. Worse, the budgetary allocation in the following year was reduced once again, even though rural distress persisted and employment options remained dire. A feature that is often forgotten is that legally speaking, the MNREGA is a demand-driven programme for which funds must be provided *by law*, so any increase in demand for work is supposed to be met with the required increases in central government funding. This means that the central government's allocations on the programme cannot be a constraint on spending on the programme: as demand for work increases, the money for this must be provided. But in reality, the government limited the employment provided by limiting the money it provides to state governments for the programme. This runs counter to the law and has acted as a brake on its potential effectiveness in periods of crisis like the pandemic.

Fiscal Restraint: The Central Government as Scrooge

The fundamental underlying problem in all of this was that the central government was simply unwilling to increase its spending

---

[16]NREGA National Tracker December 2020, Ministry of Rural Development, Government of India.

significantly in response to this calamity. The Indian government was one of the few in the world that did not increase its spending significantly during the pandemic. In the worst first phase of the pandemic, March–December 2020, total spending of the central government increased by just 8 per cent, while inflation was around 6–7 per cent over this period, so public spending increased by only around 1 per cent after taking account of inflation.[17] Indeed, for the first six months during and after the lockdown, during the worst of the economic collapse, the government actually spent *less* in real terms than it had the previous year. This was effectively a *negative* fiscal stance, with the central government adding to the contractionary tendencies in an already collapsing economy. Total public spending by central and state governments over the full fiscal year 2020–21 did increase, by around 13 per cent in real terms,[18] but even this was not enough to counter the downward economic pressures on economic activity resulting from falling mass consumption and reduced private investment.

It was argued by some that this fiscal restraint was necessary because the government revenues were also falling and therefore it did not have the resources to spend more. But this is a completely wrong way of understanding the government's role in the economy. Obviously, tax receipts fell during the lockdown-induced economic contraction. But the idea that government spending is dependent upon current revenues is mistaken: it confuses the government with a household, when a government's budget is completely unlike a household budget. Unlike individuals or families, the central government by virtue

---

[17]'Government of India Union Government Accounts at A Glance As at the End of December 2020', calculated from data of the Controller General of Accounts, Government of India, available at https://cga.nic.in/MonthlyReport/Published/12/2020-2021.aspx.

[18]Economic Survey 2021–22, Government of India, Vol. II Statistical Appendix, Table 2.6.

of controlling the central bank as issuer of currency, can always access the resources required for its spending. (Indeed, this is precisely how most countries financed their spending during the pandemic, as we saw in Chapter 1.) When the government spends, it enables more economic activity, which can counterbalance the economic decline caused by shocks like the health crisis and the lockdown. If there are supply constraints, this can lead to inflation or a larger balance of payments deficits, but some of the increased public spending can be used to ease supply constraints. It is true that open developing countries also face pressure from global financial markets, which have tended in the past to punish those running large fiscal deficits. But beyond the short run, this does not really matter, and if public spending stems economic decline, then even financial markets take a more positive view. This was certainly evident especially during the extraordinary circumstances created by the pandemic. That is why, during the Covid-19 pandemic, governments across the world in both advanced and developing countries, embarked on massive spending programmes, in addition to further loosening monetary policy.

Yet the Indian government behaved in the opposite way, making it an outlier among both developed and emerging market economies. Figure 4.1 shows the monthly pattern of total receipts and expenditure of the central government, from the year before the pandemic. It reveals an interesting—albeit shocking—pattern. In the six-month period of the first wave of the pandemic (April to September 2020) total receipts of the government declined sharply by around one-third, primarily because of the sharp decline in tax revenues as the economy contracted because of the lockdown. This was entirely predictable and occurred in most countries in the world. In most other countries, governments took steps to counteract this economic decline by ramping up their own spending. Yet spending by the central government barely increased in these six months; indeed, the Indian government actually spent *less* (₹1,479 trillion in Apr–Sep 2020, compared to ₹1,488 trillion in Apr–Sep 2019) than it had in the previous year! In other words, it was apparently so obsessed with avoiding a large fiscal deficit even in this extraordinary year that it took steps to reduce its own expenditure.

Figure 4.1

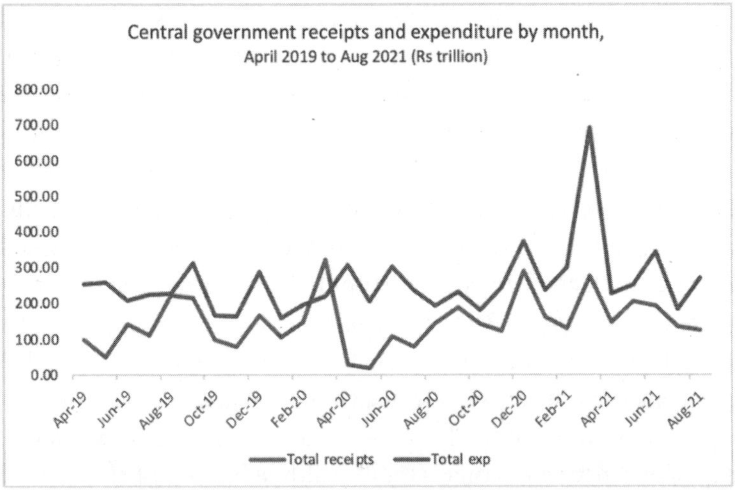

Central government receipts and expenditure by month,
April 2019 to Aug 2021 (Rs trillion)

Total receipts — Total exp

Source: Controller General of Accounts, cga.nic.in, accessed on 30 January 2022.

Essentially, the government did not treat this period of calamity as one in which it was necessary to make big increases in public spending. The large increase in the fiscal deficit that nevertheless appeared was mostly because of the significant decline in revenues during April to October 2020, and their inadequate revival thereafter. As a result, the fiscal deficit was 9.5 per cent of GDP largely because revenues declined and GDP also fell.

Obviously, this fiscal repression restricted attempts to provide basic needs and livelihood compensation or social protection to those whose income earning capacities had been destroyed, and therefore added to the material suffering of the people. It was also macroeconomically unwise, as noted above, because it worsened the tendency for the economy to contract, thereby adding to the severity of the crisis and prolonging the economic slump.[19] As households and businesses spent less, the government needed to prevent a downward spiral, provide the demand (and reduce infrastructure constraints) by spending more. Because it did not do so, it contributed to further economic contraction, and consequently even tax revenues did not recover much because economic activity remained sluggish.

Such restraint on total public spending also impacted the very sectors that really needed more government spending in this period. Health expenditure should have been the most obvious priority in what was primarily a health crisis, but this increased by only ₹8,465 crore in the eight months between April and December 2020.[20] To put that into perspective, that increase was *only 0.04 per cent of the previous year's GDP*. The central government in India has been spending only around 0.3 per cent of GDP or less on health for a while, but even in the first nine months of the fiscal year—during the worst pandemic experienced in a century—total health spending of the central government came to only 0.3 per cent of the previous year's GDP! Evidently, the pandemic was seen as significant enough for the government to shut down the economy for several months and destroy incomes of hundreds of millions of people, but not enough to warrant anything more than a trivial increase in its own spending on health.

The central government's spending on food and public

---

[19]Prabhat Patnaik, 'A matter of survival of the peasantry', *IDEAs Commentary*, December 2020.

[20]Calculated from data of the Conroller General of Accounts, Government of India, available at https://cga.nic.in/MonthlyReport/Published/12/2020-2021.aspx.

distribution did increase significantly over the financial year to end March 2021, by nearly four times compared to the previous year. Some of this was because of the provision of additional free foodgrain of 5 kilogram per month to those covered under the National Food Security Act 2014, which was continued until November 2020. But a significant part of the increase was simply an accounting change rather than an actual increase in spending on the food subsidy. For several preceding years, the central government simply had not paid the Food Corporation of India (FCI, which handles the public foodgrain procurement and distribution system) much of its dues for running the programme. This meant that some of the FCI's spending was not reported as part of the central government's food subsidy and did not show in the central government's fiscal deficit, but was instead transferred to 'off-budget' heads.[21] But this was an expensive sleight-of-hand for the public food system, because the FCI had to bear losses and take on debt to cover its costs and cope with its current expenses. This created an entirely unnecessary interest burden for the FCI, which added to its costs and even made it appear 'inefficient' for no fault of its own. It also inevitably threatened the viability of the public food system over time. Ultimately, the government was forced to pay a part of its pending dues in March 2021.

Remarkably, during the first wave of the pandemic and the national lockdown, the additional foodgrain distribution was quite limited, even though much more could easily have been provided to hungry people. Between April and December 2020, the FCI procured 91.4 million tonnes of foodgrain from

---

[21]'Report of the Comptroller and Auditor General of India on Compliance of the Fiscal Responsibility and Budget Management Act, 2003 for the year 2016-17' (Report No. 20 of 2018), available at https://cag.gov.in/uploads/download_audit_report/2018/Report_No_20_of_2018_Compliance_of_the_Fiscal_Responsibility_and_Budget_Management_Act_2003_Department_of_Economic_Affairs_Minis.pdf.

the rabi harvest[22], but distributed only 40.5 million tonnes. Because of this, the stocks held by the FCI increased from 87 million tonnes (at end March) to 104 million tonnes (at end June) and were still 86 million tonnes at the end of December 2020.[23] This was still more than three and a half times the buffer norm for stock holding of 24 million tonnes. Ironically, these excess stocks of foodgrains were expensive for the FCI to hold, estimated to cost around ₹5.70 per kilogram per year. Since stock holding increased so much beyond the storage capacity, the FCI had to take on more expensive warehousing or simply leave grain in places where it could rot or become unfit for human consumption.

The other head of expenditure that showed some increase was rural development, which increased largely because of the increased outlay of ₹40,000 crore on the rural employment programme MNREGA. This led to the central government spending more than ₹1.1 trillion on the programme[24]—but even this essentially brought the spending to levels that were required by the labour budget that had been prepared *before* the pandemic. Obviously, during the pandemic demand for work increased greatly, and therefore much more was needed, especially given the sustained rural distress and the collapse of urban employment. Several state governments requested further increases that were not forthcoming. In the Union Budget 2021–22 for the subsequent year, the allocation for MNREGA was once again brought down, to only ₹73,000 crore,[25] although

---

[22]Department of Food and Public Distribution, 'Procurement Figures', available at https://dfpd.gov.in/procurement-figures.htm.

[23]Food Corporation of India, 'Food grains Stock in Central Pool for the years 2016-2021 (Opening Balance)', available at https://fci.gov.in/stocks.php?view=46

[24]PTI, 'Highest ever spending under MNREGA during FY21: FM Sitharman', *Business Standard*, 12 February 2021.

[25]Ayshee Bhaduri, 'Centre allocates ₹73,000 crore for MGNREGA for 2021-22

rural distress continued and the programme would be a critical lifeline for people. In fact, 90 per cent of the budgetary allocation for the entire year April 2021 to March 2022 had already been spent by the end of September 2021, indicating the extent of demand for work amid continuing rural distress.[26] Since the MNREGA is supposed to be a demand-driven programme by law, the Centre should make available as much as is required, but this did not happen despite requests by several state governments, and therefore the programme continued to be underfunded relative to need.

The Spectre of Stagflation and the Role of Petrol Taxes

Unlike many other similarly placed economies, in India consumer prices began to rise in 2020. This was despite depressed mass consumption, which in other circumstances should have kept prices low. Some economists immediately (and wrongly) interpreted this as a sign of 'overheating', thereby suggesting that monetary policy should be tightened and that the scope for expansionary fiscal policy was limited. This argument is completely wrong: demand remained low because of collapses in wage income, and low private investment because of the shrinking domestic market and uncertainty about the future. The inflation in this period was not demand-driven, but rather cost-push, reflecting higher costs of some inputs, particularly of fuel.

The rising domestic price of oil throughout this period, even in the phases when global oil prices fell, was a remarkable feature of the Indian economy through 2020 and the first half of 2021. It occurred because the central government kept raising excise

---

fiscal', *Hindustan Times*, 27 July 2021.

[26]'NREGA 21-22 at mid year - What does the tracker show?', People's Action for Employment Guarantee, 21 October 2021.

duties on petroleum products domestically. In 2014, when the BJP government came to power at the centre, domestic prices were high because global oil prices were reigning high. At the time, Narendra Modi had been a vocal opponent of these high prices on the ground that hurt the poor, and used this in the electoral campaign that brought his party to power. (In 2014 he had described the hike in oil prices as 'a prime example of the failure of Congress-led UPA'.[27])

But after coming to power, the Modi government hiked excise duties repeatedly, at least eighteen times since 2014. Central taxes on petrol and diesel rose by more than three times between 2015 and 2021.[28] As a result, even though domestic oil prices were supposedly no longer 'administered' or controlled, in effect Indian consumers derived no benefit when global prices fell and suffered even more when they rose. In December 2020, excise duties on petrol were 3.5 times higher, and those on diesel nearly 9 times higher, than when Mr Modi took office in 2014.[29] This continued through the pandemic, even though the purchasing power of ordinary people had collapsed. The price of petrol in Delhi, for example, rose by more than 50 per cent between the early days of the pandemic in May 2020 and September 2021. A significant part of the rise was due to increasing central excise duties. Between 1 November 2019 and 16 October 2021, excise duty on petrol in Delhi increased by 65 per cent, from ₹19.98 per litre to ₹32.90 per litre. By June–July 2021, taxes (excise and VAT) accounted for 54 per cent of the price for petrol in Delhi.[30]

---

[27]Prabhash Dutta, 'Rising petrol prices: What Narendra Modi said before 2014 and his govt did in 4 years', *India Today,* 2 April 2018.

[28]Swati Mathur, 'Central taxes on petrol & diesel rose by 307% in last 6 years', *Times of India,* 24 March 2021.

[29]James Wilson, 'High fuel prices: blame it on high central excise which has increased manifold since 2014', *National Herald,* 19 December 2020.

[30]Ajit Dalvi, 'India saw 16 fuel price hikes in June 2021', *Autocar India,* 1 July

This became a crucial source of central government revenue: even though consumption of both petrol and diesel actually fell in the fiscal year 2020–21, central excise duty collection, dominantly from taxes on these two goods, increased by 88 per cent. The reliance on higher tax rates in fuels carried over into the following year: in the period April–August 2021, excise duty collections were already 37 per cent higher than in the same months of the previous year.[31]

It could be argued that such an oil tax would have a 'green' effect by reducing reliance on fossil fuel energy; but these increases were not accompanied by proactive measures to encourage more renewable forms of energy use. Indeed, the Modi government actively pushed more investment in fossil fuel extraction during the pandemic. From early 2020, oil and gas companies were allowed to begin drilling and other hydrocarbon exploration activities in India, without conducting the environmental impact assessment studies or public consultations that were earlier required. Later in the year, fracking was encouraged, by allowing companies to explore shale gas reserves without obtaining environmental clearances.[32] In June 2020, forty-one coal blocks were listed for auction for commercial coal mining; thirty-eight were eventually auctioned, half of which were taken by big corporate houses. Coal extraction was made more profitable for investors, by doing away with limits on ash percentages in the coal to be sold or requiring the coal to be washed before putting it into power plants. In late November 2020, coal mining was allowed before environmental and forest clearances.[33] In January 2021,

---

2021.

[31]IANS, 'Petroleum taxes to take govt's excise collections to historic high levels in FY22', *Free Press Journal,* 3 October 2021.

[32]Shashikant Yadav, 'Indian Fracking Companies Are Exploiting A Dearth of Regulation & Causing Environmental Havoc', *Green Queen,* 1 October 2020.

[33]Ayaskant Das, 'Modi government tweaks green law to allow coal extraction

it was proposed to push back the deadlines for adoption of new emission norms by coal-fired power plants (which had already been delayed from 2017 to 2022) with no final date.[34]

Clearly, environmental concerns were not behind the Modi government's hikes of excise duties on fuel—the focus was essentially on raising revenues, and it only meant that the price of the fuel went up. Since fuel is a universal intermediate that enters into all production and distribution activity, it affected costs in cultivation, manufacturing, and transport, as well as in those services with significant energy use. Much of the increase in consumer prices was due to this. The poor bore the burden of this regressive tax strategy as they faced rising prices even as their money incomes were falling.

The Squeeze on Fiscal Federalism

The push for political centralization was also associated with the undermining of financial relations between centre and states. Even before the pandemic, this had serious implications for the financial health of state governments and their ability to carry out their constitutionally mandated responsibilities. In 2015, the central government accepted the recommendation of the 14th Finance Commission, which is mandated to provide a just formula for the distribution of tax revenues between the Centre and the various state governments. This provided for a significant increase in the share of the states in total tax revenues, from 32 to 42 per cent, which would have enabled a significant increase in their spending. However, while accepting this proposal, the Modi government almost simultaneously cut plan grants and reduced the Centre's share of spending on Centrally Sponsored

sans final forest clearance', *Newsclick,* 29 December 2020.

[34]Sudarshan Varadhan, 'Power ministry proposes pushing back emission norms deadline', *Reuters,* 4 January 2021.

Schemes in health and education, neutralizing the benefit of the enhanced award for states.[35] The plan to slash the number of centrally sponsored schemes by one-third would further reduce the funds flowing to states from these schemes, many of which are designed to impact health, nutrition, and equity.[36]

The Modi government employed another legal loophole to reduce the money flowing to the states. Tax revenues have to be shared according to the Finance Commission's formula, but cesses and surcharges are exempt and can be retained entirely by the Centre. The central government has disproportionately relied on cesses and surcharges for mobilizing new revenues, making a mockery of the increase in states' share. As a result, instead of the promised 42 per cent, in 2018–19 state governments received only around 34 per cent of the tax revenues collected. Between 2011–12 and 2019–20, the Centre's cess and surcharge revenues nearly doubled, from 0.9 per cent to 1.7 per cent of GDP, while gross tax revenues that had to be shared with states declined from 10.4 per cent of GDP to 9.9 per cent in 2019–20.[37]

Covid-19 further intensified these centralizing tendencies. The national lockdown was imposed under the National Disaster Management Act that gave complete powers to the central government. However, after having announced the lockdown, the Centre did not take responsibility for managing it or dealing with the implications for public health and livelihoods. Instead, it essentially handed the problem over to the state governments to deal with. There was no sharing of strategies or (even more

---

[35]Dilasha Seth, 'State govts worry as Centre plans to trim schemes in upcoming Budget', *Business Standard*, 18 December 2020; 'Impact of the 14th Finance Commission and CSS Sharing Pattern on Health Expenditures', World Bank Group Macroeconomics and Fiscal Management.

[36]Asit Ranjan Mishra, 'Centrally funded plans face the axe', *Mint*, 3 February 2021.

[37]Suryash Tiwari and Saket Surya, *State of State Finances*, New Delhi: PRS, 2020.

importantly) financial and other resources with the state governments. As a result, state governments were forced to do all the heavy lifting of dealing with the health crisis and the economic effects of the pandemic on their own.

However, they also faced major resource gaps that were inadequately filled by the Centre. Unlike the central government, state governments in India cannot borrow freely from the RBI, and require the Centre's permission to do so, within strict limits. So they are much more sharply affected by declining revenues. A study of state finances in fiscal year 2020–21 found that between April and October 2020, revenue receipts of twenty-one states for which data were available declined by 13 per cent compared to the same period of the previous year.[38] Instead of providing more resources directly, the Centre simply raised the borrowing or fiscal deficit limit of states from 3 per cent to 4 per cent of state GDP in 2020–21, and then allowed them to frontload this debt to the first six months of the next financial year.[39] This had obvious implications for future debt burdens.

State governments were also owed significant amounts of pending dues by the Centre, which were not fully paid even during this period of great need. These dues arose because when the Goods and Services Tax was introduced in July 2017, states were enticed into agreeing to give up their revenue-raising powers by a guarantee to be paid for any loss of revenue for the first five years of the GST implementation, which came into force on 1 July 2017. GST revenues were supposed to increase by 14 per cent per year; any shortfall from this would be met by the Central government, which was to provide this amount as compensation. This promise was not honoured. GST compensation payments from the centre to the states

[38]Ibid.

[39]Prasanta Sahu, 'Front-loading: Centre allows states to borrow 75% of their annual limit in April-December', *Financial Express*, 26 April 2021.

were extensively delayed, and when the lockdown started, the states had not been paid the compensation due for the period December 2019 to March 2020.[40] Even as late as September 2020, the government admitted in Parliament that it still owed ₹151,365 crore in GST compensation to the states.[41] Although some payments were made thereafter, the shortfall for the fiscal year 2020–21 amounted to more than ₹80,000 crore.[42]

If these funds had been transferred to the states as the Centre was legally bound to do, it would have greatly alleviated the resource constraint of state governments and enabled them to spend more effectively to deal with the health and economic crises. The central government claimed that it had not received sufficient funds through the special cess on GST created for this purpose. But the agreement between Centre and States had in no way made the payment of this compensation dependent on the cess. The Centre had committed to meet any shortfall in revenue and if the cess revenues were inadequate, it could borrow money to compensate the states, and then repay that by extending the period over which the cess is levied (which is entirely up to the Centre).

There were also complaints that the BJP-ruled central government 'punished' state governments run by Opposition parties by denying them resources, such as inadequate provision for special relief measures after major floods in Kerala[43] (run by a Left Front led by the Communist Party of India Marxist),

---

[40]PTI, 'GST compensation to states pending for Dec-March FY20', *Economic Times*, 17 May 2020.

[41]PTI, 'GST compensation due to states at ₹1.51 lakh crore, Maharashtra leads', *Economic Times*, 14 September 2020.

[42]'FY21 compensation: "GST transfers to states for FY21 fell short by ₹81,179 crore"', *Financial Express*, 20 July 2021.

[43]'Centre refuses to give more funds to Kerala for flood relief', *The Hindu*, 24 January 2020.

and cyclones in West Bengal.[44] In Punjab, run by the opposition Congress Party, the Finance Minister complained in December 2021 that Centre was holding back the state's rural development fund amounting to ₹1,200 crore, possibly as 'an arm-twisting tactic' because of the state government's support for the farmers' protest.[45]

Monetary Policy and Supply Side Measures

In the absence of an expansionary fiscal stance, the government relied heavily on measures aimed at increasing liquidity in the economy: using the central bank to provide credit guarantees and access to loans at slightly lowered rates to banks, non-bank financial companies, and all sizes of business. Credit systems in India were already stressed before the pandemic, and in dire need of financial assistance. But such measures were simply not effective on their own, since in a context of declining demand, access to credit is not sufficient to increase investment or even allow consumption to recover. As could be expected, banks and non-bank lenders mostly used the cheaper funds to repair their balance sheets, rather than lend to borrowers who could eventually be unable to repay.

The monetary policy package included reducing the interest rate (by 75 basis points for the repurchase or policy rate); a decline in the cash reserve ratio applied to banks, which would allow banks to lend more; and a moratorium on interest payments for various loans including for housing, automobiles, and consumer durable purchases. These measures could have worked only if the economy would have revived enough after the moratorium was lifted, to enable borrowers to repay. Otherwise,

[44]Pranab Mondal, 'Mamata unhappy with Centre's cyclone aid, says Bengal facing repeated discrimination', *New Indian Express*, 24 May 2021.

[45]PTI, 'Withholding ₹1,200 crore of Punjab's RDF an arm twisting: Manpreet Badal', *Economic Times,* 6 January 2021.

a moratorium simply delays the problem. Unlike a debt standstill that also eliminates interest payments entirely for that period, this simply kicks the can down the road; and the can becomes bigger as it rolls because the unpaid interest gets added to the principal. This was insufficient relief for the enterprises and people whose income completely dried up during this period and did not fully recover in the year after lockdown restrictions were lifted. It was no surprise that bad loans emerged as a major problem in the Indian economy by the beginning of 2021.

Further, simply enabling banks to lend more does not mean that they will do so, especially when the economy is slumping.[46] For obvious reasons, banks are unlikely to lend to those without the means to service such debt. Nor are investors likely to seek to borrow if they do not foresee an expanding market for their production. At best, those enterprises that were only marginally affected and those who had a temporary liquidity setback would seek to access funds, and banks would be willing to lend to them. But since many banks were already burdened with significant bad loans (known as 'Non Performing Assets'), they were more likely to go slow on credit provision in any case. Also, it was found that cutting the repo rate at which banks could borrow did not translate into lower interest rates for borrowers, especially those with loans from non-bank lenders. Credit going to non-food sectors actually declined slightly between March and November 2020, while credit to industry fell by 5.2 per cent.[47]

The problem of bad loans expectedly intensified during this period. By August it was already being estimated that 40 per cent of the loans held by companies would require restructuring.[48]

---

[46]See C. P. Chandrasekhar, 'The Indian economy: Before and after the pandemic', in Rawal, Ghosh, and Chandrasekhar (eds.), *When Governments Fail*, 2020, for a more detailed argument.

[47]RBI Bulletin, 21 January 2021, available at https://www.rbi.org.in/Scripts/BS_ViewBulletin.aspx.

[48]Krishna Kant, 'Q1 results: 40% of corporate loans may require restructuring

The RBI announced a corporate restructuring scheme in early August 2020 to assist large borrowers (those with aggregate exposure of more than ₹25 crore) who had suffered losses due to the pandemic. It was estimated that around two-thirds of non-MSME borrowers would be eligible for this; but a study by CRISIL found that only one per cent of those eligible would seek this assistance, since their debt was mostly short-term, whereas the scheme focused on alleviating long-term debt, and because of fears that this would impact their future credit rating.[49] Non-bank lenders and fintech companies began to be hit by defaults from September 2020 onwards. These were mostly in the form of 'auto-debit failures' whereby loan instalments that are meant to be automatically paid from bank accounts are cancelled because of lack of funds in the accounts. More than 40 per cent (by volume) of auto-debit payments failed in October 2020.[50] Problems intensified thereafter, especially as the second wave of Covid-19 once again affected economic activity along with people's lives. By July 2021, the Reserve Bank of India warned that the proportion of non-performing loans to assets in commercial banks could increase from 7.48 per cent in March 2021 to anywhere between 9.8–11.22 per cent by March 2022.[51] The situation was even more serious for non-bank lenders and microfinance institutions, many of which reported significant increases in non-payment as the slowdown affected jobs, salaries, and small and medium sized businesses.[52]

---

by banks', *Business Standard*, 7 August 2020.

[49]Ritu Singh, '99% non-MSME companies unlikely to opt for one-time debt restructuring, says CRISIL', *CNBC*, 17 November 2020.

[50]Shayan Ghosh, 'Loan defaults hit NBFCs, fintech firms the hardest', *Mint*, 17 November 2020.

[51]Reserve Bank of India, Financial Stability Report, July 2021, available at https://www.rbi.org.in/Scripts/PublicationReportDetails.aspx?UrlPage=&ID=1174.

[52]Mimansa Verma, 'For India's finance industry, there seems to be no end to the bad loan problem', *Scroll.in*, 27 August 2021.

In September 2021, the government set up the National Asset Reconstruction Company Limited—a 'bad bank' to clean up the balance sheets of commercial banks. It was noted that this reflected the failure of the Insolvency and Bankruptcy Code to resolve the problem of bad loans without much fiscal cost, and did not create any incentives for repayment.[53]

Meanwhile, the smaller borrowers (especially the MSMEs—micro, small, and medium enterprises) as usual were given the short shrift. The government's economic package for this group of enterprises included collateral-free automatic loans of up to ₹3 lakh crore for the period up to September 2020, to be fully guaranteed by the government, as well as partial credit guarantee schemes for stressed MSMEs. These schemes were self-limiting: they explicitly excluded both first-time borrowers and those with existing bad loans, which meant that many of those who really needed such assistance were left out. Only firms that already had outstanding loans were eligible to borrow, and that too only up to 10 per cent of their outstanding debt. This came to only 7 per cent of the total estimated number of MSMEs.[54] By October 2020, when the scheme ended, only 65 per cent of the target of loans of ₹3 lakh crore had been met, and these were mainly taken by larger enterprises within the MSMEs.[55] Between April and December 2020, total credit to micro and small enterprises declined by 2.4 per cent, while that to microcredit institutions fell by more than 14 per cent. Instead of this convoluted—and ineffective—set of measures, it would have been much more effective and helpful for the MSMEs if the central government had simply repaid the dues owed to

[53]'Will a bad bank fix India's broken banking system?', *The Hindu*, 8 October 2021.

[54]Sangeeta Ghosh, 'Examining the Covid-19 relief package for MSMEs', *Economic and Political Weekly*, Vol. 55, Issue 22, 30 May 2020.

[55]PTI, 'COVID-19: Government unlikely to extend credit guarantee scheme for MSME sector beyond October', *New Indian Express*, 18 October 2020.

them, which amounted to ₹5 lakh crore![56] The decline continued into the next financial year, with a decline of 0.7 per cent in bank credit to this segment between end March and end July 2021.[57] Hopes of revival of microfinance were shattered by the impact of the second Covid-19 wave, as the April–June 2021 period saw a decline in such credit by 7 per cent compared to the already depressed levels of same months of the previous year.[58] Meanwhile, household debt also emerged as a potential problem area. Even before the pandemic, between 2012 and 2018, debt taken on by households from both formal and informal credit sources had soared by 84 per cent in rural areas and 42 per cent in urban areas.[59] Debt vulnerability of households obviously increased substantially during the pandemic, and the moratorium only postponed the problem without reducing it.

Although the real economy was in decline, people increasingly relied on cash transactions, flying in the face of the push for digital transactions that was supposed to be an aim of the ill-fated demonetization. Even though the economy contracted, currency in circulation increased by 22 per cent over 2020,[60] and the currency to GDP ratio crossed 15 per cent—the highest since Independence. There was some amount of precautionary hoarding of cash because of fears of medical or financial emergencies during the lockdown and pandemic, when access to banks and ATMs also became more difficult. But also,

---

[56]Anchal Magazine and Anil Sasi, '₹3 Lakh Crore Relief Package for MSMEs but Goverments, Private Firms Owe Them More', *Indian Express*, 15 May 2020.

[57]RBI Bulletin September 2021, Appendix Table No. 15, p. 110., available at https://rbidocs.rbi.org.in/rdocs/Bulletin/PDFs/0RBIBULLETIN2021EC0A2D2A342245A9A337CFF2ECD21B59.PDF

[58]'June quarter: Micro lending falls 6.9 per cent on 2nd wave hit', *Indian Express*, 21 October 2021.

[59]Rakshith S. Ponnathpur, 'Even Before Pandemic, Debts Had Soared By 84% In Rural & 42% In Urban India', *IndiaSpend*, 20 October 2021.

[60]'Currency in circulation jumps by 22% in 2020 despite GDP contraction', *Economic Times,* 7 January 2021.

demonetization had paradoxically led to reduced public faith in the banking system, because people were unable to withdraw cash out of their own bank accounts for several months.

A major part of the policy response of the central government was directed to medium term 'structural' reforms that bore no immediate relation either to the pandemic or to the economic havoc created by the lockdown. These reforms harked back to the well-known tropes of privatization and deregulation. While they had little or no immediate effect on economic revival, they could possibly damage economic prospects for the medium term. These measures included: laws that would deregulate agricultural markets, possibly exposing farmers to exploitation by large corporate buyers rather than empowering them—which then gave rise to massive protests by farmers; encouraging more fossil fuel extraction, especially in the coal sector, which could add to future problems of climate change and insufficient adaptation; easing environmental regulations in order to attract private investors, which could damage the ecology; bringing in four new labour codes that effectively reduced the bargaining power of workers vis-à-vis employers; privatizing public sector enterprises that could have played an important role in economic revival; opening up banking and retail trade to foreign investors; and even suggesting private involvement in space exploration! The overall thrust was to use the 'opportunity' created by the pandemic to push through neoliberal economic 'reforms' that would increase the power of big capital relative to labour and to other citizens and stakeholders. This was evident in the move by several state governments to suspend or do away with many laws designed to protect labour, on the argument that this would help to attract foreign capital.[61] Subsequently, the adoption of four Labour Codes tilted the balance of power in favour of employers

[61]Jayati Ghosh, 'Will States Diluting Labour Laws Attract More Investment?', *BloombergQuint*, 11 May 2020.

vis-à-vis workers, effectively disempowering labour, as discussed in the next chapter.

Agriculture

The pandemic and lockdown could not have come at a worse time for India's farmers, who were already facing a complex set of problems that threatened their economic viability. The months of March to June are typically the most intensive for agriculture across the subcontinent, running from the time of the rabi harvest to the beginning of sowing for the kharif crop. These are complex operations that need to be carried out quickly and respond to changes in weather and other conditions, and even slight delays can have major impacts in terms of final output and sales revenues. These are months when labour demand is at its peak because of the nature of these operations and the short window of time within which they must be performed. They require farmers to interact with a wide range of different people: workers, input suppliers, purchasers of output, suppliers of credit, and the like. The transactions associated with these operations are overwhelmingly conducted in cash or through credit rotation practices that are often informal in nature and based on trust rather than legal contracts.

The abrupt announcement of the lockdown provided most farmers with very little time to prepare or adjust to the dramatically changed circumstances. Although agricultural activities were officially exempted from the lockdown, there was much confusion on which specific activities were allowed; and the regulations on this were issued more than a week after the lockdown had commenced. Different state governments and officials at lower levels had different interpretations. Farmers found it hard to hire agricultural workers, because they could be stopped while attempting to travel to the work sites, or because the workers themselves were less willing to travel for such employment. In some cases, standing crop ready to be harvested had to be left on the ground for several weeks, susceptible to drying out or rotting. Once crops were harvested, transport to markets became an issue, with vehicles carrying crops becoming extremely expensive and liable to being stopped by an overzealous (or corrupt) local police. Most mandis failed to open in the first three weeks of lockdown, making it next to impossible for most farmers who did not have other arrangements (like co-operatives or contracts with companies) to sell their produce.[62] In the first round of lockdown, horticulture farmers were very badly affected across the country, with reports of fruit and vegetables being simply thrown away or destroyed by despairing farmers who could not recoup even a fraction of their costs of cultivation through local market sales. Significant amounts of perishable crops were sold at low prices by farmers to local traders and dealers, because they could not get them to markets.

After the initial mess, horticulture distribution was generally sorted out. But for some crops like potatoes and onions, lack of local storage facilities and inadequate distribution meant that farmers got very low prices, and affected supplies until the end of the year, when the next crop could be expected. Milk and dairy products faced significant cuts in demand because of closures of restaurants and similar food shops, which had accounted for one-fifth of milk consumption in the country before that. Farmers who kept chicken to supplement their incomes faced a terrible market with sharp price falls, as rumours of chicken being carriers of the virus and new fears of avian flu led consumers to cut down on chicken consumption.

The greater concern was with foodgrains. Wheat was

---

[62]Vikas Rawal, Manish Kumar, Ankur Verma, and Jesim Pais, 'COVID-19 Lockdown: Impact on Agriculture and Rural Economy', *Social Scientist,* Vol. 48, No. 3/6 (562–565), March–June 2020, pp. 67–82.

harvested from mid-March to mid-April in large parts of central and western India (in states like Gujarat, Madhya Pradesh, Rajasthan, and Vidarbha in Maharashtra) but public procurement operations simply did not occur in several states over this period. Farmers were often forced to sell to local traders at a fraction of the official minimum support price. By the end of the first week of April, arrivals at major mandis were only 5–10 per cent of the arrivals over the same period in the previous year.[63] Even several months after the lockdown was imposed, total arrivals in the registered mandis remained much lower than they had been in previous years.[64] But the rabi (winter) harvest was good because of favourable climate, and a good monsoon also enabled more sowing for the kharif (late summer/autumn) crop. Exports of agricultural commodities, which fell sharply in April, recovered fairly quickly thereafter. As a result, in a period when the rest of the economy was reeling under the lockdown, agriculture was perceived as the one 'bright spot', with growing crop production celebrated as a sign of the resilience of Indian cultivation despite all odds.

It was in this context the Modi government chose to suddenly bring in three new farm laws, without consulting stakeholders like the farmers themselves or state governments, which are responsible for agriculture under India's Constitution. These laws were first introduced as ordinances in early June, then rushed through parliament using the ruling party's majority, without the usual procedures like referral to a Standing Committee of Parliament, and became law in September 2020. On the face of it, these laws—the Farmers (Empowerment and Protection) Agreement on Price Assurance and Farm Services Act (FAFSA), the Farmers' Produce Trade and Commerce

---

[63]Ibid.

[64]Sen and Rawal, 'The Covid-19 pandemic impact on Indian agriculture' in Rawal, Ghosh, and Chandrasekhar (eds.), *When Governments Fail.*

(Promotion and Facilitation) Act (FPTCA), and the Essential Commodities (Amendment) Act (ECAA)—appeared to be harmless or even beneficial for farmers. They relaxed restrictions on the interstate purchase, sale, and transport of farm produce, removed constraints on stockpiling under the 1955 Essential Commodities Act, and enabled contract farming based on written agreements. The government's declared purpose was to create 'an ecosystem where farmers and traders enjoy freedom of choice', with 'competitive alternative trading channels' that 'promote efficient, transparent, and barrier-free' trade.

But there were many concerns about these laws, which would dramatically change the existing arrangements for selling farm produce that allowed farmers (at least in some parts of the country) access to regulated markets with minimum crop prices. With the new laws, private traders would be allowed to set up private market yards or electronic trading platforms and price fixation would be left entirely to 'mutual consent' between the buyer and the seller without any regulation. The state government could not mediate to ensure fair prices for farmers; the regulated market yards run by state governments were barred from imposing any levies, cess, or taxes on trade. Private stock holding norms were made so high that they could enable hoarding and speculation by traders. In effect, the laws deregulated farm-produce transactions, contract farming, and stock holding in ways that would harm farmers.[65]

Farmers' organizations expressed fears that these 'modernizing' laws would pave the way for the predatory corporate commercialization of Indian agriculture, with some politically connected tycoons already expressing interest, and that small and marginal farmers would be the worst affected,

---

[65]Sudha Narayanan, 'The Three Farm Bills: Is This the Market Reform Indian Agriculture Needs?', *India Forum*, 27 November 2020.

without even access to the normal legal channels.[66] These fears eventually spilled over by November 2020 into some of the most widespread public protests seen since the anti-CAA law protests that had begun sweeping across the country nearly a year earlier. Farmers were particularly skeptical because of previous unkept promises of the Modi government. For example, Modi had promised to double their incomes in five years by offering minimum support prices (MSPs) for their produce (sold to the public food-procurement agency) that were 50 per cent above total cultivation costs; but then sought to change the measurement of costs to a lower estimate. As a result, procurement prices of crops under the Modi regime have been even lower relative to costs of production than they had been under the previous government.[67]

Farmers also suspected that the new laws would sound the death knell for the public food-procurement system, which, though imperfect, still provided them with some basic protection against the vagaries of the market. Farmers from states like Punjab and Haryana where the state procurement process is reasonably robust, were concerned that they would meet with a fate similar to their counterparts in Bihar. Similar reforms had been implemented in Bihar several years ago, ending the monopoly of regulated market yards, and farmers there receive much lower prices for their crops than their counterparts in Punjab and Haryana, well below the Minimum Support Prices announced by the government.[68] The greater power of large buyers relative to cultivators is well known, so farmers were concerned about power and bargaining imbalances once large

---

[66]P. Sainath, 'And you thought it's only about farmers?', PARI, 10 December 2020.

[67]Himanshu, 'India's Farm Crisis: Decades Old and with Deep Roots', *India Forum*, 5 April 2019.

[68]Parth M. N./PARI, 'Farm Laws: Fate of Farmers in Bihar Points To What Those Across India Might Soon Face', *The Wire*, 26 February 2021.

corporates entered agricultural marketing.

One of the new laws aimed to do away with 'middlemen' like commission agents—but farmers claimed they would rather interact with such people, and potentially develop a human relationship that allows for some flexibility and concessions when required, than deal with faceless, intractable corporations that can use various means like 'quality control' during purchase to deprive them of their due.[69] There is global experience of farmers switching to cultivating crops that are demanded by big buyers, and eventually being forced to sell at prices dictated by those buyers, with losses when 'quality' is deemed by the buyer to be below par. Farmers in Punjab, who had unpleasant experiences with potato cultivation for the multinational Pepsico, were very aware of this possibility.[70] Exposing farmers to the full blast of commercialized production without any protection from the state through regulation of agricultural markets could even lead to the destruction of the peasantry.[71] The utilization of land and cropping would in effect be dictated by demand in the world market, because of the superior purchasing power of advanced countries reproducing the colonial pattern. This could lead to a shift away from foodgrains to cash crops, leading over time to renewed import dependence for basic food, as occurred more recently in several African countries. Farmers' fears that they would be at the mercy of large corporations could be justified by both history and international experience: small farmers producing cash crops inevitably lose out with global price volatility, not gaining that much with higher prices and facing losses and losing out in years of low prices, often getting indebted to the point at which they could lose ownership of their land.

[69]Shreya Sinha, 'The Agrarian Crisis in Punjab and the Making of the Anti-Farm Law Protests', *The India Forum,* 28 November 2020.

[70]Shinzani Jain, 'Tried, tested, failed: Why Punjab farmers are against contract farming', *Newsclick,* 20 December 2020.

[71]Patnaik, 'A matter of survival of the peasantry'.

Similarly, the amendment to the Essential Commodities Act weakened provisions for imposing limits on stockholdings by various operations in the food supply chain, to the point of almost doing away with them. The new legislation allows for government regulation only in extraordinary circumstances, such as war, famine, natural calamities, or extraordinary rises in prices. It also made special concessions for exporters even beyond this: stock limits are not applicable if the stocks are less than the installed capacity of an agro-processing company or projected export demand.[72] While the effectiveness of the ECA in ensuring smooth supply and reducing price volatility of essential commodities in the past has been questionable, the new law would effectively remove this ability to any meaningful extent.

Farmers' organizations also expressed concerns about ecological constraints and soil degradation resulting from ever greater reliance on chemical agriculture, scarce and contaminated water, and climate change reflected in adverse weather events and changing rainfall patterns. Deregulation and the shift away from any state protection of farmers' interests would likely worsen these problems. Several state governments also expressed concerns, not only that these laws would inhibit their ability to ensure good conditions in agriculture—which is still a state subject in the Indian Constitution—but that they were not even consulted about this legislation and not allowed to express their views.[73]

The protesting farmers understood another problem with these laws that had wider implications for all citizens: the removal of legal recourse in the event of disputes. Section 13 of the Farmers' Produce Trade and Commerce (Promotion

---

[72]Sen and Rawal, 'The Covid-19 pandemic impact on Indian agriculture'.

[73]T. K. Rajalakshmi, 'State governments in Punjab, Chhattisgarh, and Rajasthan get their acts together and pass amended farm Bills in their State Assemblies', *Hindu Frontline,* 4 December 2020.

and Facilitation) Act, 2020 (now better known as the APMC Bypass Act) states that 'No suit, prosecution or other legal proceedings shall lie against the Central Government or the State Government, or any officer of the Central Government or the State Government or any other person in respect of anything which is in good faith done or intended to be done under this Act or of any rules or orders made thereunder.' Decisions about what is good faith and the adjudication are all to be made by the local bureaucrat. As noted by Sainath, 'It's not just farmers who cannot sue. Nobody else can, either. It applies to public interest litigation too. Nor can non-profit groups, or farm unions, or any citizen.'[74] This clearly anti-democratic stipulation gave sweeping powers to corporates entering the field who could easily influence the local bureaucracy.

The impasse continued through most of 2021: farmers were adamant that they would not stop their protest until all three laws were withdrawn; and the central government was equally determined to press on with these, with at best minor revisions. This rigidity on the part of the state could have been because, in an overall context of economic stagnation and declining consumer demand, large capital is desperately searching for new frontiers for profitability. The digital space, including telecom-driven connectivity and digital entertainment and marketing, provides one such new avenue; the opening up of agricultural markets, enabling profits to be squeezed out of both producers and consumers for essential commodities like food, could have been seen as another. The corporate pressure on the Modi government to enact laws that would give them free access and untrammelled powers in this area, was therefore immense.[75] Nevertheless, the central government was ultimately

---

[74]Sainath, 'And you thought it's only about farmers?'.

[75]Arindam Banerjee, 'New farm laws: Corporate euphoria, farmers' discontent', *Newsclick*, 2 October 2020.

forced to capitulate in the face of this prolonged peaceful mass protest by farmers that was receiving more and more public support across the country. On 19 November 2021, in a rare retreat, Prime Minister Modi announced that he would repeal the farm laws, and the Parliament followed suit in January 2022 with a formal repeal, once again without any discussion despite Opposition requests.[76] While this move may have been related to the upcoming state assembly elections in several important states (including populous Uttar Pradesh) it did not result in the dissolution of the farmers' movement, which then moved on to other demands for making cultivation more viable, including ensuring more remunerative crop prices.

Industry and Services

Expectedly, industrial production (which had been largely stagnant already over the previous year) fell sharply in April 2020 and continued to stay low in the subsequent months. When the lockdown was progressively lifted, industrial production also appeared to limp back, driven by the necessities of survival faced by businesses. The government, which had been so unwilling to provide transport to migrant workers seeking to return to their homes during the initial phases of the lockdown, proved to be far more supportive of employers who wanted to get their workers back into factories. Manufacturing and electricity tended to recover more rapidly, especially from late 2020, but even this was highly uneven, and within that most sectors continued to languish. By July 2021, only intermediate goods production was higher (by 12.4 per cent) than the pre-pandemic level of January 2020. All other categories were still lower than in January 2020, with capital goods and consumer durables showing the

[76]Roshni Kapur, 'The Problem With Modi's Repeal of India's Farm Laws', *The Diplomat*, 12 January 2022.

biggest declines, such that they were lower by nearly ten per cent compared to January 2020. Even as late as July–September 2021, manufacturing ouput was below its pre-pandemic level of January–March 2020.[77]

Figure 4.2

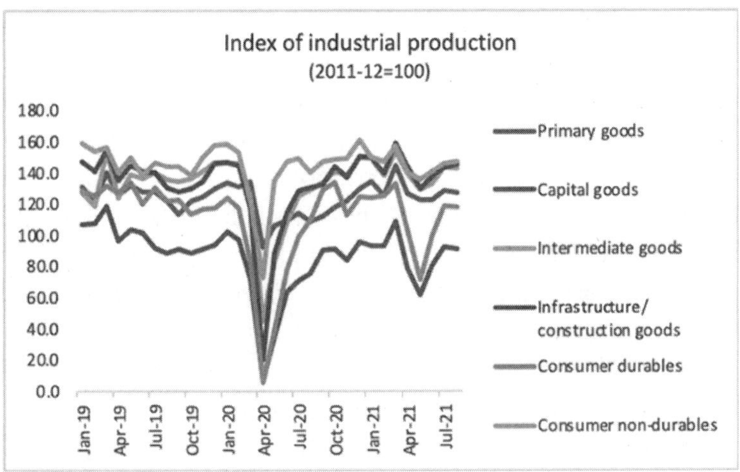

Source: Index of Industrial Production, mospi.nic.in/iip, accessed on 20 October 2021.

While the second pandemic wave could have resulted in the evident drops in production in April and May 2021, the recovery in production had already been muted before that. Falling and then stagnant domestic demand was certainly an important reason for this, but supply factors also played a role. The unplanned and disorganized disruption of supply chains brought about by the national lockdown affected large and small enterprises, including some of India's most well-known brands

[77]National Statistical Office, 'Press Note on Second Advance Estimates of National Income 2021-22 and Quarterly Estimates of Gross Domestic Product for the Third Quarter (Q3) of 2021–22', 28 February 2022.

in the formal sector. When the lockdown was announced, many businesses simply did not open, and those who did found it difficult to access inputs to transport their goods to sale points. Officially, essential goods and services were spared, but there was confusion about what was included in 'essential', and different states and local authorities made their own decisions.

Consider what happened to one of the most well-known companies in India, producing fast-moving processed food goods.[78] Parle-G biscuits are the most widely consumed biscuits in the country, accessible in small packets to the poor who eat them and relatively cheap as a quick source of energy when cooked food is not possible or hard to obtain, and also consumed by the rich in luxury hotels. At first, after the imposition of the lockdown, all the 135 factories across India that produced a billion packets of Parle-G biscuits every month were closed. After some days, the managers were able to clarify that the biscuits came under the category of essential goods and the company could start production again. But then permission was also required for all those producing and transporting the raw materials; permits were required for all the workers (100,000 directly employed and 50,000 indirectly working for the company) to enable them to come to work, for the distributors transporting the biscuit packets and the millions of retail stores and final vendors. The process of getting permits was so laborious and time-consuming that even in late June many were still awaiting their permits. In the meantime, an elaborate supply system had effectively unravelled, and it took several months—and the 'unlocking' of the economy—for it to recover. Yet Parle Biscuits was among the more fortunate companies, as demand for its products actually grew. Migrant workers seeking easy digestible food to stave off hunger during their long journeys back home, as well as others

[78]Alia Allana, 'India's Comfort Food Tells the Story of Its Pandemic', *The Atlantic*, 13 June 2020.

impoverished by the collapse of employment and livelihoods, increasingly relied on these as substitutes for more nutritious but unaffordable food. Most industrial enterprises were not so lucky: they were hit by the fearsome combination of demand collapse along with supply chain disruption and transport and logistics failures. Many—especially the smaller ones that were already operating at razor-thin margins—have simply not recovered.

In general, industrial employment was much more adversely hit than production. A parliamentary committee suggested that in the automobile industry alone—which accounts for a significant proportion of production and employment in the consumer durables sector—around 345,000 jobs were lost by November 2020, as the industry suffered losses of ₹2,300 crore per day in the wake of the lockdown.[79] Production was cut by 18–20 per cent as demand dropped. Nearly 300 auto dealers also closed down. The committee report predicted that the automobile industry would go through at least two consecutive years of severe contraction, leading to low levels of capacity utilization, lack of future capital investment, high risk of bankruptcy, and resulting job losses across the entire automotive value chain. In addition to slower increases in manufacturing and continued declines in organized sector employment, there was already much anecdotal evidence of employers seeking to go in for more mechanized techniques that would prevent the dependence on human labour that could be affected in future outbreaks. Further, construction—hitherto the biggest and most dynamic employer within industry—was very badly affected, in terms of both output and employment.

Remarkably, amidst all the general gloom and economic downswing, corporate profits increased. In the period July–September 2020, corporate profits increased by more than 300

[79]PTI, 'Lockdown impact: Automotive industry suffered ₹2,300 crore loss per day, says par panel', *Economic Times*, 15 December 2020.

per cent compared to the previous year, even as the value of sales declined more than 6 per cent.[80] Over April to October 2020, the period of the worst spread the pandemic, corporate profits increased by ₹86,348 crore even though corporate income fell by ₹5,741 crore.[81] This was essentially because, even though sales declined, costs declined even more, through a combination of falling prices of raw materials and intermediates, reduced costs of holding inventories (as firms chose to draw down on inventories rather than increase production) and falling wage and salary costs.[82] This extended beyond the firms known to have benefited from the pandemic, like telecom and e-commerce companies; it also included some manufacturing firms, even though overall demand for products was down and sales revenues fell. The profits of listed companies increased by 58 per cent[83] with the most favoured companies showing even greater gains, even as overall corporate sales declined. This points to one more way in which organized firms increased their clout vis-à-vis small producers, which were more likely to be among the suppliers of these raw materials and intermediate goods, and workers, who faced an even more adverse labour market than before.

This was also a period of intense concentration within the Indian corporate sector, in both industry and services sectors. The telecom sector was one obvious arena for such concentration, which accelerated earlier with the entry of the Reliance Jio network of Mukesh Ambani. Jio was also the foremost recipient of foreign direct investment in this period,

[80]Niti Kiran, 'India Inc's Q2 profit grows 3x to record ₹1.45 lakh cr; sales down 6.3%', *Business Today,* 17 November 2020.

[81]Rohit Azad, Subhanil Chowdhury, and Zico Dasgupta, 'A profit-led recession', *Indian Economy Lab,* 30 January 2021.

[82]Mahesh Vyas, 'Why profits rose sharply in the lockdown', *CMIE,* 3 December 2020.

[83]Krishna Kant, 'Corporate profit to GDP ratio hits 10-year high of 2.63% in FY21', *Business Standard,* 31 May 2021.

which allowed it to reduce and almost eliminate the debts it had taken on in its aggressive expansion.[84] Both FDI and FPI into Reliance and Jio contributed to vertical and horizontal concentration, enabling the group to expand from broadband provision into sectors like e-commerce and pharmaceutical distribution, while the group also had control over a significant part of the media and entertainment industry. It is worth noting that the Reliance Group, along with the Adani Group, had also expressed interest in expanding into commercial agriculture through both contract farming and agricultural marketing and was explicitly named by the protesting farmers opposing corporate power in agriculture.

In this context, some of the most important capitalists with close ties to the ruling regime benefited greatly individually, despite overall economic decline. The wealth of a relatively small number of super-rich individuals skyrocketed by an estimated 35 per cent during the pandemic;[85] the number of Indian dollar billionaires increased from 102 to 140 in 2020, with just three people adding a further $100 billion to their individual wealth.[86] Several international studies pointed to India as showing one of the highest increases in inequality during the pandemic.[87]

Labour Codes and Other Policies Affecting Workers

The central government used the disruptions created by the pandemic to push through various legislative and regulatory

[84]'From Facebook to Google: Full list of investors who helped Reliance Jio raise ₹1,52,055.45 crore', *Free Press Journal,* 15 July 2020.

[85]IANS, 'Indian billionaires saw their wealth go up by ₹12.97 trn during Covid-19', *Business Standard,* 25 January 2021.

[86]Tenzin Zompa, 'Despite Covid, India adds 38 billionaires in 2021, Ambani & Adani retain top 2 spots', *The Print,* 8 April 2021.

[87]See the World Inequality Report 2022 and the Oxfam Briefing Paper, 'Inequality Kills', January 2022.

measures that would otherwise have faced much more public scrutiny and pushback. In addition to the farm laws, new Labour Codes were introduced and rushed through Parliament in record time in September 2020, without any discussion. In the case of the Labour Codes, the haste and lack of discussion were all the more surprising because these actually *replaced* bills that had already been placed before Parliament by the same Modi government in 2019 to simplify the system of existing labour laws, about which the Parliamentary Standing Committee on Labour had submitted reports to be discussed by Parliament.[88]

The codes are broad and open-ended, giving huge power to the executive that will frame the rules. The silences in the Codes are deafening, particularly with respect to labour standards like working hours, occupational safety, working conditions, and even for social security. The new laws allow the government to exempt any establishment from the laws 'in the public interest'. The Code on Industrial Relations, 2020, gives greater freedom from regulatory control to factory owners and limits the role of trade unions, giving even greater bargaining power to employers. The Code on Social Security effectively makes the provision of social security dependent upon the goodwill of employers and does not even insist on common minimum mandatory entitlements across states, so that workers can have portability of their benefits. The Code on Occupational Safety, Health, and Working Conditions, 2020, increases the scope for employers to hire contract labour. Clearly, the thrust of these new labour laws is to disempower workers in various ways. The underlying principle seems to be that this is necessary for attracting more private investment, since the current laws are complex and hard to enforce. This move of the central government followed upon similar moves of several state governments—notably the BJP-

[88]Atul Sood, 'The silent takeover of labour rights', *India Forum*, 20 November 2020.

ruled states of Uttar Pradesh, Madhya Pradesh, Gujarat, and Assam, all of which are seen as 'labour surplus' and send migrant workers to other states.

Together, these legislative changes would further undermine workers' rights, in a context of greatly weakened bargaining power of labour. Consider what just some of these changes would mean for workers. It has been noted by Sood[89] that the laws contain no requirements for employers to provide any of these: ventilation in worksites, toilets for workers, periodic breaks in the working day, ability of workers to sit, weekly holidays, provision for food during working hours that can now go up to 72 hours per week. No need for employers to follow basic safety norms in factories, or ensure minimal working conditions, or to compensate workers for industrial accidents. Because trade union activity and the right to organize are also constrained by these laws, workers would be restricted in mobilizing to improve such conditions. The new laws have been contested by trade unions. Several national strikes and other protests from November 2020 onwards[90] added to the protests by farmers to create a more general sense of growing popular tensions and concerns with the government's economic policies.

These extreme measures have little economic justification; they reflect the political power of employers' lobbies in a context in which the central government is desperate to kickstart economic activity through further deregulation in favour of private capital. The argument that weakening labour protection attracts more private investment is deeply flawed, with much recent research revealing the logical fallacies and the poor empirical basis of such arguments.[91] Some argue that labour

---

[89]Ibid.

[90]See for example, 'India: Over 250 million workers joined protesting farmers in one of the biggest nationwide strikes ever', Business & Human Rights Resource Centre, 26 November 2020.

[91]See Servaas Storm, 'The Bogus Paper That Gutted Workers' Rights', Institute

laws are anyway poorly implemented, so it's all right to abolish them. But enforcement has been poor because of lack of political will and tolerance of corruption of inspectors. Abolishing labour protection on grounds of poor enforcement is akin to saying that if traffic rules are not followed, we can simply dump them altogether and allow road chaos and accidents to occur freely.

High labour costs are not the factor that is holding back private investment in India, which already has one of the cheapest and most exploited labour forces in the world, and among the lowest wages in South Asia.[92] State governments like Rajasthan, Andhra Pradesh, Haryana, and UP that went in for such labour 'reforms' did not succeed in attracting big investments, or boost industrialization or job creation.[93] Such an outcome should have been obvious. After all, for four decades India has had lower wages and less worker protection than China,[94] yet India did not attract even a small fraction of the FDI flowing into China, despite liberalizing rules and providing various other concessions. Even now, as companies seek to move out of China, they move to countries like Vietnam and Thailand, both of which have higher wages and more effective and comprehensive worker protection

---

for New Economic Thinking, 6 February 2019; and Aditya Bhattacharjea, 'Labour market flexibility in Indian manufacturing: A critical survey of the literature', *International Labour Review*, Vol. 160, Issue 2, June 2021, pp. 197–217.

[92]ILO, *Global Wage Report 2020-21,* available at www.ilo.org/wcmsp5/groups/public/---dgreports/---dcomm/---publ/documents/publication/wcms_762534.pdf.

[93]Sanjay Upadhyay and Pankaj Kumar, 'Amendments in Labour Laws and Other Labour Reform Initiatives Undertaken by State Governments of Rajasthan, Andhra Pradesh, Haryana and U.P. An Analytical Impact Assessment', *NLI Research Studies Series No. 122/2017*, Noida: V. V. Giri National Labour Institute, 2017.

[94]Baijayanta Mukhopadhyay, Chunbao Liu, and Jody Heymann, *The Work, Family, and Equity Index. Setting the Global Floor: a comparative study of labour standards in India and China*, Institute for Health and Social Policy, Montreal, Canada: McGill University, 2009.

than India. Companies invest looking at decent infrastructure, efficient logistics, a vibrant domestic market, transparent official procedures; and they prefer a healthy, educated workforce that can deliver higher productivity and therefore lower unit wage costs. Also, suppressing wage incomes and damaging workers' protection reduces their ability to demand goods and services, which reduces the size of the domestic market, and the possible capacity to operate at efficient scales of production.

The External Sector

One explanation for the complete absence of fiscal response from the Indian government in the face of one of the biggest economic crises ever faced, is that the central government was concerned about its external vulnerability. A large increase in public spending could generate higher imports, thereby worsening the trade deficit at a time when volatile capital flows have already made the balance of payments vulnerable. Indeed, this was explicitly cited by some officials as well as some economic commentators.[95]

Was this fear justified? India's external sector has been weak and vulnerable for some time now, and a dramatic exodus of foreign capital from all emerging markets including India in April 2020 was yet another indication of the fickle behaviour of international capital markets. But trade in merchandise showed a different tendency—the trade deficit shrank significantly over the period of the pandemic, as indicated in Figure 5.4. In the financial year April 2020 to March 2021, the deficit was only $102 bn, compared to $157 bn in the previous financial year. This reflected a collapse in imports, which fell much more sharply

[95]For example, see Ila Patnaik and Rajeswari Sengupta, 'Impact of Covid-19 on the Indian Economy: An Analysis of Fiscal Scenarios', Working Paper 20/319, New Delhi: National Institute of Public Finance and Policy, 2020.

than exports during the first wave. Within total imports, oil imports recorded the most significant declines. Some of this was obviously related to the curbs on travel, transport, and production during the lockdown, and the domestic slump in economic activity following upon that lockdown. But it was also related to the collapse of global oil prices: crude oil prices fell to less than $10 per barrel in April 2020, and even in December 2020 oil prices were nearly 40 per cent lower than a year earlier.[96] The increase in the total import bill from early 2021 similarly reflects the increase in global oil prices, which went up quite sharply from January 2021. The recovery of non-oil imports was partly due to the increase in production after the 'unlocking'; however, rising imports also replaced domestic production, especially from micro and small enterprises that were destroyed by the lockdown.

Figure 4.3

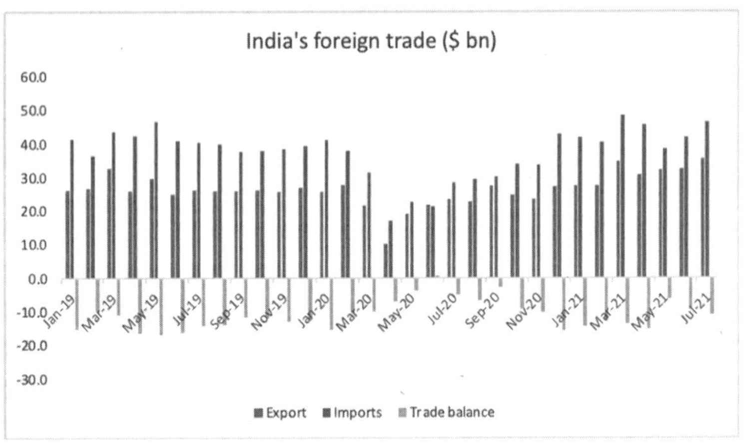

Source: RBI, dbie.rbi.org.in/DBIE/dbie.rbi?site=publications, accessed on 24 Oct 2021.

[96]Primary Commodity Price System, IMF Data, available at https://data.imf.org/?sk=471DDDF8-D8A7-499A-81BA-5B332C01F8B9&sId=1547558078595.

The decline in the trade deficit helped the current account to move from deficit to minor surplus in the January–March 2020 quarter. Over the financial year April 2020 to March 2021, India recorded a current account surplus of 0.9 per cent of GDP, compared to a deficit of 0.9 per cent of GDP in the previous year.[97] This was also because remittances from overseas migrant workers and exports of software services remained high enough to balance other outflows of profits and dividends and outward remittances of resident Indians.

As in other emerging markets, cross-border capital flows were very volatile over this period. There was massive outflow of foreign portfolio capital in March and April 2020, and subsequently a minor recovery as the massive infusions of liquidity in the advanced economies created yet another surge of footloose capital looking to benefit from easy access to cheap finance by investing in developing countries with higher interest rates. This peaked in August 2020, but the inherently unstable character of such flows was evident in September, when there was once again a net outflow.

There was also a large surge in foreign direct investment in August 2020. The main recipient was Jio Platforms, the telecom subsidiary of Reliance Industries, in which Google alone invested \$4.5 billion,[98] while an earlier \$5.7 billion deal Jio had made with Facebook probably also fructified around this time. Jio also received other investments, including from private equity. Reliance also sold around 10 per cent stake in its retail sales unit to foreign investors for around \$6.7 billion.[99] These foreign investment inflows were part of a broader tendency towards

---

[97]RBI, 'Developments in India's Balance of Payments during the Fourth Quarter (January-March) of 2020-21', available at www.rbi.org.in/Scripts/BS_PressReleaseDisplay.aspx?prid=51820.

[98]'16% surge in FDI inflows till August', *The Hindu,* 20 October 2020.

[99]PTI, 'Reliance Retail completes ₹47,265 crore fundraise from 10.09 per cent stake sale', *Times of India,* 19 November 2020.

vertical and horizontal concentration in the Indian corporate sector, in which organized industry and services are increasingly coming under the control of a few key oligopolistic players with strong links to the ruling governments at centre and state levels.

Another constraint to enhanced public spending is often presented in terms of the public debt and fears of it increasing to unsustainable levels. In developing countries, that is most often expressed in the concerns about external public debt. But in India, such fears are completely misplaced. In March 2020, India's external debt amounted to $55.8 billion, of which $48 billion was government borrowing (46 per cent of which was taken on concessional terms with lower rates of interest). A year later, in March 2021, it had increased marginally to $57.9 billion—still only 21 per cent of GDP, well below any levels that could be seen as a cause of concern.[100] So the external constraint should not have led to the evident reticence in central government spending. (Total public debt to GDP is currently higher, at nearly 90 per cent of GDP, but since that is dominantly denominated in rupee terms and owed to Indian residents, repayment is not an issue for a government that still has the power, through the central bank, of issuing its own currency.)

So, while the external sector was not in good shape and did not provide much source of optimism, it did not really constrain expenditure by the central government. This was evident in the growth of foreign exchange reserves, which increased by nearly 40 per cent during the period of the pandemic, from $461 billion in January 2020 to $637 billion in October 2021.[101] Taking the imports for 2020–21, this amounted to nearly two years' worth of imports of all goods and services, far in excess of what is usually

---

[100]RBI, 'Handbook of Statistics on the Indian Economy', 15 September 2021.

[101]RBI, 'RBI Data on Indian Economy', *Banking-Performance Indicators*, 5 March 2019, available at https://dbie.rbi.org.in/BOE/OpenDocument/1608101729/OpenDocument/opendoc/openDocument.faces?logonSuccessful=true&shareId=2.

seen as the maximal prudent requirement (typically six months' worth of imports). This suggests that the government could easily have spent a significant amount more within the economy to enable recovery of employment and provide some income compensation to the people, without running into balance of payments difficulties. It did not do so, apparently because of fears that larger fiscal deficits could lead to downgrading by global credit rating agencies and therefore capital flight.

The Intensification of Inequality

All of these economic forces led to significant increases in wealth and income inequality in a country that had already become significantly more unequal since 2000, as shown by Lucas Chancel and Thomas Piketty.[102] The share of the top 1 per cent in total national incomes increased from around 6 per cent in 1980 to 15 per cent in 2000 to more than 20 per cent in 2015. In 2012, the top 10 per cent of the population owned at least 63 per cent of total wealth; within that group, the richest 1 per cent captured 30 per cent of total wealth in the country.[103] Since then and until 2019, there was even more income and wealth concentration, actively aided by various government policies. But even in that very unequal context, the sharp increases in inequality during the pandemic were startling.

Over the course of the pandemic, inequality worsened across the world—but in India the trend was especially stark. The economy collapsed, millions lost jobs, hundreds of millions saw their incomes decline sharply, and at least half the population faced significantly reduced access to food. Yet the very rich did

---

[102]Lucas Chancel and Thomas Piketty, 'From British Raj to Billionaire Raj? Indian income inequality 1922-2015', *Review of Income and Wealth*, (forthcoming) published as a World Inequality Lab working paper in July 2017.

[103]Nitin Bharti, 'Wealth Inequality, Caste and Class in India 1961–2012', WID. world working paper 2018/14, 2018.

rather well over these months: the Forbes list of the 100 richest individuals showed that half of them showed wealth gains in 2020.[104] The wealth of Indian billionaires increased by 35 per cent during the lockdown, while the net wealth of just the top 100 richest people increased by 14 per cent,[105] largely through stock market gains that defied gravity and seemed to diverge completely from the harsh and worsening reality of the real economy. There was even polarization among the very rich, as those with stakes in digital, pharma, and media businesses got much richer. More than half of the total wealth gains of the top 100 richest individuals came from one man alone: Mukesh Ambani, whose wealth increased by 73 per cent to reach $88.7 billion.[106] Between the start of the lockdown and the end of September, it was estimated that his wealth increased on average by an additional ₹90 crore *every hour*. The next richest man, Gautam Adani, saw his wealth increase by 61 per cent to $25.2 billion. The period of lockdown and pandemic proved to be especially remunerative: according to the Billionaires Insights Report, the combined net worth of India's dollar billionaires rose by more than a third between April and July 2020.[107] Just the *increase* in wealth of the top 11 billionaires over this period—an estimated ₹13 lakh crore—would be enough to pay for the central government's health budget for a decade.

The conditions of the vast majority of the Indian population, by contrast, deteriorated dramatically—as much of this book has already illustrated, and as will be evident in the following

[104]'Forbes India Rich List 2021: Mukesh Ambani wealthiest for 14th consecutive year', *Indian Express*, 7 October 2021.

[105]Oxfam, 'Inequality Kills, India Supplement 2022', available at https://www.oxfam.org/en/research/inequality-kills.

[106]'Forbes List Of India's 100 Richest Shows Gains In Wealth Despite Pandemic', *Forbes*, 7 October 2020.

[107]Mahima Kapoor, 'Indian billionaires' wealth rose by a third in just four months', *BloombergQuint*, 14 October 2020.

chapter. Inequalities increased across almost all dimensions. Take what happened in the formal sector. Even as total income of corporate India fell by ₹52,000, corporate profits increased by more than ₹86,000 crore—essentially because companies reduced raw material costs by squeezing their smaller suppliers, and cut wage and salary bills.[108] So corporations facing falling sales did rather well on the whole, because they reduced payments to their workers and to the small and often informal enterprises who supplied them with inputs. MSMEs, by contrast, mostly faced truly dreadful circumstances and many had to close, shedding labour in the process. In the labour market, there were sharp differences between those employed with formal contracts and informal workers who had no social or legal protections over this period. Within formal workers, there was a divide between those who could keep their jobs and continue to be paid the same, and those who lost their jobs or faced lower wages. Even among those who kept their jobs, differences in conditions and risk depended on whether workers could safely work from home or were forced to attend their work places and expose themselves to health risks after lockdown restrictions were lifted. Therefore, the gap between protected regular workers (essentially white collar and professional workers) who could benefit from digital technologies and all other workers increased hugely.

While incomes at the top grew through this crisis, there was significantly more distress at the lower end of the spectrum. Surveys by CMIE estimate that the average Indian household lost about ₹25,000 over the first six months of the pandemic, compared to the same period of the previous year, and in October 2020 average household incomes were 12 per cent lower than they were a year earlier.[109] But the greatest losses

---

[108]Rohit Azad and Shouvik Chakravarty, 'A tale of two Indias', *The India Forum*, 22 January 2022.

[109]Mahesh Vyas, 'Avoid a fresh lockdown', Centre for Monitoring Indian Economy, 29 March 2021.

were borne by the poorest: in rural areas, the poorest 10 per cent of households lost 54 per cent of their incomes, while the top 10 per cent lost only 16 per cent. In urban areas, the bottom decile lost 39 per cent of their previous incomes, while the top decile lost 21 per cent.[110]

Inequality increased across other dimensions as well. In terms of housing, there was from the start a clear distinction between those for whom sheltering in place to avoid infection was possible and even comfortable, and those whose living conditions were crowded, congested, unhealthy, and uncomfortable, for whom physical distancing was neither possible nor particularly effective. The homeless, who were not considered at all in official policy during this period, were possibly the worst affected. There were major differences in how men and boys were affected, in work and living conditions, compared to women and girls and transgender people. There were also growing inequalities of access: to food, to education, to health care, which are discussed in the next chapter. The growing reliance on digital means of accessing many services exacerbated the digital divide. And government policy combined with political goals of the ruling party at the centre to create growing divisions even according to religion and caste, despite the supposed 'universality' of the virus spread.

All this points to a situation of serious mismanagement of the Indian economy over this period, which created a serious economic contraction well beyond what was warranted by the pandemic per se and generated many other unfortunate economic and social consequences. Some of this was driven by unwarranted fiscal reticence and unwillingness of the central government to spend more even in the face of severe economic crisis. In addition to the immediate adverse effects, this had

---

[110]Rahul Lahoti, Mrinalini Jha, and Amit Basole, 'What 2020 did to India's inequality', *Mint*, 19 January 2021.

serious implications for the future potential for investment, economic activity, and employment. And the associated decline of livelihoods impacted several other aspects of life, as discussed in the next chapter.

chapter 5

THE IMPACT ON WORKERS, LIVELIHOODS, AND LIVES

What Happened to Employment?

Of all the economic indicators that were already weak even before the pandemic, employment was probably the weakest—and then it suffered the most during the pandemic. During the lockdown, the impact was especially brutal because enforced closure left the majority of Indian workers without any income from wages or self-employment, and the absence of social protection meant no compensatory incomes either. Even after the lockdown was progressively lifted, demand for workers recovered only partially, and then was hit once again by the second wave of the pandemic.

The official Periodic Labour Force Surveys provide some information on patterns of employment in the immediate aftermath of the lockdown. We can compare this with the data derived from the large private surveys conducted by the CMIE, to get some idea of what happened to recognized employment in the first phase of the pandemic.[1] The differences between the two estimates across men and women in urban and rural India are quite significant, and probably related to sampling methodology techniques and the nature of the questions posed in the two surveys.[2] Nevertheless, the short-term tendencies

---

[1]Vikas Rawal and Jesim Pais, 'An Assessment of the Recent PLFS Data and Provisional Analysis of the Impact of the COVID-19 Lockdown on Employment and Poverty in India', *SSER Working Paper*, New Delhi, 2021.

[2]See Jesim Pais and Vikas Rawal's assessment of the CMIE-CPHS survey and

for total employment are similar in both. It is worth noting that aggregate employment was already declining in January–March 2020 compared to the previous quarter, *before* the impact of the lockdown and pandemic was really felt. The period of lockdown inevitably resulted in a further and significant decline in employment, such that it fell by around 20 per cent in April–June 2020 relative to October–December 2019, amounting to around 88 million workers who were rendered completely jobless or without any livelihood. (Both surveys include casual, part-time, and sporadic work, including in the form of self-employment, in total employment—so any kind of paid work is captured.) The CMIE surveys also cover later periods, and suggest that employment recovered partially from September 2020 onwards, but collapsed again at the peak of the second wave of the pandemic from March to June 2021. The recovery in employment in September 2021 was mostly a rural phenomenon, reflecting demand for labour for agricultural operations.[3]

The dramatic decline in employment mostly affected informal workers who typically had no other means of support. The recovery of employment that occurred as lockdown measures were eased was largely because the paucity of relief measures meant that most people were forced to seek some employment, however meagre the payment, simply to survive. This continued until employment peaked at 398 million in September; thereafter it declined, to 388 million in December as the 'recovery' ran out of steam, and seasonal jobs were shed in agriculture.[4]

---

database. 'CMIE's Consumer Pyramids Household Surveys: An Assessment', *India Forum*, 3 September 2021.

[3]See Mahesh Vyas, 'Employment increases in rural India', CMIE, 4 October 2021.

[4]Mahesh Vyas, 'Labour markets disappoint in Dec', *Business Standard,* 5 January 2020.

Figure 5.1: Estimates of total quarterly employment in rural and urban areas, by sex (million persons)

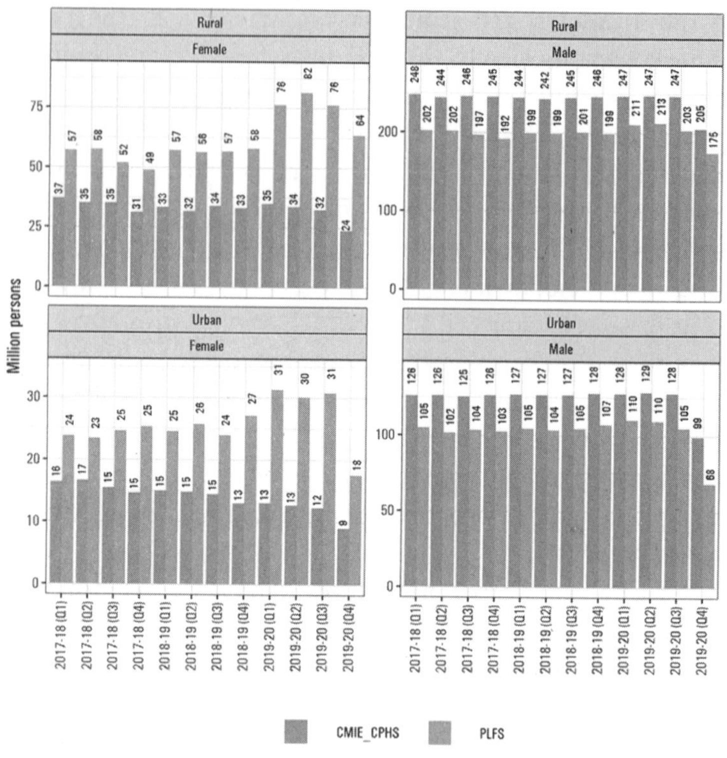

Source: Rawal and Pais, 'An Assessment of the Recent PLFS Data and Provisional Analysis of the Impact of the COVID-19 Lockdown on Employment and Poverty in India', p. 8, figure 2.

Women's employment was particularly badly affected. Women's recognized employment fell more sharply (in proportionate terms) than that of men.[5] Furthermore, it did not recover

[5]Ashwini Despande, 'The COVID-19 Pandemic and Gendered Division of Paid and Unpaid Work: evidence from India', IZA Discussion Papers, No. 13815, Institute of Labor Economics (IZA), Bonn, October 2020.

thereafter, even when more men found jobs once again. Data from the CMIE surveys (which admittedly do not capture women's employment fully, though this should not affect the time trend) suggest that the recognized work participation rate of women did not recover even after the lockdown was lifted, but continued to decline to probably the lowest rates in the world, as low as 9 per cent.[6]

Other surveys also found dramatic job losses during and in the immediate aftermath of the lockdown. A survey of MSMEs found that around 25–30 million jobs were lost in these enterprises alone during May–June 2020, with another 10–15 million job cuts in August.[7] Quite often, these layoffs were sudden, without prior notice and without any termination benefits being given to workers. For example, 1,300 women garment workers in a town in Karnataka were informed on a Saturday evening in June that they would be laid off with immediate effect, and paid only half their monthly wages—because the owners decided that the decline in export orders made it viable to run only one of their factories.[8] That this violated all the existing labour laws did not seem to be a problem for the employers. Many job losses persisted through the year and then worsened once again during the second pandemic wave. A survey of nearly 2,000 households in the capital city of Delhi found that 65 per cent of them had no source of employment at all during April–May 2021, one year after the lockdown of the first phase. The proportion of those without income was even worse for casual workers.[9]

---

[6]Mahesh Vyas, 'Female workforce shrinks in economic shocks', CMIE, 14 December 2020.

[7]Indivjal Dhasmana, '25-30 million lost jobs in MSMEs during March-June, says survey', *Business Standard,* 28 July 2020.

[8]Prajwal Bhat, '1300 garment workers in Karnataka lose their jobs overnight', *News Minute*, 7 June 2020.

[9]'Results of the Survey on the Impact of COVID-19 Second Wave in Delhi-NCR Region', Communist Party of India (Marxist), New Delhi, 2021.

Labour force participation rates (which show employed workers and would-be workers as a proportion of the total population) fell, either because the lockdown prevented many from seeking employment, or because would-be workers were simply discouraged from trying to find work and so just stopped trying. The number of 'discouraged workers' (who might have taken up paid work if it was available and provided more than a pittance for wages, but counted themselves out of the labour force because they had stopped looking for work) was estimated to have nearly doubled to 22.6 million people by November 2020.[10]

These declines in employment obviously showed significant deterioration of an already weak labour market, so the bargaining power of workers declined further and forced workers to accept wages even lower than those they had been receiving before the pandemic. Even after the lockdown was lifted, demand remained low, so after an initial spurt of recovery, both employment and wages fell again. Rural wage data from the Labour Bureau, which had indicated real wage declines between October 2019 and March 2020, indicated some revival for non-agricultural wages in September and October, but declines thereafter for all types of rural labour. By December 2020, rural real wages were lower than they had been even two years earlier.[11] Total wage incomes declined even more than wages, because paid work was typically available for fewer days per month than before. Even formal sector workers were affected: a survey of employees in formal employment found that 40 per cent of them faced reductions in their pay, sometimes substantial.[12]

---

[10]Mahesh Vyas, 'Why unusually high number of people aren't actively looking for jobs', *Times of India*, 9 December 2020.

[11]Vineet Sachdeva and Abhishek Jha, 'Is there deferred stress in rural labour markets?', *Hindustan Times*, 7 January 2021.

[12]PTI, '40% India employees witnessed reduction in pay due to COVID pandemic: Survey', *Mint*, 30 June 2021.

The employment crisis was particularly acute for women workers and young people. Many studies found that workers from disadvantaged communities (like Scheduled Castes and Muslims) were also more likely to lose employment, as the intersecting inequalities in the labour market got aggravated during this period. Some of this could have been the unfortunate fallout of the attempts to impart a communal flavour to the disease, described in Chapter 2. Consider the plight of a domestic worker in Latur, Maharashtra who lost her job of thirty years as 'the whispers telling people to stay away from Muslims travelled like fire.... My son-in-law said I lost the jobs because of the Jamaat. But how am I related to it?'[13] In addition, because the pandemic reinforced existing caste/class prejudices in Indian society, already disadvantaged groups suffered disproportionately.

High rates of open unemployment among youth well before the pandemic showed how India was not just wasting its 'demographic dividend' but even turning it into a demographic disaster, as more and more young people (more of whom now had some tertiary education) entered the labour market, only to find that there were no jobs to be had. The halting and inadequate nature of the employment generation during the pandemic and apparent economic 'recovery' meant that there could be a 'lost generation' of young people facing a frightening future without paid employment. A study of vacancies in an online job portal relating to largely formal sector jobs found a dramatic decline in job opportunities, which especially affected young, female, and less educated job seekers.[14] The proportion of entry level jobs (requiring less than one year's experience) declined and the minimum experience required for a job increased by two-fifths,

---

[13]Ira Deolgaonkar, 'How do I earn, what do I eat?', PARI, 15 April 2021.

[14]Gaurav Chiplunkar, Erin M. Kelley, and Gregory Lane, 'Which jobs were "lost" during India's Covid-19 lockdown? Evidence from online vacancy postings', *Ideas for India*, 8 September 2020.

obviously affecting the employability of first-time job seekers. Even those who had jobs and could keep them or were somehow able to find employment in this disastrous period suffered. A survey of nearly 10,000 young working people across 203 urban centres in October and November 2020 found that more than three quarters of them had experienced financial stress, one third had to borrow money to meet expenses and around half had to dip into their savings.[15]

Perhaps the cruellest was the destruction of dreams and aspirations of the youth striving to somehow achieve a middle-class existence. These aspirations, which were among the factors propelling Narendra Modi to his first national electoral victory, had already been battered by the falls in total employment and worsening labour market conditions for educated youth during the Modi government's first tenure. But the pandemic's impact was even more direct and brutal. One study of joblessness among younger workers in the low-income states of Bihar, Jharkhand, and Uttar Pradesh found that in January–March 2021, nearly a year after the first lockdown, 40 per cent of the sample had no work or pay, 8 per cent who had lost their jobs continued to be out of work, while another 8 per cent were working zero hours. The younger and poorer workers were the worst affected even among this group: nearly half of those aged eighteen to twenty-five years who already had lower than median wages before the pandemic had no work or pay.[16]

Take the case of the young man from rural Uttar Pradesh who used his diploma in plastics technology to get a job in a plant in Maharashtra making plastic boxes for branded confectionary items. He hoped to start his own business recycling plastic to

---

[15]YouGov-Mint-CPR Millennial Survey, reported in 'A post-pandemic crisis of income uncertainty', *Mint*, 28 December 2020.

[16]Swati Dhingra and Fjolla Kondirolli, 'City of dreams no more, a year on: worklessness and active labour market policies in urban India', Centre for Economic Performance, July 2021.

make products for daily use. But the lockdown meant that the factory closed and he was out of work and without pay. This had allowed him to send back more than half his monthly salary of ₹13,000 to his home village, supporting his younger brother's education to become a lawyer. The factory reopened in early May, but without taking the required safety and health precautions, so he did not feel it safe to return to work. He kept searching for alternate employment but could not find any. When his money ran out in June, he was forced to join the estimated 131,000 migrant workers who returned to his district of Gonda in that month, no longer able to contribute to meeting his family's expenses and putting his brother's future education under threat.[17]

As described in Chapter 2, around 95 per cent of workers in India are informal, without legal or social protection. They were more or less left to their own devices, forced to rely on savings and then borrowing to tide over this period. A livelihood survey conducted by researchers at Azim Premji University[18] of nearly 5,000 self-employed, casual, and regular wage workers across twelve states of India, conducted between 13 April and 23 May found that there was a massive increase in unemployment and an equally dramatic fall in earnings. Two-thirds of those surveyed had lost work. The few who were still employed during the lockdown experienced wage declines of more than half. In general, urban residents and migrants were more impacted, but some who were already vulnerable were disproportionately badly affected: Muslims, Dalits, women, and those with lower levels of education. Because there were hardly any forms of social safety net in operation, and the government's response was so meagre, workers faced the consequences directly. The survey found that

[17]Saurabh Sharma and Devjyot Ghoshal, 'Back to the paddy fields: Covid smashes Indian middle class dreams', *Reuters*, 17 August 2020.
[18]'Covid-19 Livelihoods Survey: Compilation of Findings', Centre for Sustainable Employment, Hyderabad: Azim Premji University, 2020.

nearly eight out of ten workers and their families were eating less than before, nearly two-thirds did not have enough money to cover a week's worth of essential purchases, and more than one-third had already taken loans to cover their basic expenses. Furthermore, very few of them had received any benefit from the meagre official relief packages, including those entitled to 5 kilogram per month of free foodgrain ration and the tiny ₹500 cash transfer to women holders of Jan Dhan accounts.[19]

A substantial proportion of workers—more than half in agriculture and slightly less than half in non-agriculture—are self-employed. Indeed, most enterprises in the broad category of MSMEs in India are what are described as 'own account enterprises', essentially self-employment. This tends to be forgotten in much of the public policy discussion, as 'the private sector' is typically conflated with the private corporate sector, when the greater bulk of private activity in terms of employment actually occurs within tiny and micro enterprises. In some ways, these workers tend to be among the most vulnerable, other than the minority of highly qualified professional workers like doctors, lawyers, accountants, etc. Farming is obviously a high risk and difficult occupation, and its difficulties were described in Chapter 4. But even in industry and services, the bulk of the self-employed tend to operate at the very margin of survival, in informal economic activities. They bear all the risks of production and because they lack both access and bargaining power in input, output, and credit markets, they tend to be exploited and marginalized in all of them, resulting in lower margins and much greater fragility of livelihoods.

Many self-employed workers faced multiple whammies: their markets collapsed, the supply chains that enabled them

[19]'Only a third of the respondents received the Jan Dhan cash transfer. Half of the respondents reported not receiving any cash transfer'. Azim Premji University, 'Covid-19 Livelihoods Survey: Compilation of Findings'.

to access inputs broke down, they could not get credit to keep afloat, and then they were forced to repay interest on loans once the moratorium on repayment ended by September 2020. This situation was particularly harsh for borrowers from microfinance institutions (MFIs), who were dominantly women. MFIs typically target those without collateral: small and marginal farmers, very petty traders, landless labourers in rural areas and those without assets in urban areas, who would find it difficult if not impossible to get loans from banks. Most MFIs proved to be extremely aggressive in demanding repayment, even during the period of declared moratorium on repayment, which they typically claimed did not apply to them. Even those with an excellent earlier history of timely repayment were not spared when they found themselves without any income during the pandemic. Stories abounded of MFIs demanding payment and threatening to take away whatever little assets the households possessed, even when there were no possibilities of earning either wage or self-employed incomes.[20] Perhaps these pressures contributed to the apparent loan recovery of MFIs across India as a whole, from next to nil in April and May to up to 60–80 per cent by July.[21] But one year later, the stress in microfinance persisted, as income earning opportunities remained low for women who had taken such loans, and by July 2021, defaults on microfinance loans were surging once again.[22]

Workers in traditional and handicraft industries—many of whom were already struggling because of declining demand and increased competition from imports (such as from China) were

---

[20] Parth M. N., 'MFI loans: Fear and loathing in lockdown times', PARI, 4 May 2020.

[21] Sayantan Bera, 'Stories of distress from small borrowers', *Mint*, 17 August 2020.

[22] 'India's Microfinance Sector Hit As Defaults Surge In COVID-19', *NDTV.com*, 14 July 2021.

affected by both the lockdown and the subsequent restrictions that reduced large celebrations and kept festival and marriage spending low. This affected small producers who would have typically provided goods and services for festivals and events, from traditional weavers to performers at marriage venues. This extended well beyond the lockdown period, as the major festivals of Ganesh Chaturthi, Durga Puja/Dussehra, and Diwali in the period August to November witnessed collapsing demand for many of the artefacts typically sold during the celebrations, affecting potters across the country.[23] Some of these traditional, highly skilled crafts could simply die out as those who are essential to making them survive by passing on their skills faced not just income losses but even starvation in the absence of official support. Since this is a sector dominated by self-employed artisans or daily wage workers with no social protection, the material damage was immense.[24]

In rural areas, non-crop incomes of both men and women workers were affected. The fall in demand for milk across the country as restaurants, tea shops, and catering activities closed affected both volumes and prices of the milk sold by dairy cooperatives. Many small producers who operated through cooperatives of Self Help Groups for marketing their products were similarly devastated by the collapse in demand and the breakdown of earlier marketing channels, many of which have simply not revived. Adivasi women of Sambalpur district of Odisha, who used to get two-thirds of their household income by selling minor forest produce like mahua flowers, siali leaf plates, and various forest seeds through marketing cooperatives, found that both prices and volumes of their sales contracted by around four times, making survival a real concern.[25] Fisher

[23]Srishti Verma, 'A melting pot of lockdown losses', PARI, 17 August 2020.

[24]'Impact of the Pandemic on Indian Artisans & Handicrafts and the Revival Strategies', *IndianRetailer.com*, 12 August 2021.

[25]Archana Soreng and Ranjita Pattanaik, 'Adivasi women's collectives in Odisha

people were prevented from going out to sea, and fish processing and marketing (in which more women workers are involved) could not occur.

The Trauma of 'Migrant Workers' and the Forced Reverse Migration

Migrant workers were possibly the worst affected. No one can say for sure how many 'migrants' there are in India: that is, those who have travelled to live and work within the country in some place other than their home. The 2011 census of India estimated around 51 million migrants who moved for economic reasons, of whom 3.5 million had moved in the previous one year, and of whom over 80 per cent were men. But these referred to 'permanent migrants', whereas it is generally accepted that 'circular migration' dominates in India. There are many kinds of migrants even in urban areas: those who came from elsewhere (rural or other urban areas) for a permanent shift; those who stay mostly in urban areas but go back once or twice a year, for a month or more, to their village or home town; those who are seasonal migrants, coming for work during lean employment seasons to their place of origin; sporadic migrants, especially those working for contractors who organize specific periods of work. There are also many rural–rural migrants, often even less recognized; indeed, sowing and harvesting activities across many parts of India would be impossible without migrant workers, while brick kilns across the country and small industries especially in peri-urban areas rely heavily on migrant workers. These 'hunters and gatherers of work' (as Jan Breman has described them[26]) had in some circumstances

hit hard by Covid-19 and Amphan', *Behanbox.com*, 22 June 2020.

[26]Jan Breman, *Wage Hunters and Gatherers: Search for Work in the Urban and Rural Economy of South Gujarat*, OUP, 1994.

even become scavengers of work in the already depressed pre-pandemic Indian labour markets of early 2020: scrounging for any small wages, taking on several different activities even in the course of one day, to somehow eke out a living.

There are many reasons to believe that the number of migrant workers estimated in 2011 was a significant underestimate. Various estimates suggested that the number of migrants exceeded 100 million even then.[27] Thereafter, in the absence of any new survey data, the Government of India's Economic Survey even used net annual flows of unreserved passenger travel as a proxy for work-related migrant flow. This showed that in the five years after 2011–12, net flows averaged 9 million per year,[28] which suggests that by 2020, the number of economic migrants in different parts of India would be around 180 million, even excluding short-term and seasonal migrants. The economic contributions of these migrant workers are immense, incalculable—and hidden: they build India's cities and towns; serve in the factories, mostly as labour to draw upon whenever required, without any formal contracts; make up the crucial labour required in sowing and harvesting seasons for most crops; provide all sorts of essential and non-essential services as self-employed people or workers in small enterprises. Like the unpaid women who subsidize the economy by providing essential care and domestic services for free within their households, their contribution generally tends to be little recognized and mostly taken for granted.

Of all the informal workers whose lives and livelihood were upended by the lockdown, these migrant workers and their families emerged as among the most vulnerable. Like the rest

[27]P. Deshingkar and S. Akter, 'Migration and Human Development in India, Human Development Research Paper 2009/13', New York: United Nations Development Programme, 2009.

[28]Economic Survey 2016-17, Volume I, Chapter 12, Government of India, Ministry of Finance, Government of India, New Delhi.

of the population, they were given no advance warning of the lockdown that would so dramatically affect economic activity. Overnight, the self-employed lost the opportunity to earn their own living; casual workers lost the tenuous employment that provided them some wages by the day, week, or fortnight; piece-rate and home-based workers either did not get any more orders or could not fulfil or deliver their work for payment. Women among such migrant workers were inevitably the most vulnerable, not only those who were working themselves, but those who had moved with their families for the duration of the employment.

At first, the absence of any clear idea of how long the lockdown would last meant that many workers were prepared to survive the three weeks initially announced by running down their savings and borrowing, largely from informal sources. But the situation became increasingly difficult by the end of the first week, because so many migrants are paid by fortnight or week, and many did not receive dues even for the time they had worked; while those on daily wages and the self-employed did not receive any incomes. Many found it difficult to meet rental and other payments; soon, even affording necessities became a problem. A survey of distressed workers at the end of the first phase (three weeks of lockdown) by the Stranded Workers Action Network[29] covered around 10,000 migrant workers in several states including destination states like Maharashtra, Delhi, Karnataka, and origin states like Uttar Pradesh, Bihar Jharkhand, and West Bengal. It found that half the workers had enough food rations left for only one more day, while 72 per cent only had enough for two more days. This was despite eating frugally over the period: a group of 240 workers in Bengaluru

[29]'21 Days and Counting: COVID-19 Lockdown, Migrant Workers, and the Inadequacy of Welfare Measures in India', Stranded Workers Action Network, 15 April 2020.

had been having only one meal a day to conserve their meagre supplies of food. Of those surveyed, 89 per cent had not been paid at all by their employers during the lockdown, including for work already performed and 78 per cent had only ₹500 left with them, creating conditions whereby babies had to be fed with sugar water instead of milk. State assistance was almost non-existent: the survey found that 96 per cent of the migrants had received no food rations from the government and 70 per cent had not received any cooked food either.[30] A second survey a month later between 14 and 26 April, found that food distress remained high and public intervention was still very inadequate: 80 per cent still had no access to government food rations and 68 per cent had not received any cooked food. There was marginal improvement in food support in Karnataka, but no improvement in Maharashtra, Delhi, and Haryana—other states with large numbers of stranded workers. Cash in hand was even more limited—nearly two-thirds of the workers had less than ₹100 left with them, and more than 97 per cent had not received any cash relief from the government. Volunteers of the network continued to receive 'SOS calls' from people on the verge of starvation who had not eaten anything for more than a day or more.

The dramatically worsening material conditions, insecurity, and desperation led to the greatest forced migration witnessed in India since the Partition of 1947. These movements of people were made more dangerous and dehumanizing by the approach of the central government and many state governments to pandemic control; not as a public health concern, but a law-and-order problem, enforced like military curfews.[31] At the start

[30]This survey covered only workers who reached out to volunteers offering food and other assistance, and therefore was not a random survey. Nevertheless, it captures the extent of the distress.

[31]By 28 May 2020, the media group India Today had documented details of 238 migrant workers who died while trying to reach their homes. Analysis

of the lockdown, many workers wished to go home but were prevented by the sudden and complete stoppage of all public transport facilities and the closure of interstate borders. Those who nevertheless attempted to make the long arduous journeys by foot in the first few weeks were intimidated and abused on the roads, some faced lathis or were sprayed with dangerous 'disinfectant' chemicals.[32] Many were locked up at state and district borders (supposedly to reduce possibilities of infection), in detention camps of varying degrees of discomfort, by overzealous police and officials.[33] The fear and paranoia created among the citizenry because of the containment measures also led to stigma and abuse of the migrants, even without any evidence that they could be carriers of the disease. Despite this, as the weeks progressed and it became near impossible to ensure even physical survival, more and more migrants sought all possible means to return to their homes.

The period from mid-April 2020 onwards saw this initial trickle become a flood of tragic proportions. The stories and terrible graphic evidence multiplied: people trudging for hundreds of kilometres, often without food; some dying of exhaustion and hunger before they reached their homes, including the twelve-year-old girl from Jharkhand who collapsed and died just a short distance from her home after walking 360 kilometres in three days; others killed by accidents on the road,

---

of this data shows that the reasons for migrant workers' deaths during their homeward journeys included: getting burnt to death in forest fires, being hit or crushed by truck/bus/trains, exhaustion, heart attack, among others. This database was prepared by collating media reports. Mukesh Rawat, 'Migrant workers' deaths: Govt says it has no data. But didn't people die? Here is a list', *India Today*, 16 September 2020.

[32]'Coronavirus: Anger as migrants sprayed with disinfectant in India', *BBC.com*, 31 March 2020.

[33]Swapnil Rawal, Pankaj Jaiswal, and Avinash Kumar, 'Coronavirus lockdown: Millions in migrant camps battle despair about uncertain future', *Hindustan Times*, 9 April 2020.

such as the fourteen men who were run over by a freight train as they slept on a railway line in the mistaken belief that no trains were running; families carrying small children in their arms and a few possessions on their heads as they walked through immense heat over journeys that could take days if not weeks; a heavily pregnant young woman on a 1,000 kilometre journey who gave birth on the roadside and then walked another 160 kilometres to reach her village; people reduced to travelling in a cement mixer.

None of these tragedies were necessary, and all could have very easily been avoided. The Indian Railways has the capacity to move 23 million passengers every day, and the decision to shut it down completely other than for freight movement was a bizarre one since it was done when there were relatively few cases of infection. If the railways had been pressed into service before or even during the first week of the lockdown, while barring all other non-essential travel, to allow migrants to go back to their homes, this could have enabled all or most of those who wished to get back to their homes to do so within a few days. Yet it took more than a month—after the number of Covid-19 positive cases had already increased exponentially and therefore chances for infection were much greater—for the government to announce a few Shramik Sewa trains to transport some migrants back to their home states. These trains were woefully inadequate in number, and to add insult to injury, they also required workers who had received no incomes for more than a month and were already close to destitution, to pay the full fare, with a small additional surcharge.[34] In response to criticism on this, the central government made the claim that it was covering 85 per cent of the cost—a spurious claim based on the fact that tickets typically cover around half the cost of all railway journeys even in

[34]Gopi Maniar Ghanghar, 'Covid-19 lockdown: Migrants in Gujarat pay ₹700 for train ticket as BJP claims opposition charging labour', *India Today*, 4 May 2020.

normal times, and because of Covid-19, fewer passengers could be taken in each coach.[35] The fact remains that people had to pay prices that were sometimes even higher than normal full fares to undertake this travel, when the journeys should really have been provided for free for all returning migrant workers. Notably, several reports emerged that physical distancing norms were poorly followed at the time of ticket distribution, during the boarding of trains, during travel as well as at arrival—making the official insistence on subsequent quarantine of the travellers slightly farcical. Indeed, the conditions on these trains were so poor—and they were so congested and uncaring of the health of the travellers—that they became known as 'virus trains'. Several instances of Covid-19 infections being contracted on these trains were reported, with tragic outcomes for already desperate migrants and their families.[36] In just two weeks between 9 and 27 May, eighty deaths on board were reported on such trains for stranded migrant workers.[37]

Even the lockdown rules, ostensibly neutral, were harsher for the migrant workers forced to travel on foot. Until 31 May, there was a national curfew between 7 p.m. and 7 a.m. This could not possibly have a public health purpose, since the virus does not have a daily timetable for transmission that makes it more deadly at night. This forced those who were trudging desperately to their homes to walk only during the days, often in scorching

[35]Since these special trains for migrant workers were supposed to carry not more than 1,200 passengers, even with passengers paying full fare, the 'subsidy' to the Railways amounted to 85 per cent. But this did not mean that the centre covered 85 per cent of the ticket price, as the passengers were still charged the ticket price for 'normal' trains. See 'Fact Check: No, the Centre Isn't Paying for Migrant Workers' Train Journeys Home', *The Wire*, 6 May 2020.

[36]Jeffrey Gettleman, Suhasini Raj, Sameer Yasir, and Karan Deep Singh, 'The virus trains: How lockdown chaos spread Covid-19 across India', *New York Times*, 15 December 2020.

[37]Anisha Dutta, 'Railway Protection Force reports 80 deaths on Shramik trains', *Hindustan Times*, 30 May 2020.

temperatures in excess of 40 degrees.

In addition to these unnecessarily cruel outcomes, public apathy and even aggression towards migrant workers who did not fit into recognized official categories was stark. Take the case of the couple with three young children who had to travel from Delhi to Lamgarha in Rajasthan carrying all their belongings—but had no 'home' to go to because they belonged to 'nomadic tribes' and the lockdown simply had not planned for such people, all 100 million of them. When they arrived, they were 'quarantined', which meant locking them into an empty school building some distance from the town, with no food or milk for the children, no medicines for the sick, not even a matchstick to light a fire. They could not go out and buy anything since they were locked in. Like millions of Indians, this couple did not have any of the currently 'official' proofs of identity like Aadhaar cards, voter IDs, bank accounts. This was not treated as a failure of the system, but their own fault: they were not provided shelter but had to live under a tree, under the vigilance of a local official who would not even let them gather firewood or see a doctor because there was nothing in the 'instructions' about dealing with people like this.[38]

The class bias of the central government became even more evident when, even as trains for migrant workers remained well below the need, more trains were allowed that could only be afforded by the middle classes, like the fast air-conditioned trains that had more expensive seats.[39] The central government placed the responsibility of providing buses for migrants upon the resource-constrained state governments—without providing them any additional funds for this purpose. Once again, such

[38]'Citizens and the Sovereign Stories from the largest human exodus in contemporary Indian history', A Migrant Workers Solidarity Network publication, November 2020.

[39]Shine Jacob, 'Covid-19 lockdown: Passenger trains to be back on tracks from Tuesday', *Business Standard*, 11 May 2020.

buses were completely insufficient to meet the demand, and many could not even afford the tickets, so for many workers walking became the only option to get home. In late May, a migrant worker sheltering under a Ghazipur flyover en route to Pratapgarh, 400 kilometres from Delhi (where he had worked as an AC repairman), explained why he and others had chosen this arduous and demanding route. 'You think walking was our first choice? We know all about the government facilities, but they are using a mug to water a sugarcane field. The process to register for tickets is complicated, the fares are unaffordable, and the number of trains is too few.'[40]

Yet when they finally reached their homes, many migrants had to face cold welcomes, because of the panic created by official and media descriptions of these workers as carriers of disease. Aggressively implemented 'institutional quarantines' in poor conditions often enhanced the anxieties of already exhausted and enervated migrants, leading to extreme reactions: in Sitamarhi in UP, for example, there was a report of a person being lynched to death after he informed local authorities about possibly Covid-positive returning migrants in his neighbourhood.[41] Certainly, one major result of these massive movements of people was the further spread of infection to towns and villages where health infrastructure is even less developed than in India's big cities. On 18 May, the government of Bihar (a state with pre-existing very poor health indicators) randomly tested 8,337 samples of returning migrant workers and found around 8 per cent of them to be Covid-19 positive, while 26 per cent of the migrants from Delhi tested positive.[42] Obviously, they would spread the disease

---

[40]Quoted in Yashee, 'Why migrants are walking home: We know of government schemes, they won't help', *Indian Express*, 20 May 2020.

[41]Calcutta Research Group, *Borders of an Epidemic: Covid-19 and Migrant Workers*, Kolkata: Mahanirban Calcutta Research Group, 2020.

[42]'As Bihar Finds 26% of Returning Delhi Migrants Infected, Doubts Cast on NCR's COVID Count', *The Wire*, 20 May 2020.

in their home locations, where testing facilities were generally non-existent and treatment possibilities negligible. As a result, this forced migration resulting from the brutal lockdown had the adverse public health impact of spreading the disease, just the opposite of what was intended.

The economic outcomes of this massive reverse migration are hard to fathom immediately, but they could be profound and long-lasting. Rural distress and lack of income opportunities, and the needs of survival and hope for creating a better life by earning and saving by working elsewhere, drove millions of people to towns and cities, and to other rural areas for seasonal agricultural activities. But the shock dealt out by the central government dealt multiple blows to these goals. Migrant workers and their families were prevented from working and earning their living; in many cases they were not just denied wages during the lockdown but did not even receive their dues for work already done; they were mostly denied any official relief or compensation for this government decision to lock down, with only a tiny proportion receiving any food assistance and even fewer receiving any cash; many of them were thrown out of their homes because of inability to pay rent, which landlords demanded despite gentle exhortations from the Home Ministry; they were effectively reduced to being paupers having to beg for the means of survival, thereby undermining their dignity; and then, in the unkindest cut of all, they were prevented from even returning home. In extreme cases, as in Karnataka, the state government even cancelled some trains after requests from the local construction industry that wanted to keep its workers, before being forced to backtrack because of public outcry.

The urge to return home was not confined to rural–urban migrants: even in rural destination areas, there was evidence of the desire to return home. For example, by 16 May, 180,000 workers had left Punjab on trains, while more than one million more were in the queue, having registered to leave.[43] This would clearly affect sowing operations in the forthcoming kharif season, making it likely that farmers would search for mechanised alternatives. And this option, if it became widespread, could sharply alter labour demand in Indian agriculture in coming years.

But this terrible phase and its aftermath could also alter patterns of labour supply across the country in the medium term. The enormity of the betrayal experienced by working people may not be easily forgotten, and could affect future decisions to migrate or to return, whatever be the conditions in the place of origin. There were more than a hundred reported protests, involving hundreds of thousands of migrant workers in different parts of the country, between the start of the lockdown and the middle of May.[44] Many reports suggested that a significant proportion of returning migrants and their families no longer felt the allure of big cities. It was not only the state that let down the workers so comprehensively; it was also, in far too many cases, their employers and their neighbours. Workers could be justified in feeling betrayed and being treated as little more than bonded labour. The consequent absence of feelings of social solidarity and the fracturing of the trust that must typically underlie any successful development process can have economic effects that play out in complex ways over longer time periods. Reduced inclination to resume exploitative and insecure employment in urban areas could mean that one assured source of workers for urbanization and industrialization may no longer be so easily available. Indeed, a survey in Madhya Pradesh found that more than half of the migrants who had returned home did not wish to go back to work in the cities.[45]

---

[43]SNS, '1.80 lakh migrants leave Punjab, over 10 lakh more in queue', *The Statesman*, 16 May 2020.

[44]'Documenting Migrant Workers' Resistance across India', Migrant Workers Resistance Map, available at www.mwsn.in/resistancemap/.

[45]Rahul Noronha, 'Study on migrant labourers who returned shows half of

Women as Paid and Unpaid Workers

Women—and especially young women—were the worst casualties of the employment crisis generated by pandemic and lockdown. Work participation rates of women collapsed to unimaginably low levels from what were already some of the lowest rates in the world.[46] Women were disproportionately more likely to lose employment during the lockdown, in both urban and rural areas. Worse, unlike for men, women's employment did not recover at all when the lockdown was lifted, but continued to decline. Women self-employed workers were badly affected by the collapse of markets for their products and services, and also by the insistence of most microfinance institutions on repayment throughout this period. In general, studies found that women, Dalits, and Muslim workers were the worst affected in labour markets.[47]

This was reflected in many ground reports. A study of more than 5,000 informal workers across the country conducted by the Azim Premji University found that 71 per cent of women casual workers in rural areas lost their jobs, compared to 59 per cent of men. A survey of informal women workers in the National Capital Region of Delhi two months into the lockdown found that 83 per cent of the surveyed women workers faced severe income drops.[48] This was especially marked among construction workers, all of whom lost their jobs and got no pay, while only 6 per cent got any relief from the welfare boards specifically

---

them do not want to go back', *India Today*, 8 June 2020.

[46]Deshpande, 'The COVID-19 Pandemic and Gendered Division of Paid and Unpaid Work: Evidence from India'.

[47]See, for example, Surbhi Kesar, Rosa Abraham, Rahul Lahoti, et al., 'Pandemic, informality, and vulnerability: Impact of COVID-19 on livelihoods in India', CSE, Hyderabad: Azim Premji University, June 2020.

[48]Shiney Chakraborty, 'Increased Care Work, Reduced Wages: Informal Women Workers Are Barely Getting By', *The Wire*, 25 May 2020.

set up for construction workers. It was also found that 97 per cent of street vendors faced complete loss of income, and since many of them had taken loans from informal moneylenders to procure their wares, repayment had become a major concern. Women waste pickers lost income because they faced greater difficulties not only in collecting waste, but segregating and selling it, and they were forced to sell at significantly reduced prices because only a few dealers were still operating during the lockdown. Home-based workers, who typically did piece-rate work under contract for suppliers, reported that their payments for work already were being withheld, while new orders were not coming in because of disruptions in supply chains. Domestic workers mostly did not get paid during the lockdown period, as restrictions prevented them from getting into employers' homes. Those who did manage to keep their jobs had to confront falling wages: more than four out of five women informal workers interviewed experienced lower money wages.

Meanwhile, as is typical in gender-blind public policy in India, the lack of recognition of women farmers meant that they were particularly disadvantaged during the lockdown. A survey by SEWA Bharat[49] found that, since very few women farmers have independent means of transport, they were unable to procure the required passes for transporting goods. This meant that they were unable to sell their produce in the larger markets. Therefore, they were forced to sell at much lower prices than they otherwise would have, and also lower than men farmers who could get their produce to the more remunerative markets. Many women who were small landholders even shifted to subsistence farming, because of reduced market access.

As noted in Chapter 2, most of women's work in India is unpaid, and gender norms dictate massive disparities in unpaid

[49]SEWA Bharat, 'Gendered precarity in the lockdown', All India Federation of Self Employed Women's Association, May 2020.

work time by gender. The pandemic led to increases in the unpaid work done by women, even during the lockdown when men were also largely confined to their homes and therefore some more domestic work burden could have been shared. Existing divisions of care work responsibilities did not seem to change. Most studies suggested increasing unpaid work burdens for women at home, particularly for child care and elderly care.[50] A significant proportion also highlighted greater difficulties in provisioning food due to the lockdown, more time spent standing in queues to access food rations, and concerns about meeting physical distancing norms while collecting food or water. Most surveyed women did not get any help from male household members in doing all this.

The decline in access to food described below affected women and girls even more than men and boys within households. But there were several other ways in which both the existing patterns of gender discrimination and the gender insensitivity of public policy and administration combined to worsen the conditions women faced. The greater difficulties of accessing proper care during pregnancy and childbirth were described in Chapter 3. Across the world, domestic violence was on the increase during lockdowns, even leading the United Nations to describe it as 'the shadow pandemic'. In the first three weeks of the lockdown alone, calls for help to the National Commission for Women from desperate women facing spousal violence more than doubled from earlier rates. Loss of livelihood, anger, and frustration at being confined to homes, as well as alcohol abuse, all contributed to the violence. One study using data on reported violence found that increases in domestic violence and cybercrime were most concentrated in districts that saw the

[50]See Chakraborty, 'Increased Care Work, Reduced Wages'; SEWA Bharat, 'Gendered precarity in the lockdown', All India Federation of Self Employed Women's Association, May 2020.

strictest lockdown measures.[51] In the same period, however, rape and sexual assault complaints outside the home fell, largely because of decreased mobility in public spaces, public transport, and workplaces. Beyond income and job losses, poorer women also suffered in health terms because of the disruption in regular health services and Anganwadi centres. One study estimated that the closure of family planning services could result in nearly 3 million unintended pregnancies, nearly 2 million abortions (more than half of them unsafe), and several thousand more maternal deaths.[52]

As of 30 November 2020, reported cases of domestic violence rose by almost 60 per cent over the previous twelve months. But these reported cases represented only a minuscule proportion of the actual extent of violence. It is not common in India for women to report violence committed by spouses or family members: the National Family Health Survey (NFHS-4) revealed that more than three-quarters of the women who had experienced physical or sexual violence had never reported it to anyone. Most women typically do not dare to call authorities or even NGOs or any 'outsiders' for multiple reasons; but they were even less likely to do so when they were effectively trapped inside their homes with their oppressors. Even working women like frontline care workers faced such violence, often not only from their spouses but from in-laws who feared they could pick up the virus during their work and transmit it to the rest of the household.

In any case, pleas for help did not necessarily result in protection. Typically, the women had to remain at home with

---

[51]Saravana Ravindran and Manisha Shah, 'Unintended Consequences of Lockdowns: COVID-19 and the Shadow Pandemic', *NBER Working Paper* 27562, Cambridge, MA: National Bureau of Economic Research, July 2020, Revised March 2021.

[52]Study by Foundation for Reproductive Health Services of India, quoted in Sadhika Tewari, 'Lack of contraceptives during lockdown could lead to unsafe abortions, maternal deaths', *IndiaSpend*, 12 May 2020.

an even more enraged spouse, with only 'counselling' from patriarchal policemen. The statement of a Superintendent of Police in Mahoba, Uttar Pradesh typifies the attitude: 'We usually do not arrest the accused in domestic violence cases on the first or even second complaint. Initially we counsel them. In fact, we do counselling of both accused and victim once, twice or even thrice. Only when we find that the situation is not getting better, do we file the FIR.'[53] This was the general pattern, which was obviously not conducive to more reporting of violence; but things got even worse during the lockdown, when emergency calls were less likely to be responded to.[54]

The lockdown, the destruction of livelihoods, and the increase in economic insecurity had particularly adverse implications for older girls and young women as many were forced into early marriages. There were reports from across the country of a spike in child marriages.[55] Sometimes, this was sought to be controlled by the local administration: for example, in one district of Maharashtra alone, 208 child marriages were stopped by district authorities in just the four months between April and July 2020.[56]

The Increase in Hunger

The collapse in employment and wage incomes during and after the lockdown, combined with the completely inadequate relief measures, had direct and dire effects on the extent of hunger in the country. This exacerbated one of the more obvious failures of

---

[53]Quoted in Jigyasa Mishra, 'Lockdown has hit UP women hard, literally', PARI, 23 June 2020.

[54]Lyla Bavadam, 'At home but not safe', *Frontline*, 22 May 2020.

[55]Sophie Cousins, '2.5 million more child marriages due to Covid-19 pandemic', *The Lancet*, 7 October 2020.

[56]Sushmita Pathak and Lauren Frayer, 'Child Marriages Are Up In The Pandemic. Here's How India Tries to Stop Them', *NPR*, 7 October 2020.

India's much-storied economic boom, the continued presence of widespread hunger and undernutrition. One study[57] showed that even in 2011, at the peak of the boom, nutritious diets were so expensive relative to unskilled wages (at 80–90 per cent of female wages and 50–60 per cent of male wages) of casual labourers, that between 63–76 per cent of the rural poor could not afford the recommended minimum diet. Thereafter, despite the National Food Security Act that was designed to ensure that everyone in the country got enough essential foodgrain for survival, there was significant exclusion from the public distribution system (PDS) of food. Khera and Somanchi[58] found that *despite the expansion of the PDS and some state government providing 'top-ups' beyond central support, over 400 million people were excluded.* Of these, at least 100 million could be considered income-poor, unable to buy the required food out of their own incomes.[59]

At least half the population—and probably more—were already food-insecure before the lockdown was announced. Thereafter, the massive decline in incomes from wages and self-employment during the lockdown and in subsequent months meant that many millions more were unable to afford even their earlier inadequate levels of food consumption. The result was a truly horrifying increase in the number of people facing absolute hunger, and in cutbacks in diets among the bulk of the population, with people eating fewer meals per day, children being denied milk or eggs, families going without pulses (the basic source of protein) or vegetables. Even in India's capital city, there were accounts of children who had to sleep without food for seven nights in a row, as the parents were without livelihood

---

[57]Kalyani Raghunathan, Derek Heady, and Anna Henforth, 'Affordability of nutritious diets in rural India', *Food Policy*, Volume 99, February 2021.

[58]Reetika Khera and Anmol Somanchi, 'A review of the coverage of PDS', *Ideas for India,* 19 August 2020.

[59]'More than 100mn excluded from PDS as govt uses outdated Census 2011 data', *IndiaSpend*, 16 April 2020.

and had to borrow to be able to eat even one meal during the day; of asthma patients (common in highly polluted Delhi) who previously earned wages, just lying by the road begging for food because they had no savings left and could not travel to the nearest community kitchen and wait for hours standing in the queue; of single mothers with hungry children who were given water mixed with some sugar as a substitute when they cried for milk.[60]

Food deprivation very quickly brings on desperation and the loss of dignity, which came quite suddenly to hundreds of millions of workers who had earlier managed to eke out a living, however simple and basic, and provide for their families. When they were prevented from doing this by the draconian lockdown, it was expected that the government would at least ensure minimum food access for all the people. In the first stimulus package announced on 26 March 2020, the 'PM Garib Kalyan Anna Yojana' (PMGKAY), it was claimed that 800 million individuals (around two-thirds of India's population) would be provided double of their entitlement of 5 kilograms of wheat or rice per month over next the three months, with the additional amount free of cost. This was subsequently extended several times, to March 2022. This number of 800 million was based on the National Food Security Act eligibility criteria, even though at least 100 million eligible people had been excluded from the NFSA list because it relied on outdated 2011 data.

In the event, much less was actually distributed. The government was not able to double the amount of subsidized grain that was distributed to the states: data from the Food Corporation of India show that while the government distributed about 4.3 million tonnes of grain every month under NFSA, the distribution of grain through PMGKAY was significantly lower

[60]Astha Savyasachi, 'I had to give them sugar water when they cried for milk', *The Citizen*, 18 June 2020.

from April through September 2020.[61] This was not only because the government did not take any serious steps to expand the coverage of public distribution of food; it also reflected serious weaknesses in the functioning of the distribution system and the central government's failure to use the existing system effectively despite the dramatically increased need. A subsequent scheme for enabling migrant workers to access some free food under the public distribution was largely unsuccessful: while the government promised to cover 80 million workers, lack of any design in the scheme, poor specification of beneficiaries, along with tardy and lacklustre efforts at implementation meant that by July 2020 only 13 per cent of the allocated free foodgrain was handed out to returning migrant workers, with eleven states not even covering one per cent of such workers.[62]

The government's attitude to food procurement and distribution in this crisis displayed remarkable cynicism and lack of concern about the massive increase in hunger, especially because it had sufficient surplus foodgrain stocks to provide many times more than the amount it actually distributed. In recent years, public food stocks increased continuously to be more than three times the buffer stock norm. By 1 May 2020, before the procurement season for rabi 2020 started, the government had 87 million tonnes of grain (including wheat, rice, and unmilled paddy), which was 67 million tonnes in excess of the stocking norms. By July, the amount held *increased* to 81 million tonnes as the rabi (winter) procurement was added. Then even more foodgrain was procured in the kharif (autumn) season while distribution was not increased in tandem, so that by December 2020, more than 85 million tonnes of foodgrain was being held in the public storage facilities.[63] This larger stockholding meant

[61]Sen and Rawal, 'The Covid-19 pandemic impact on Indian agriculture'.

[62]Harikishan Sharma, 'Only 13% of allocated free food grain handed out to returning migrant workers, reveals govt data', *Indian Express,* 2 July 2020.

[63]'Food grains Stock in Central Pool for the years 2016-2021 (Opening

more costs for the FCI (around ₹6 per kilogram) and it would have been the most obvious solution to reduce the massive excess stocks of grain and distribute the surplus grain free to state governments. This would have countered the tremendous increase in hunger among people brought about by the pandemic and lockdown to ensure that everyone had access to at least basic food—but this opportunity was inexplicably missed.

Many observers had called for additional free 10 kilograms per person per month to be distributed over the year, as the pandemic showed no signs of abating and the livelihood crisis intensified, but that call was not heeded. The government could also have allowed some part of the wages under the MNREGA to be paid in the form of foodgrain—a demand made by many workers in the programme, especially women. Instead, the central government allowed the FCI to engage in some sales through the Open Market Sales Scheme, which state governments could also access if they wanted to add to the meagre amount being distributed. And since the amount of food stocks continued to increase even as stories of starvation grew, there were real—and subsequently justified—concerns that at least some of it was being stored in ways that could cause it to rot, get eaten by rodents, or otherwise become unfit for human consumption.[64]

Because of this central hoarding of foodgrain, subsidized foodgrains remained out of reach for the millions of households that became vulnerable to food insecurity due to loss of livelihoods following the lockdown.[65] Some state governments, such as Delhi, Rajasthan, and Odisha tried to cover some of the yawning gap and address the problem of growing hunger by

Balance)', Food Corporation of India.

[64]Vikas Rawal, Manish Kumar, Ankur Verma, and Jesim Pais, 'India let 65 lakh tonnes of grain go to waste in four months, even as the poor went hungry', *Scroll.in*, 3 June 2020.

[65]Priscilla Jebaraj, '30% of ration card holders yet to get PMGKAY benefit for May', *The Hindu*, 4 June 2021.

issuing new temporary ration cards, and meeting the additional requirement through their own open-market purchases of grain from the FCI.[66] But they were also constrained by lack of fiscal resources, as described in Chapter 4, and therefore the public distribution was simply inadequate to meet the need.

In consequence, tragic stories of the fallout of growing hunger proliferated. Even several months after the lockdown had ended, a survey by the Right to Food Campaign covering 3,500 households across eleven states in October and November 2020[67] found that while things had improved slightly after the really desperate month of April and May, they were still much worse than before the lockdown. One third of respondents reported having to skip meals often or at least sometimes. People had reduced both the quantity and quality of their diets. While there was lower consumption of staples like rice and wheat, there was significantly reduced consumption of pulses (the main source of protein) for two-thirds of those surveyed, and three-quarters were consuming fewer green vegetables. A later survey conducted between December 2021 and January 2022[68] found that very little had improved in terms of pervasive undernutrition. Nearly two years after the pandemic first broke, eight in ten of the surveyed households reported some form of food insecurity during the pandemic and a quarter reported severe food insecurity. More than two-fifths reported a deterioration in the nutritional quality of their diet compared to pre-pandemic consumption.

What this meant for malnourishment of ordinary people whose lives and livelihoods were shattered by the brutal

---

[66]Reetika Khera and Anmol Somanchi, 'A review of the coverage of PDS', *Ideas for India*, 19 August 2020.

[67]Dipa Sinha and Rajendran Narayanan, 'Hunger, nutrition worse than before lockdown', *Indian Express*, 26 November 2020.

[68]Right to Food and Centre for Equity Studies survey, quoted in '8 out of 10 Indian households faced food insecurity last year despite free ration relief: Survey', *Gaon Connection*, 24 February 2022.

lockdown is evident from the stories of people living in Domari, a village 'adopted' in 2018 by no less than Prime Minister Narendra Modi, under the 'model village' scheme for members of Parliament.[69] It is situated just across the river from Benaras, within his parliamentary constituency of Varanasi. The wife and three young children of a boatman were malnourished as they could buy only one-third of the milk they purchased earlier, and often had to do without any, relying on 'meals' composed of just sago and water. But they were still better off than the fifty-five-year-old single man who had to trudge 6 kilometres every day to beg at the Ashwamedha Ghat in Benaras to get something to fill his stomach; or the domestic worker, a single mother with six children, who was reduced to any odd jobs or alms she could gather because her employers in Benaras simply stopped paying her. The village is supposedly under a universal public distribution system, but not one of these very vulnerable people was covered. And while it is striking that they were supposed beneficiaries of the prime minister's interest in their village, their stories were hardly exceptional; millions of people across India experienced similar hunger.

The consequences of hunger for the young are of special concern, because lack of nutrition at an early age has terrible and lasting consequences on health and physical and mental development through the rest of life. The school closures associated with lockdown, and the fact that most schools remained closed thereafter until early 2022, had very severe implications for child nutrition because it meant that the Mid-Day Meal programme was effectively suspended. This affected around 80 per cent of primary school students, or around 144 million children. The closure of Anganwadis under the Integrated Child Development Scheme (ICDS) was another

[69]Supriya Sharma, 'In Varanasi village adopted by Prime Minister Modi, people went hungry during the lockdown', *Scroll.in,* 8 June 2020.

calamity. This caters to pregnant and lactating mothers as well as infant children, providing supplementary nutrition in the form of take-home rations and cooked meals, but somehow this was not deemed to be an 'essential service' by those in power. This suspension had very severe and potentially lasting consequences. Remember that this closure came in the wake of a stagnant trend in child nutrition revealed by the latest National Family Health Survey, which suggested that India was one of the worst performing countries in the world. It is estimated that around 100 million pregnant and lactating mothers relied on this,[70] mostly those already in conditions of precarious food security. There were heart rending stories of infant children weakened by lack of nutrition dying because the Anganwadi centres where mothers could previously access food were closed, and no alternative arrangements were made by the government.[71] This was even true in urban areas, like the shop assistant in Delhi who had lost his job, whose infant son died because the mother got no nutrition support, even as the parents worried about the life of their young daughter as they were simply unable to feed her (or themselves) adequately.[72]

The increase in hunger was also captured by the Global Hunger Index, which found a worsening of India's number and rank among countries to one of the lowest in the world (101 out of 116 countries), and lower than most other countries in South Asia.[73] The government's attempts to dismiss this internationally

---

[70]Muzna Alvi and Manavi Gupta, 'Learning in times of lockdown: how Covid-19 is affecting education and food security in India', *Food Security*, Vol. 12, No. 4, 2020, pp. 793–96.

[71]Sadhika Tiwari and Shrinkhala Pandey, 'Malnutrition Could Cost Children's Health & Lives for Years After COVID Crisis, Experts Warn', *IndiaSpend*, 6 June 2020.

[72]Radhika Bordia, 'Hunger Threatens India. Malls Open, But Anganwadis Stay Shut', *Article 14*, 9 September 2020.

[73]'India', Global Index Hunger, available at www.globalhungerindex.org/india.html.

respected report on the grounds that it was based on a telephonic survey were unjustified: the index uses data on the extent of undernourishment from the Food and Agriculture Organization, and data on stunting, wasting, and under-five mortality from the government's own official surveys. Indeed, the first results of the National Family Health Survey for 2019–20 indicated that stunting and wasting indicators have stagnated or declined for most states for which the data were available.[74] While foodgrain distribution was inadequate, rising prices of other food items like edible oils and pulses made healthy diets less affordable, especially in a context of declining money incomes. And the central government actually reduced its budgetary allocation for 2021–22 for schemes like the Integrated Child Development Services (ICDS) and Mid-Day Meals in schools, which would be central to reducing hunger especially among vulnerable populations.

The Role of the Rural Employment Programme

In the context of overall decline in employment opportunities, the Mahatma Gandhi National Rural Employment Guarantee Act (MNREGA—earlier declared by Prime Minister Modi as an emblem of failure of the previous government[75]) was perhaps the only saving grace. It became an important form of support for the rural poor, providing perhaps the only cushion enabling consumption beyond the limited provision of foodgrain, and acting as an automatic macroeconomic stabilizer in the period of downswing.

The MNREGA was one of the more historic pieces of legislation in independent India, based on two interlinked

[74]Dipa Sinha, 'A reminder that India still trails in the hunger fight', *The Hindu*, 27 October 2021.

[75]ANI, 'MNREGA epitome of Congress' failure: PM Modi', *Business Standard*, 27 June 2015.

concepts.[76] First, ensuring livelihood security to rural residents by providing at least 100 days of guaranteed wage employment in a financial year to every household whose adult members volunteer to do unskilled manual work. Secondly, utilizing the programme for the mobilization of existing surplus labour in the countryside so as to unleash productive forces and generate more economic growth in the rural areas. Because wage and work norms are legally defined in the programme, it has the potential to bring other rural wages at least close to the legal minimum, to reduce extremely exploitative working conditions, and provide work on more equal terms to women and other marginalized groups like SC/STs who are routinely discriminated against in rural labour markets. Women workers have been participating heavily in the programme even in states with low women's work participation overall—even though the work is physically arduous and essential legal requirements like worksite crèches are frequently not made available—simply because it offers wages that are mostly on par with male workers.

The MNREGA therefore is much more than 'social protection' through some livelihood stability and poverty reduction. Because it can be an automatic stabilizer—with expansion when demand for work goes up because of a shock or economic crisis—it can help in a revival of economic activity. Providing wage employment puts money in the hands of local people who demand local goods and services, thereby enabling some recovery of local small industries and services.

All these features would have made it an ideal candidate for significant expansion to provide some employment support during the lockdown and subsequent economic crisis. There

---

[76]This section draws on Jayati Ghosh, 'The role of labour market and sectoral policies in promoting more and better jobs in low and middle income countries: issues, evidence and policy options: the case of India', *Employment Working Paper No. 206*, Geneva: International Labour Office, 2016.

were many demands from independent analysts and state governments to increase the number of days per household and to extend the employment guarantee to urban households. Yet, as was noted in Chapter 3, the central government provided only a limited increase in the budget for this programme, much less than the requirement, and by the end of the year this was already leading to significant shortages and the likelihood that the functioning of the programme would be affected. In any case, every year around one-fifth of the budget allocation had to be spent simply for dealing with the pending liabilities carried over from the previous year, because the central government has been routinely not providing the required resources.[77]

After the lockdown was announced, the employment programme suffered in the following month (despite massive need generated by the lockdown) because of confusion about whether such works would be allowed, and the distancing and other norms that were required to be followed. When the programme picked up in May, the massive demand for work meant that work days generated exceeded the approved number of labour days, and this continued throughout the subsequent months. By the end of December 2020, over 83 per cent of funds had been utilized, with less than 12 per cent of the approved labour budget remaining for the next three months.[78] These were clearly insufficient funds to generate the required employment in the last three months, which meant that once again there would be very large pending liabilities for the next financial year. Because state governments did not receive the funds they had already spent on the programme, they tended to restrict their

---

[77]Chetan Chauhan, 'Centre left with mere 10% NREGA funds as scheme sees 243% jump in Corona times', *Hindustan Times*, 11 December 2020; 'Budget: Centre allocates ₹73,000 crore to MGNREGA – 34% less than revised estimate for 2020-21', *Scroll.in*, 2 February 2021.

[78]People's Action for Employment Guarantee, MNREGA Tracker, December 2020.

spending, even though the Act specifies that budgets cannot be a constraint.

By the end of the fiscal year in March 2021, many states had negative balances, which meant that they had spent more than they received from the central government, even though they were not able to fully meet the demand for work.[79] A survey conducted by Gaon Connection and CSDS-Lokniti suggested that only 20 per cent of the willing households got work. About 45.6 lakh households were not issued cards and the demands of 97 lakh households were not met during the year.[80] This restrictive attitude of the central government to the MNREGA persisted through the following year. The allocation for the programme in the Union Budget for 2021–22 was 34 per cent less than what was spent the previous year, and nearly a quarter of it was already covered by pending liabilities from the previous year. The same pattern repeated itself in the next fiscal year, with the Centre allocating very inadequate funds, such that the allocated funds did not even cover the expenditures already made in the programme by state governments, so that they did not have the funds required to continue with the work.[81] The Union Budget for 2022–23 allocated so little to the programme that, after pending dues were adjusted for, it would provide only around twenty days of work over the year for the millions of households that had registered for the programme.[82]

Given the lack of any other form of social protection and the huge reliance of the rural poor on the programme during this

---

[79]People's Action for Employment Guarantee, MNREGA Tracker, September 2021

[80]Kushal Mishra, 'Only one in five rural households availed work under MGNREGA during the lockdown: Gaon Connection survey', *Gaon Connection*, 11 September 2020.

[81]People's Action for Employment Guarantee, MNREGA Tracker, January 2022.

[82]Laavanya Tamang and Anuj Goyal, 'Questions on MNREGA Budget estimation', *The Hindu,* 22 February 2022

crisis, it was obvious that the programme needed to be expanded and extended to cover at least 150 (ideally 200) days of work per household—something that could be done entirely through executive decision. In addition, rolling out an urban employment guarantee (something several states were already attempting, albeit with very limited resources) would be important. Yet there was no evidence of either strategy being actively considered by the central government.

In addition, major problems of implementation persisted and even grew over this period. A survey conducted by LibTech India among nearly 2,000 workers in Andhra Pradesh, Rajasthan, and Jharkhand revealed serious concerns about last-mile delivery. Nearly half the workers had to visit banks multiple times to access their wages and an estimated 40 per cent of banking correspondents users made multiple trips due to biometric failures; the average cost incurred while visiting a bank to withdraw wages was ₹31. Workers paid about ₹11 while accessing their wages from banking correspondents and ₹67 when they visited an ATM; 57 per cent of the respondents reported that their passbooks don't get updated; an estimated 42 per cent of workers in Jharkhand and 38 per cent in Rajasthan took more than four hours to access wages from banks, while an estimated 18 per cent of bank users were denied wages and asked to visit the banking correspondents instead.[83]

The Impact on Education

The impact of school closures on education—and on intensifying inequalities of learning outcomes based on existing advantages (or lack of them) of students—has been evident across the world during the pandemic. In India, where the digital divide

---

[83]Quoted in Debmalya Nandy, 'MGNREGA: rural welfare on crutches', *The Hindu*, 1 January 2020.

is so marked, these effects have been very sharply evident. The disruptions in education created by the lockdowns and the continuing closure of pre-schools, schools, and tertiary education institutions affected a very large number of children and older students. Educationists agree that learning outcomes will be affected not only for the period of closure but subsequently, as much lost ground will have to be regained. There is evidence that short-term disruptions in schooling are also more likely to lead to eventual dropout, especially among the poor and among girl students.[84]

The approach of the central government and many states in response to lockdown and pandemic-induced school closures was essentially to substitute face-to-face learning with online education. In May 2020, the government launched the scheme PM e-VIDYA, that includes various platforms to enable education to continue through the pandemic. Some of the platforms were only for children of Class 9 and above, while most of them required apps accessible only on smartphones.[85]

This ignored the basic realities of education in India. Digital education is much more difficult in India than perhaps in any other large country, because so many students are effectively excluded from access. It has been estimated by UNESCO that around 320 million students in schools and higher education institutions were affected by closures, 84 per cent of whom live in rural areas, with 70 per cent attending government schools.[86] Only a very small fraction of them had access to the basic means for enabling online education, which depends not

---

[84] A. N. Reddy and S. Sinha, 'School dropouts or pushouts? Overcoming barriers for the right to education', Report number: PTA 40 Affiliation: Consortium for Educational Access, Transitions and Equity (CREATE) & NUEPA, July 2010.

[85] 'PM e-Vidya: All You Need to Know About the Govt Online Learning Platform', *News18.com*, 31 May 2021.

[86] 'Education: From disruption to recovery', UNESCO, available at https://en.unesco.org/covid19/educationresponse.

only on access to and ability to operate internet-enabled devices like smartphone, tablets, and computers, but also sufficient internet connectivity to attend classes and participate in them. The official report on infrastructure in school education (UDISE 2019–20) found that only 39 per cent of schools had computers and only 22 per cent had internet connections.[87] The National Sample Survey 75th Round conducted in 2017–18 found that less than 5 per cent of rural households and less than 15 per cent of urban households had a computer. Access to the internet (which can occur through smartphones and tablets as well) was possible for only 15 per cent of rural households, compared to 42 per cent of urban households. But this rural–urban divide is only the tip of the iceberg, with some categories (economically and socially disadvantaged groups and girls within these) facing extreme lack of access.

The sudden shift to digital learning when the pandemic struck was undertaken without any attempt to train teachers, almost all of whom had no experience of such pedagogy and no understanding of how it can be made effective. There was also no attempt to reorient the curriculum to make it amenable to online learning. Therefore, online classes were simply treated in most cases the same as regular classes; in other words, simply not enough to ensure learning. The lack of a connected instrument (such as a smartphone or tablet) effectively amounted to exclusion from education, once educational institutions decided to shift to this mode without making adequate provision for those who did not have and could not afford to buy them. As a result, there were accounts of low-income parents going into debt or selling assets like cattle to purchase smartphones that would enable their children to access online classes.[88] Most

[87] PTI, 'Only 39% Schools In India Had Computers, 22% Had Internet In 2019-20: Report', *NDTV.com*, 30 June 2021.

[88] Kundan Pandey, 'COVID-19 lockdown highlights India's great digital divide', *Down To Earth*, 30 July 2020.

families with smartphones had only one instrument, typically under the control of the (male) head of household. With online classes, which child could get access to the phone became an issue for families with more than one child. The gender divide was important here, as it is known that wives and daughters get the least access, and girls typically tend to be deprived when there is scarcity.

A survey of 3,176 households across five states (Assam, Bihar, Uttar Pradesh, Telangana, and Delhi) found that school education was very badly hit, with children affected in multiple ways.[89] Importantly, the mere presence of devices did not ensure access, and within households there was a clearly gendered pattern to such access. While 52 of the children reported having a TV at home, only 11 per cent reported ever viewing or listening to educational broadcasts on TV or radio. Similarly, even when there was a phone at home, in 71 per cent of cases, phones were owned by a male family member, and only 30 per cent of children reported access (26 per cent of girls compared to 37 per cent of boys). In households facing financial difficulties, only 38 per cent of such children were confident about having access to a phone whenever needed for schooling.

Another study based on a survey of teachers and parents in five states (Chhattisgarh, Madhya Pradesh, Rajasthan, Uttarakhand, Karnataka) similarly found that online schooling was not providing any real learning opportunities, given all the constraints. Overwhelmingly, teachers reported that it was impossible for them to maintain any emotional connect with students in this mode; no meaningful assessment of children's learning was possible in online classes; and children were unable to complete the assignments shared during online classes, creating

---

[89]Neha Ghatak, Achala S. Yareseeme, and Jyotsna Jha, 'Life in the time of Covid-19: Mapping the impact of Covid-19 on the lives of school-going children especially girls in India', Centre for Budget and Policy Studies and India Champions for Girls' Education, 26 November 2020.

significant learning gaps. In any case, 60 per cent of students could not really make use of online learning opportunities because of absence of a smartphone, multiple siblings sharing a smartphone, and/or difficulty in using the available apps. Seventy per cent of parents felt that their children were not learning from online classes; and 90 per cent were willing to send their children to in-person school with necessary health safeguards.[90]

Even when the students did have some instruments they could use, connectivity was a very big concern. Despite the central government's push for digitalization in many spheres, internet penetration in India is neither wide nor deep enough. Consider this description from a tribal village in a rural part of Gujarat: 'if you see a group of boys in Dongari sitting under a tree, it's a safe bet that the spot has some semblance of network. One or two among the group would have a smartphone, while the rest would be staring at it in excitement. And yes, they would be boys. It's hard to find girls here who own a smartphone.'[91] Even in urban areas and big cities, connectivity can be poor and inadequate for the requirement, while electricity supply can be poor and fluctuating. Also, mobile data can be expensive, so that poor families cannot afford to allow their children to stream or download classes. A survey of school-aged children in two areas of the city of Jaipur, Rajasthan, found that most children did not have access to smartphones or phones at all for online 'classes', and even those who did, had major problems of poor connectivity.[92] Several of the children surveyed had forgotten everything they had learned earlier.

---

[90]Azim Premji University, *Myths of Online Education*, Field Studies in Education, APU Hyderabad, September 2020.

[91]Parth M. N., 'Schoolkids: Digital divide to digital partition', PARI, 29 June 2020.

[92]Mohit Verma and Navya Poonia, 'Notes from Jaipur on How School Closures Impacted Children from Marginalised Communities', *The Wire*, 23 October 2021.

That is why, in most such situations—accounting for the greater part of all students at all levels of education—everything effectively stopped, with no teaching or extracurricular activity for the students. The fig leaf of online education really created more of a digital apartheid, which has denied the bulk of students in the country the opportunity for anything resembling real education. There was massive damage to actual learning because of such prolonged school closures, which by October 2021 amounted to an average of sixty-nine weeks across all the states, among the longest in the world. This could lead to erasing whatever knowledge had been gained in the past—definitely in rural areas, but also in urban areas among children from less-privileged households.

The disruption of education also created an increase in child labour, in both recognized employment and unpaid domestic work. Investigators conducting field surveys in July 2020 (for example in Bihar) were not able to interview most of the boys during the day times, because they had started working in the field or in other activities, while girls were rarely seen outside as they were all working in their homes.[93] Of the 3,000 children who could be interviewed, 80 per cent said that their lives had got worse—and more than 40 per cent (especially girls) were uncertain about returning to school when it would reopen, because of economic distress and social norms. All children suffered nutritionally because school closures affected their access to food provided through the Mid-Day Meal programme, and girls were pushed into more household labour, which affected their ability to study, even when they could access online teaching.

The economic and social devastation faced by the majority of Indians during this period was extreme, but none of this was

---

[93]Jyotsna Jha, 'A nightmare for our poor that we must wake up to', *Mint*, 7 January 2021.

really necessary despite the pandemic, and much could have been done differently at each point, to alleviate distress and prevent such outcomes. By early 2022, despite some recovery in aggregate GDP measures, there was less of a recovery in the economic situation of most people: the conditions of life remained fragile and difficult for the majority of people. It was evident that a substantial shift in economic strategy would be necessary to undo some of the damage and provide conditions for future economic and social progress. Some possible routes to such a recovery are considered in the next, final chapter.

chapter 6

GETTING OUT OF THE MESS A POSITIVE AGENDA

This has not been a pretty story thus far. There was much that was wrong with the Indian economy, society, and polity before the pandemic struck; and this book has suggested that much more has gone wrong since. It is easy to feel horror at the inequalities exposed and accentuated by governmental and societal responses to the pandemic, despair at the apparently widespread loss of moral compass and minimum ethical considerations especially among those in positions of power, and anger at the unnecessary human tragedies that have unfolded as a result.

Yet there is still much that can be done to remedy and improve the situation; and there are signs of hope on the horizon. The famous Cambridge economist Joan Robinson, who was a frequent visitor to India in her later years, once remarked that 'for everything that can be said about India, the opposite is also true.'[1] Perhaps this is only to be expected in this vast and diverse country, but there is no doubt that both the Indian economy and Indian politics have at different times confounded sceptics, proven both optimists and pessimists wrong in different ways, and shown patterns of change that were not always expected. Within India, however strong the current pulls in the opposite direction, there is still tremendous progressive energy and desire for change towards a more just economy and a more inclusive

[1]Quoted in Eric Weiner, 'India's chaotic lesson in letting go', *BBC.com*, 16 September 2015.

yet diverse society. This belief in the capacity of the country to step back from the brink and change course in economic strategy, so as to enable people's livelihoods to recover and enlarge human capabilities, underlies the proposals that follow in the rest of this chapter.

So what can be done? Two major concerns have been highlighted throughout this book: the weak fiscal response and inadequate public spending, which have added to contractionary tendencies within the economy and have very severe implications for the future economic trajectory; and the near-absence of meaningful social protection, which renders the vast bulk of the population completely vulnerable to external or internal shocks. These concerns are related, as are the solutions. Since the pandemic was just the first major shock in what is likely to be a very uncertain future in a country already affected by climate change, ensuring resilience must be a central goal of economic policies. This means that all future strategies have to be evaluated in terms of environmental costs and benefits, with a strong focus on pollution reduction and strategies to mitigate climate change. Employment generation strategies will need to be linked to the restoration and creation of ecological commons in urban and rural areas.

Proactive Fiscal Policy

At the moment, as described in the previous chapters, we are dealing with an economy in decline, where the 'output recovery' is weak and confined to the upper strata, while employment, wage, and self-employed incomes and mass consumption languish at levels much lower than before the pandemic. It is urgent and essential to raise public spending, particularly in employment-intensive sectors. The widespread increase in absolute hunger and decline in access to nutritious diets means that alleviating hunger has to be a central plank of economic policy, both through direct public provision and by providing income transfers and wage incomes to enable private food purchase. In addition, employment revival is essential, and this too can be done through a combination of direct public employment and support for MSMEs that provide the bulk of employment opportunities in India. The health crisis is acute, well beyond the specific concerns with Covid-19, and this too requires immediate policy attention, through direct public provision.

A Social Protection Floor for India

In a country like India, with a vast informal labour force, the social protection floor should consist of the following four elements: universal access to basic nutrition; universal access to good quality basic services such as health, sanitation, and education; universal access to basic employment through an employment guarantee scheme in both rural and urban areas; and universal state-provided non-contributory pensions for those who cannot work, and do not receive pensions from other sources. This combination would be more suited to the specific requirements of Indian society, than the Universal Basic Income (UBI) that is often advocated, for several reasons. First, the amounts provided as cash transfers for a UBI in India are likely to be very small if they are truly universal, while targeting such cash would give rise to the well-known problems of unjustified exclusion and unwarranted inclusion. Second, even these small amounts of cash could be rapidly eroded by inflation. Third, in India there is a real concern that such cash transfers would be seen as a *substitute* for publicly provided essential services, rather than an *addition*, as they are in most countries. Indeed, there are already plenty of indications in previous statements of the central government, suggesting precisely such a substitution. This would drastically undermine equity, inclusion, and the quality of essential services. Fourth, the only employment benefits of cash transfers are indirect, operating through the impact on demand.

By contrast, a social protection floor consisting of the combination of food, universal basic services, employment programmes, and pensions would directly generate significantly more employment (through the employment guarantee and because social services in health, care, and education are all labour-intensive activities) and create more secondary employment through the multiplier effects of spending by those who receive the wage incomes. It would improve the quality of life and the health and skills of the population, which are essential for future progress. The employment schemes would self-select those in need, rather than requiring various administrative attempts at exclusion. Cash transfers would be in the form of pensions (ideally at half the minimum wage) for those who cannot work for reasons of age, disability, or other constraints.

Universal public food distribution is now an essential requirement. In the current situation, because of the continuing crisis of livelihoods and reduced food access, there should be free provision of 10 kilograms of wheat/rice to every person for six months, without requiring ration cards. This is essential to combat hunger and ensure basic nutrition without excluding some of the most needy and vulnerable people. Biometric identification of beneficiaries, which has generated significant exclusion of the really needy, must be abolished, and alternative ways of ensuring access (some of which are already being experimented with by some state governments) must be developed. Universality does not mean that everyone will avail of this; various studies suggest that such free foodgrain from the Public Distribution System would be taken up by at most 80 per cent of the population. With an estimated population of 1.3 billion, providing this for 6 months would require 62.4 million tonnes of grain. This is a maximal estimate: the actual requirement would be lower. In early 2022, the FCI was holding 85 million tonnes of foodgrain stocks, nearly four times the buffer stock norms of 24 million tonnes, and would soon procure more after the 2022 rabi harvest. Therefore, such free food distribution would be easily possible even while maintaining the required buffer stock. Apart from cereals, some pulses, cooking oil, and other necessities should also be provided over this period. Where Mid-Day Meals and cooked food in Anganwadi centres cannot be provided, there should be arrangements to deliver food to people's homes. There should be expansion of community kitchens, canteens, and other such arrangements to provide free or heavily subsidized cooked food for those (homeless and others) who are not in a position to cook food themselves.

Since the economy had not been creating jobs well before the pandemic, it is clear that the government must actively undertake employment generation programmes itself, in addition to creating conditions conducive for good quality job creation by private employers. The rural employment guarantee scheme must be expanded to offer 150 days of employment to *all* willing adults. It should be expanded to cover the possibilities of training and some skilled work, and extend beyond creation of basic rural infrastructure (as at present) to include all activities that improve the well-being and living conditions of people. A new urban employment programme, which includes caregiving and building water-supply, sanitation, and shelter for the urban poor, must be created and put into place; useful templates for this already exist, including those being instituted by some state governments.

The need for massive increases in health spending should now be more than obvious; a tripling of the government's health budget to 3 per cent of GDP is required for India even to reach the level of other similarly placed economies. This has been promised for years by successive governments (including the present one). These resources should be dominantly passed on to state governments, since health remains primarily the state governments' responsibility. Some of the health spending should be devoted to expansion, improvement, and repair of health infrastructure, but most of all, significant additional expenditure is required on more and better paid public health workers. In addition to filling all the vacancies in public health employment, all 'scheme workers' providing health care in different forms should be regularized, treated as government employees, and paid at least the state minimum wages and more. The other facilities that would allow them to function effectively, such as social security, transport, and communication assistance on the job, etc., must be provided. Similarly, sanitation workers must be treated as regular employees with all benefits and accorded proper respect and protection with adequate safety precautions at work. All these features of public health and sanitation employment are taken for granted in most other countries, yet in India these are still seen as extreme demands.

The massive gaps in education that became evident during the pandemic were not confined to the digital divide; they extended to all sorts of infrastructure, facilities, and personnel. Once again, the earlier promise of providing at least 6 per cent of GDP as public spending on education has not been honoured. But it is essential, not just for greater equity and inclusion, but also if India is to come even close to getting any advantage out of the much-hyped demographic dividend of a population bulge of young people. The expansion of health and education services should go along with expansion of other much-needed public services, such as in agricultural extension, livestock management, and different types of care services adjusted to the specific needs of the population. Ultimately, public employment should not be seen simply as a fiscal cost, but as essential for a just, healthy, equitable, and peaceful society, and playing a hugely important role in economic revival. The significance of care services as a major employment generator of the future must not be overlooked: this is one of the activities, being fundamentally relational, that can be assisted but not substituted by automation, unlike many other sectors.

Employment and the Environment

Medium, small, and micro enterprises, which employ the overwhelming proportion of India's workers, have been the most badly damaged by the pandemic-related policies and the subsequent demand stagnation that has affected their markets. They will necessarily require substantial additional support in the form of both input and credit packages. For most such enterprises, the moratorium on repayment obviously needs to be extended until their markets recover, and ideally converted into debt standstills (whereby the interest for the period does not keep adding up for later repayment). Employment generation in rural areas could also benefit from the active encouragement of cooperatives (for example using the Kudumbashree model in Kerala or the SEWA model in Gujarat) as well as small panchayat-owned village-level enterprises in a number of fields, such as processing local products. This would require, in addition to bank credit, assistance in design, input access, and marketing, at least in the initial stages.

Many measures are required for agriculture, where the problem of farming becoming unremunerative has reached crisis proportions. The overhang of farmers' debt needs to be addressed, especially for small cultivators. Research and extension services as well as input provision need to be developed much more, particularly to encourage more environmentally sustainable forms of cultivation and to reduce reliance on water and chemical inputs. The farmers' protests have highlighted the importance of protecting agriculturalists from very volatile crop prices and assuring stable remunerative crop prices. The need for ensuring remunerative procurement prices, including through the extension of procurement operations to cash crops, has been repeated by successive official reports, but not properly acted upon. In the volatile international economy, it is necessary to use flexible tariffs to insulate domestic prices from world price fluctuations. Land reforms that involve the distribution of ceiling surplus land to the landless, starting with plantations that have unused land, still have a lot of scope. The recognition of the rights of forest-dwellers who have been cultivating land for generations has still not been properly achieved despite legislation. All of these necessarily involve active public investment and intervention; they cannot be achieved by changes in regulation that simply grant more freedom and power to large corporations engaged in agribusiness, as the new farm laws propose. The (required) medium term shift of the work force to higher value added activities cannot be achieved by simply destroying the viability of cultivation, which is counterproductive. It requires the creation and expansion of productive employment opportunities outside agriculture, which is much more likely if these employment-generating measures work to expand the domestic market.

Both climate change and ecological devastation are already wreaking havoc on people's lives and livelihoods across the subcontinent. 'Greening' of the economy is now an urgent imperative, with several dimensions: stopping or reducing the devastation and over-exploitation of nature; reducing atmospheric and water pollution; climate change mitigation efforts, including reduction of greenhouse gas emissions and fossil fuel use; strategies to enable adaptation to climate change; dealing with people and activities displaced by climate-related events and processes as well as other environmental damage like desertification; and preventing the ongoing processes from disproportionately impacting the poor. This is a medium-to-long-term goal that will require significant resources, as well as new regulatory practices in order to overhaul production, consumption, and distribution to make them all more sustainable and less ecologically destructive. New urbanization patterns will also need to be developed: the existing framework of 'Smart Cities' has not delivered on its promises and must be completely transformed.

Raising Public Resources and Addressing Financial Concerns

Of course, all this requires significantly enhanced public spending, and the usual question is then posed: where is the money? For some of the most immediate spending requirements, such as for food, employment programmes and other social protection, the government should simply spend, and finance through borrowing from the Reserve Bank of India. In the situation of depressed demand prevalent in India today, more public spending is unlikely to be inflationary, especially if some of the spending is devoted to addressing whatever supply bottlenecks are evident. More spending is likely to generate much more economic activity, which will also lead to higher tax revenues over time, so that the increased spending will not all be deficit spending of the government. The increased inflationary pressures being felt globally and in India are essentially the result of supply factors, and these must be addressed, instead of knee-jerk measures like raising interest rates. Meanwhile, as was seen in Chapter 4, the balance of payments is not a constraint at present: the current account deficit is small and shrinking (because of falling imports); foreign exchange reserves have grown substantially. The fear of capital flight persists, but that can be addressed through measures outlined below. So very little prevents the central government from significantly increasing its spending other than its own ideological blinkers.

However, in the medium term, obviously, more resources must be raised. The most obvious source of revenue generation is through taxes, but tax policy is a crucial tool that has been very inadequately utilised by the central government. India's tax mix is regressive and narrow in design, with a high and growing dependence on indirect taxes that disproportionately burden the poor. India's tax-GDP ratio (16–17 per cent) is low when compared with tax-GDP ratios across various developed and developing countries. In addition to most of the developed countries, other emerging economies such as Brazil, Turkey, South Africa, and China perform much better than India in terms of the tax-GDP ratio.

There are some obvious areas in which direct tax collections could be raised, which would also address (even if only to a limited extent) the sharp increases in inequality in the recent past. India's wealth and inheritance taxes were scrapped in 2015, but in any case, at rates of less than 0.01 per cent, they produced pitiful amounts of revenue. There is a case for a higher wealth tax, of say 4 per cent, but imposed on *only* the very richest individuals and families, the dollar billionaires or the top 0.01 per cent of the population. This could generate up to 2 per cent of GDP—double the current health spending of central and state governments taken together. Similarly, an inheritance tax of around 30 per cent, once again imposed on the very rich, would be at rates similar to several other Asian countries, and less than many European countries.

Taxation of multinationals at the same rate as domestic companies provides another potential source of revenue. Currently, MNCs are able to avoid taxation by shifting their profits abroad to low-tax jurisdictions, so they pay low or no tax for their activities within India. Instead of this, if a unitary system of taxation were brought in, whereby an MNC would be treated as one global unit, then the Indian government could tax India's share of their global profits (according to a formula based on sales or users for digital companies, employment, assets) at the prevailing rate for corporate taxes. Such a measure is being negotiated globally, but given the inadequate nature of the global compromises on this after several years of discussions, there is a strong case for independent action on this front. Similarly, even a slightly higher turnover tax on all financial transactions as well as on foreign exchange transactions would not only provide more tax revenues, but also curb speculative trades based on high volumes and low margins.

Within India's national economy, there are enormous variations across states on many key indicators such as total and per capita income, rates of employment, levels of education, participation of women in the economy, as well as impact of and response to the pandemic. These differences are inherent in the very structure of the Indian polity. However, federal fiscal relations have been badly damaged by a number of recent central government moves, as described in earlier chapters. In addition to the GST and its problematic fallout, the replacement of the Planning Commission by the NITI Aayog has reduced states' voice in expenditure decisions and allocations of the central government. These tendencies have unfortunate implications for the federal structure, and need to be reversed to ensure the future political and economic stability of the country. Centre–state relations need to be carefully and sensitively rebuilt. The centre must eschew its continuing efforts to grab greater shares of fiscal resources by imposing cesses and surcharges that are not shared with the states. It must engage with and consult the states on all important matters and take such decisions jointly, unlike the present situation in which state governments are not consulted or even informed about major policy decisions and have to learn about them through the media. The Inter-State Council, which has not even met for several years now, must be revived and given greater voice and powers.

The current problems facing commercial banks suggest that some restructuring of bad loans and recapitalization of banks will be inevitable. But this must be accompanied by a special focus on providing credit to underserved groups, and concerted and serious action against large corporate defaulters, who need to be publicly named, shamed, and made to pay. In addition, development banking, which had been dismantled in the early 1990s, needs to be brought in as an essential part of the public agenda, to enable investment in infrastructure and projects with long term and strategic value. Priority lending to agriculture and micro and small enterprises must be revived and properly implemented.

If policies such as proposed above are indeed implemented, the possibility of knee-jerk movements of finance capital out of the country cannot be wished away. Such inflows have not really contributed to domestic investment (in the recent past they have mainly added to the foreign exchange reserves) but they do have the potential to destabilize the economy. Initial capital outflows could well be reversed once the positive impact of these measures on the domestic economy becomes evident, but the immediate effect of even announcing such measures could well be capital flight, leading to rapid currency depreciation and associated instability. Therefore, it would be necessary to institute some prudential and other capital controls, to reduce volatile flows of hot money and speculative capital.

Clearly, given the interdependence of all economies today and the strong impact of the international trade and finance architecture on domestic policy making, the external environment is also important. However, some of this architecture can also be affected by Indian intervention. While the Indian government initially blocked the proposal in the IMF for a new issuance of SDRs (a global unit of account and form of liquidity created by the IMF) to the tune of $650 billion, it has since accepted the proposal. This provided much-needed foreign exchange to developing countries in accordance with their IMF quotas. India should now argue for further increases in SDR allocations, especially to provide much-needed climate finance to developing countries. Unlike all loans, including the Swap Lines of the US Federal Reserve Board, the SDRs are non-discriminatory, non-discretionary, interest-free, non-repayable, and do not entail either any 'conditionalities' or any arm-twisting. Therefore, they would also be of benefit to India if it does go in for policies to expand domestic economic activity, and would provide it with greater policy flexibility.

The Urgency of Change

This is one possible blueprint for recovery and construction of a better framework for the economy; of course, there may be others. To counter those who will argue that this set of proposals is too ambitious or unrealistic in the current political context, I will mention just two points. First, ideas can and must predate the political and social mobilization required to put them into practice; without an alternative agenda being available, accessible, and widely known, it is unlikely that changes in economic policies will come about even when political conditions are more favourable for them. Secondly, the implications of 'business as usual', of carrying on as if mere tinkering with existing policies with a lack of substantial change, are too dire to contemplate. The extent of the deep economic crisis that is affecting the bulk of the Indian population has been described in previous chapters, and it should be evident that the current trajectory is simply not sustainable, in economic, political, social, or environmental terms. Doing nothing, or doing very little while pretending to do more, are no longer viable options for the medium term.

ACKNOWLEDGEMENTS

It is usual when writing acknowledgements to provide a disclaimer absolving those named from any responsibility for the contents. But my work has been so closely influenced over the years by discussion, exchange, and collaboration with colleagues, friends, and students, that in some ways I believe that they must be complicit in this book, even though I should not hold them responsible for its flaws.

Intense collaboration in academic research and organizational activities along with continuing discussions over decades with C. P. Chandrasekhar have moulded my thinking and sharpened my perspectives, besides getting me into the habit of dealing with lots of work and frequent deadlines. Along with him, some friends and colleagues provided valuable suggestions and advice on earlier drafts. Robert Pollin, Ranjana Sengupta, Zoya Hasan, and Amrita Basu carefully read through the entire draft of an earlier version and made many suggestions that resulted (I hope) in a more organized and accessible book. Prabhat Patnaik prevented me from making logical fallacies. Abhijit Sen told me off on some points that forced me to hone my arguments. Vikas Rawal clarified several issues and provided important insights on agriculture. Dipa Sinha provided important correctives to some of the discussion on health and women's employment. Gerald Epstein helped me to contextualize the Indian experience in comparison to other more advanced economies.

Over the years, discussions on different aspects of the Indian economy with those already named, along with Smita Gupta, Praveen Jha, Rohit Azad, Himanshu, Nikhil Dey, Aruna Roy, Anjali Bharadwaj, Prashant Bhushan, Harsh Mander, Ritu

Dewan, Amiya Bagchi, Pronab Sen, S. Subramanian, Biswajit Dhar, Surajit Mazumdar, Sunanda Sen, and Utsa Patnaik, have enriched my understanding. Jahnavi Sen has reminded me constantly of the world beyond the economy; and she, C. S. R. Shankar, Vipulya Chari, Trina Shankar, Isha Vallari, Ragini Jha, Sandhya and Mallika Vishwanathan, and their friends also helped me to appreciate that world and laugh about some of it. Aditi Mehta, Ayesha Kagal, Ayesha Kidwai, Angelie Multani, Ram Ramaswamy, Kajori Sen, and other friends made the world more bearable in general. Robert Pollin and Sigrid Miller Pollin, with their incredible generosity, provided much more than a home away from home: at a critical time, they gave of their friendship, empathy, and intellectual stimulation. Heena Dey took over domestic responsibilities that freed me to do other things. Anil Mani helped to ease other practical aspects of professional life.

The idea for this book was first proposed to me by Pallavi Goswami of Aleph Book Company. I am thankful to her for suggesting it and then keeping me on track despite various changes in professional and personal life that could have distracted me. Tanvi Sharma, Hitasha Sharma, and Pavitra Kanagaraj assisted in updating some parts of the manuscript over a rapidly changing period.

The book has been written quickly, but still, I believe, carefully—because the assessment of this most fateful period in the evolution of the Indian economy demands nothing less than serious and careful consideration.

This is a challenging time in many ways for those who wish not only to preserve a certain idea of India in all its plurality, but to see it emerge as a true and just democracy. This book is dedicated to the young Indians, especially young women, who continue to strive for that against truly difficult odds. I was fortunate to call some of them my students, and there are others from whom I have learned and continue to learn: for their honesty, wisdom, courage, humour, and resilience. It's really because of them that I continue to have hope for the future of India.

REFERENCES

Allana, Alia, 'India's Comfort Food Tells the Story of Its Pandemic', *The Atlantic*, 13 June 2020.

Alvi, Muzna and Gupta, Manavi, 'Learning in times of lockdown: How Covid-19 is affecting education and food security in India', *Food Security*, December 2020, pp. 793–96.

Anand, Abhishek, Sandefur, Justin, and Subramanian, Arvind, 'Three New Estimates of India's All Cause Excess Mortality during the COVID-19 Pandemic', Center for Global Development Working Paper 589, July 2021, available at https://www.cgdev.org/sites/default/files/three-new-estimates-indias-all-cause-excess-mortality-during-covid-19-pandemic.pdf.

Azad, Rohit, Chakraborty, Shouvik, Ramani, Srinivasan, and Sinha, Dipa (eds.), *A Quantum Leap in the Wrong Direction?*, Hyderabad: Orient Blackswan, 2019.

Azim Premji University, *Covid-19 Livelihoods Survey: Compilation of Findings*, Centre for Sustainable Employment, Hyderabad: Azim Premji University, 2020, available at https://cse.azimpremjiuniversity.edu.in/wp-content/uploads/2020/06/Compilation-of-findings-APU-COVID-19-Livelihoods-Survey_Final.pdf.

———, *State of Working India 2021,* Centre for Sustainable Employment, Hyderabad: Azim Premji University, 2021, available at https://cse.azimpremjiuniversity.edu.in/wp-content/uploads/2021/06/SWI2021_Web_25June.pdf.

Balarajan, Y., Selvaraj, S., and Subramanian, S. V., 'Health care and equity in India, *The Lancet*, 11 January 2011.

Banaji, Murad and Gupta, Aashish, 'Estimates of pandemic excess mortality in India based on civil registration data', *MedRxiv*, 1 October 2021.

Barbosa-Filho, Nelson H. and Izurieta, Alex, 'The Risk of a Second Wave of Post-Crisis Frailty in the World Economy', *International Journal of Political Economy,* Vol. 49, No. 4, November 2020, pp. 278–303.

Bharti, Nitin, 'Wealth Inequality, Caste and Class in India 1961-2012', WID.world working paper 2018/14, 2018.

Calcutta Research Group, *Borders of an Epidemic: Covid-19 and Migrant Workers,* Kolkata: Mahanirban Calcutta Research Group, 2020.

Chakraborty, Shiney, 'Increased Care Work, Reduced Wages: Informal Women Workers Are Barely Getting By', *The Wire,* 25 May 2020, available at www.thewire.in/women/women-informal-workers-lockdown.

Chancel, Lucas and Piketty, Thomas, 'From British Raj to Billionaire Raj? Indian income inequality 1922-2015', *Review of Income and Wealth,* (forthcoming) published as a WID.world working paper 2017/11, 2019.

CBGA, *Numbers on the Edge: Assessing India's fiscal response to Covid-19,* New Delhi: Centre for Budget and Governance Accountability, 29 May 2020.

Chandrasekhar, C. P., 'The Indian economy: Before and after the pandemic', in Rawal, Vikas, Ghosh, Jayati, and Chandrasekhar, C. P. (eds.), *When Governments Fail: A Pandemic and Its Aftermath,* Tulika Books and Columbia University Press, 2021.

Chatterjee, Patralekha, 'Is India missing Covid-19 deaths?', *The Lancet,* 5 September 2020, available at https://doi.org/10.1016/S0140-6736(20)31857-2.

Chiplunkar, Gaurav, M. Kelley, Erin, and Lane, Gregory, 'Which jobs were "lost" during India's Covid-19 lockdown? Evidence from online vacancy postings', *Ideas For India,* 8 September 2020.

Deshingkar, P. and Akter, S., Migration and Human Development in India, Human Development Research Paper 2009/13, New York: United Nations Development Programme, 2009.

Deshpande, Ashwini, 'The COVID-19 Pandemic and Gendered Division of Paid and Unpaid Work: Evidence from India', *IZA Discussion Papers,* No. 13815, Institute of Labor

Economics (IZA), Bonn, 2020, available at www.econstor.eu/bitstream/10419/227342/1/dp13815.pdf.

Biswajit, Dhar and Joseph, Reji K., 'The Challenges, Opportunities and Performance of the Indian Pharmaceutical Industry Post-TRIPS', in Liu, K. C. and Racherla, U. (eds.), *Innovation, Economic Development, and Intellectual Property in India and China*, ARCIALA Series on Intellectual Assets and Law in Asia, Singapore: Springer, https://doi.org/10.1007/978-981-13-8102-7_13.

Dholakia, Ravindra, Nagaraj, R., and Pandya, Manish, 'Manufacturing Output in New GDP Series: Some Methodological Issues', *Economic and Political Weekly*, Vol. LIII, No. 35, 1 September 2018.

Drèze, Jean, Gupta, Aashish, Parashar, Sai Anki, and Sharma, Kanika, 'Pauses and Reversals of Infant Mortality Decline in India in 2017 and 2018', SSRN, 8 November 2020, available at https://papers.ssrn.com/sol3/papers.cfm?abstract_id=3727001.

Drèze, Jean, Khera, Reetika, and Mungikar, Meghna, 2020, available at www.indiaspend.com/more-than-100mn-excluded-from-pds-as-govt-uses-outdated-census-2011-data.

Drèze, Jean and Somanchi, Anmol, 'The Covid-19 crisis and food security', *Ideas For India*, 21 June 2021, available at www.ideasforindia.in/topics/poverty-inequality/the-covid-19-crisis-and-food-security.html.

Duggal, Ravi, 'A new health policy for health sector reforms', Mumbai: Centre for Enquiry into Health and Allied Themes (Cehat), available at www.cehat.org/cehat/uploads/files/a87.pdf.

Gangolli, Leena V., Ravi Duggal, and Abhay Shukla, *Review of Healthcare in India*, Mumbai: Centre for Enquiry into Health and Allied Themes (Cehat), 2005.

Ghatak, Neha, Yareseeme, Achala S., and Jha, Jyotsna, 'Life in the time of Covid-19: Mapping the impact of Covid-19 on the lives of school-going children especially girls in India', Centre for Budget and Policy Studies (www.cbps.in) and India Champions for Girls' Education, 2020.

Ghosh, Jayati, 'Growth, industrialisation and inequality in India', *Journal of the Asia Pacific Economy*, Vol. 20, No. 1, 2015, pp. 42–56, available at https://doi.org/10.1080/13547860.2014.974316.

———, 'Public employment for public purpose', *India Exclusion Report 2019-20*, New Delhi: Centre for Equity Studies, 2020, pp. 243–260, available at http://centreforequitystudies.org/wp-content/uploads/2021/01/India-Exclusion-Report-2019-20-e-copy.pdf.

———, 'The role of labour market and sectoral policies in promoting more and better jobs in low and middle income countries: issues, evidence and policy options: the case of India', *Employment Working Paper*, No. 206, Geneva: International Labour Office, 2016.

———, Chandrasekhar, C. P., and Patnaik, Prabhat, *Demonetisation Decoded: A Critique of India's Monetary Experiment*, New Delhi: Routledge Taylor and Francis Publishers, 2017.

———, *Never Done and Poorly Paid: Women's Work in Globalising India*, New Delhi: Women Unlimited, 2009.

Ghosh, Sangeeta, 'Examining the Covid-19 relief package for MSMEs', *Economic and Political Weekly*, Vol. 55, Issue 22, 30 May 2020, available at www.epw.in/journal/2020/22/commentary/examining-covid-19-relief-package-msmes.html.

Himanshu, 'India's farm crisis: Decades old and with deep roots', *The India Forum*, 29 April 2019, available at www.theindiaforum.in/article/farm-crisis-runs-deep-higher-msps-and-cash-handouts-are-not-enough.

Horton, Richard and Das, Pam, 'Indian Health: The Path from Crisis to Progress', *The Lancet*, Vol. 377, No. 9761, 2011, pp. 181–183, available at www.thelancet.com/journals/lancet/article/PIIS0140-6736(10)62179-4/fulltext.

IHD and UNICEF, *Assessing impact of the Covid-19 pandemic on socio-economic impact of vulnerable populations through community-based monitoring*, New Delhi: Institute for Human Development and UNICEF, 2021, available at www.ihdindia.org/pdf/Book-Covid-UNICEF-Report_2021.pdf.

ILO, *India Wage Report 2018*, New Delhi: International Labour Office, www.ilo.org/wcmsp5/groups/public/---asia/---ro-bangkok/---sro-new_delhi/documents/publication/wcms_638305.pdf.

Ioannides, John P., 'Infection fatality rate of COVID-19 inferred from seroprevalence data', *WHO Bulletin*, January 2021, Vol. 99, pp. 19–33.

Jha, Ravinder, 'Prices of new pharmaceuticals in India: A cross-section study', *Economic and Political Weekly*, Vol. 45, No. 10, 6 March 2010, available at www.epw.in/journal/2010/10/special-articles/prices-new-pharmaceuticals-india-cross-section-study.html.

John, Jacob and Kang, Gagandeep, 'Tracking SARS=CoV-2 infection in India with serology', *The Lancet,* 27 January 2021, available at www.thelancet.com/journals/langlo/article/PIIS2214-109X(20)30546-5/fulltext.

Joseph, Reji K., *Pharmaceutical Industry and Public Policy in Post-reform India*, New Delhi: Routledge India, 2015.

Kapoor, Radhicka, 'Understanding India's Jobs Challenge', *The India Forum,* 10 September 2019, available at www.theindiaforum.in/article/what-periodic-labour-force-survey-telling-us-about-employment-and-unemployment-india.

Kregel, Jan A., *Economic Development and Financial Instability: Selected Essays*, Rainer Kattel (ed.), Anthem Press, 2014.

Khera, Reetika and Somanchi, Anmol, 'A review of the coverage of PDS', *Ideas for India*, 2020, available at www.ideasforindia.in/topics/poverty-inequality/a-review-of-the-coverage-of-pds.html.

Leffler, Christopher T., Lykins V, Joseph D., and Yang, Edward, 'Preliminary Analysis of Excess Mortality in India During the Covid-19 Pandemic', *MedRxiv*, updated 26 September 2021, available at https://doi.org/10.1101/2021.08.04.21261604.

London School of Economics, *City of dreams no more, a year on: worklessness and active labour market policies in urban India,* Centre for Economic Performance, LSE, 2021, available at https://cep.lse.ac.uk/pubs/download/cepcovid-19-022.pdf.

Lustig, Nora, Martinez, V., Sanz, F., and Younger, S., *The impact of COVID-19 Lockdowns and Expanded Social Assistance on Inequality, Poverty and Mobility in Argentina, Brazil, Colombia and Mexico*, 2020, available at https://ideas.repec.org/p/inq/inqwps/ecineq2020-558.html.

Mazumdar, Surajit, 'The Coronavirus and India's Economic Crisis: Continuity and Change', MPRA Paper 104969, University Library of Munich, Germany, revised 20 December 2020, available at https://mpra.ub.uni-muenchen.de/104969/.

Mehrotra, Santosh and Parida, Jajati, 'India's Employment Crisis: Rising

Education Levels and Falling Non-agricultural Job Growth', *CSE Working Paper 2019-04*, 2019, Hyderabad: Azim Premji University.

Migrant Workers Solidarity Network, *Citizens and the Sovereign: Stories from the Largest Human Exodus in Contemporary Indian History*, November 2020.

Ministry of Health and Family Welfare, *Report of the National Commission on Macroeconomics and Health*, New Delhi: Government of India, 2005.

Mukhopadhyay, Baijayanta, Liu, Chunbao, and Heymann, Jody, *The Work, Family, and Equity Index. Setting the Global Floor: a comparative study of labour standards in India and China*, Institute for Health and Social Policy, McGill University, Montreal, Canada, 2009, available at www.mcgill.ca/ihsp/files/ihsp/world_equity_india_and_china.pdf.

Mukhopadhaya, Indranil, and Sinha, Dipa, 'Painting a picture of ill-health', in Rohit Azad et al. (eds.), *A Quantum Leap in the Wrong Direction?*, Hyderabad: Orient Blackswan, 2019, pp. 155–179.

Mustafa, Seema (ed.), *Shaheen Bagh and the Idea of India*, New Delhi: Speaking Tiger Books, 2020.

Nagaraj, R. 'Seeds of Doubt on New GDP Numbers: Private Corporate Sector Overestimated?', *Economic & Political Weekly*, Vol. 50, No. 13, 2015, pp. 14–17.

———, 'GDP Conundrum: A synoptic view', *Ideas for India*, 20 November, 2016, available at www.ideasforindia.in/topics/macroeconomics/gdp-conundrum-a-synoptic-view.html.

Narayanan, Sudha, 'How India's agrifood supply chains fared during the COVID-19 lockdown, from farm to fork', IFPRI, New Delhi, 20 July 2020, available at www.ifpri.org/blog/how-indias-agrifood-supply-chains-fared-during-covid-19-lockdown-farm-fork?s=09.

———, 'The Three Farm Bills: Is This the Market Reform Indian Agriculture Needs?', *The India Forum*, 27 November 2020, available at www.theindiaforum.in/article/three-farm-bills.

NITI Aayog, *Healthy States, Progressive India: Report on the Ranks of States and Union Territories*, New Delhi: Government of India, 2019.

Patnaik, Ila and Sengupta, Rajeswari, 'Impact of Covid-19 on the Indian Economy: An Analysis of Fiscal Scenarios', *Working Paper*

20/319, New Delhi: National Institute of Public Finance and Policy, 2020.

Patnaik, Prabhat, 'A matter of survival of the peasantry', *IDEAs Commentary*, December 2020, available at www.networkideas.org/news-analysis/2020/12/a-matter-of-survival-of-the-peasantry.

People's Action for Employment Guarantee, *All India NREGA Tracker, May 2021*, New Delhi, 2021.

———, *NREGA National Tracker at Mid-Year, April-September 2021*, New Delhi, 2021.

Pew Research Centre, *In the Pandemic India's middle class shrinks and poverty spreads while China sees smaller changes*, 2021, available at www.pewresearch.org/fact-tank/2021/03/18/in-the-pandemic-indias-middle-class-shrinks-and-poverty-spreads-while-china-sees-smaller-changes.

Pulla, Priyanka, 'What counts as a Covid-19 death?', *British Medical Journal*, Vol. 370, No. 2859, 17 July 2020, available at https://doi.org/10.1136/bmj.m2859.

Purkayastha, Soumik, Kundu, Ritoban, Bhaduri, Ritwik, et al., 'Estimating the wave 1 and wave 2 infection fatality rates from SARS-CoV-2 in India', *BMC Research Notes*, Vol. 14, No. 262, 2021, available at https://doi.org/10.1186/s13104-021-05652-2.

Raghavan, Vijay, 'Prisons and the pandemic: the panopticon plays out', *Journal of Social and Economic Development*, 7 December 2020, available at https://doi-org.silk.library.umass.edu/10.1007/s40847-020-00127-9.

Raghunathan, Kalyani, Heady, Derek, and Henforth, Anna, 'Affordability of nutritious diets in rural India', *Food Policy*, 11 October 2020, available at www.sciencedirect.com/science/article/pii/S030691922030186X.

Rahman, Sabina Yasmin, '"Social distancing" during COVID-19: The metaphors and politics of pandemic response in India', *Health Sociology Review*, June 2020, available at https://doi.org/10.1080/14461242.2020.1790404.

Rajshekhar, M. 2020 *Despite the State: Why India Lets Its People Down and How They Cope*, New Delhi: Context (Westland Books), 2020.

Rao, Mohan, Rao, Krishna D., Kumar, A. K. Shiva, et al., 'Human resources for health in India', *The Lancet*, 12 January 2011, available at https://doi.org/10.1016/S0140-6736(10)61888-0.

Ravindran, Saravana and Shah, Manisha, 'Unintended consequences of lockdowns: Covid-19 and the shadow pandemic', *NBER Working Paper 27562*, 2020, available at www.nber.org/papers/w27562.

Rawal, Vikas and Pais, Jesim, 'An Assessment of the Recent PLFS Data and Provisional Analysis of the Impact of the COVID-19 Lockdown on Employment and Poverty in India', *SSER Working Paper*, 2021.

Ray, D. and Subramanian, S., 'Is There a Reasonable Alternative to a Comprehensive Lockdown?', *Ideas for India*, 2020, available at www.ideasforindia.in/topics/macroeconomics/is-there-a-reasonable-alternative-to-a-comprehensive-lockdown.html.

———, 'India's Response to Covid-19 is a Humanitarian Disaster', *The Boston Review*, July 16 2020, available at bostonreview.net/global-justice/debraj-ray-s-subramanian-indias-response-covid-19-humanitarian-disaster.

Ray, D., Subramanian, S., and Vandewalle, L., 'India's Lockdown', *Center for Economic Policy Reasearch Policy Insight No. 102*, April 2020, available at https://cepr.org/sites/default/files/policy_insights/PolicyInsight102.pdf.

Reddy, C. Rammanohar, *Demonetisation and Black Money*, Hyderabad: Orient Blackswan, 2017.

Reddy, A. N., and Sinha, S., 'School dropouts or pushouts? Overcoming barriers for the right to education', CREATE, 2010, available at www.create-rpc.org.

Saha, Debdulal and Roychowdhury, Anamitra, 'Indian Labour Market in the Time of COVID-19 Pandemic: Issues, Experience and Policy', *The Indian Economic Journal*, Vol. 69, No. 3, 2021, pp. 369–376.

Sainath, P., 'And you thought it's only about farmers?', PARI, December 2020, available at https://ruralindiaonline.org/articles/and-you-thought-its-only-about-farmers/?s=03.

Sanyal, Meera, *The Big Reverse: How Demonetisation Knocked India Out*, Mumbai: Harper Business, 2018.

Sen, Pronab, 'The Covid-19 shock: Learnings from the past, addressing the present - III', *Ideas for India*, 7 June 2020, 7 June 2020, available at www.ideasforindia.in/topics/macroeconomics/the-covid-19-shock-learnings-from-the-past-addressing-the-present-iii.html.

SEWA Bharat, *Gendered Precarity in the Lockdown*, All India Federation of Self Employed Women's Association, May 2020.

Siddharth, K. J., Karpagam, Sylvia, and D'Souza, Alwyn Prakash, *Working at the Margins: A Report on the Conditions of Invisibilized Frontline Workers*, Bengaluru: Ashirwad Centre for Social Concern, 2020.

Sinha, Dipa, *Women, Public Services and Health in India: Why Are States Different?*, New Delhi: Routledge India, 2016.

Sinha, Shreya, 'The Agrarian Crisis in Punjab and the Making of the Anti-Farm Law Protests', *The India Forum*, 28 November 2020, available at www.theindiaforum.in/article/agrarian-crisis-punjab-and-making-anti-farm-law-protests.

Sood, Atul, 'The silent takeover of labour rights', *The India Forum*, 20 November 2020, available at www.theindiaforum.in/article/silent-takeover-labour-rights.

Srivastava, Ravi S. and Padhi, Balkrishna, 'Collapse in Wage/Salary Income Growth in India, 2011-12 to 2017-18', *CES Working Paper 01/2020*, New Delhi: Institute for Human Development, 2020.

Stiglitz, Joseph E., 'Markets, Market Failures, and Development', *American Economic Review*, Vol. 79, No. 2, 2989, pp. 197–203.

Subramanian, Arvind, 'India's GDP Mis-estimation: Likelihood, Magnitudes, Mechanisms, and Implications', CID Faculty Working Paper No. 354, Harvard University, 2019, available at www.hks.harvard.edu/centers/cid/publications/faculty-working-papers/india-gdp-overestimate.

Subramanian, S., 'What is Happening to Rural Welfare, Poverty, and Inequality in India?', *The India Forum*, 12 December 2019, available at www.theindiaforum.in/article/what-happened-rural-welfare-poverty-and-inequality-india-between-2011-12-and-2017-18.

Debraj, Ray and Subramanian, S., 'Covid-19 and other diseases: An "Animal Farm" perspective', 23 February 2021, available at www.ideasforindia.in/topics/human-development/covid-19-and-other-diseases-an-animal-farm-perspective.html.

SWAN, '21 Days and Counting: COVID-19 Lockdown, Migrant Workers, and the Inadequacy of Welfare Measures in India', Stranded

Workers Action Network, 15 April 2020, available at https://ruralindiaonline.org/en/library/resource/21-days-and-counting-covid-19-lockdown-migrant-workers-and-the-inadequacy-of-welfare-measures-in-india.

———, '32 Days and Counting: COVID-19 Lockdown, Migrant Workers, and the Inadequacy of Welfare Measures in India', Stranded Workers Action Network, 1 May 2020, available at https://ruralindiaonline.org/en/library/resource/32-days-and-counting-covid-19-lockdown-migrant-workers-and-the-inadequacy-of-welfare-measures-in-india.

Tewari, Suryash and Surya, Saket, *State of State Finances*, New Delhi: PRS, 2020.

Upadhyay, Sanjay and Kumar, Pankaj, 'Amendments in Labour laws and other labour reform initiatives undertaken by state government of Rajasthan, Andhra Pradesh, Haryana and Uttar Pradesh', VV Giri National Labour Institute Working Paper, 2017, available at https://vvgnli.gov.in/sites/default/files/122-2017%20-%20Sanjay%20Upadhyaya.pdf.

Us Salam, Ziya and Ausaf, Uzma, *Shaheen Bagh: From a Protest to a Movement*, New Delhi: Bloomsbury India, 2020.

World Bank, *Global Economic Prospects 2021*, Washington, D.C.: The World Bank Group, 2021.

World Health Organization, *Global Spending on Health 2020: Weathering the Storm*, Geneva: World Health Organization, 2020, available at https://apps.who.int/iris/handle/10665/337859.

INDEX